PLANNING IN EUROPE

PLANNING IN EUROPE

Edited by
JACK HAYWARD and OLGA A. NARKIEWICZ

ST MARTIN'S PRESS   NEW YORK

All rights reserved. For information write:
St. Martin's Press Inc., 175 Fifth Avenue, New York, N.Y. 10010
Printed in Great Britain
Library of Congress Catalog Card Number: 77-25975
ISBN 0-312-61406-3
First published in the United States of America in 1978

Library of Congress Cataloging in Publication Data
Main entry under title:
Planning in Europe.
    Bibliography: p. 193
    Includes Index.
    1. Europe—Economic policy—Addresses, essays,
lectures. 2. Europe—Social policy—Addresses, essays,
lectures. 3. Planning—Addresses, essays, lectures. I.
Hayward, Jack Ernest Shalom.
II. Narkiewicz, Olga A.
HC240.P573   338.94   77-25975
ISBN 0-312-61406-3

CONTENTS

PREFACE

The connection between the social, economic, political and physical aspects of development is well known, but difficult to analyse in a precise and systematic fashion. For some time now, many scholars have been perturbed by the lack of links between different sectors of development and by an absence of inter-disciplinary studies which would bring these aspects together. One of the ways in which this state of affairs can be remedied is by setting up studies on planning. Despite the extensive literature it has already generated, planning as a discipline is relatively new but it is one which lends itself well to devising an integrated way of studying development. The growing problems of development in Europe make the setting up of such studies ever more urgent.

This book is the result of a preparatory meeting of some twenty-five specialists in planning (both academic and practitioners) from East and West Europe who discussed the analytical problems of conducting such studies. The papers which were given, though primarily of a descriptive nature, are devoted to the search for solutions. Some of the contributors are already distinguished in their field, either in an academic or administrative capacity; others are at the beginning of their careers. They are all convinced that, given the will, it would be possible to improve the institutional and environmental conditions in such a way as to ameliorate the quality of life of all Europeans.

The papers are arranged in an order which gives priority to economic and financial planning, followed by industrial and administrative planning, and social and spatial aspects of planning. The Western European papers draw predominantly upon French and British experience, France being the country which has attained an impressive degree of success in the perilous venture of planning, while Britain has more to teach from its misadventures than from its attainments. One of the editors (Jack Hayward) has primarily been concerned with the study of economic planning in Western Europe, while the other (Olga Narkiewicz) has been more especially involved in the Eastern European aspects of social and environmental planning. There is an element of continuity between this book and the study of planning in three West European countries, *Planning, Politics and Public Policy*, as they not only share a co-editor but two other contributors (Bruno Jobert and Stephen Young). While this is necessarily a less complete study because of its more comprehensive coverage, it does offer the possibility of comparing planning in both Communist and non-Communist polities. Each of the editors has contributed a chapter, a mainly retrospective introduction and a forward-looking conclusion, which serve as a setting for the papers.

What distinguishes this from most other symposia is the fact that the papers address themselves to European problems on an all-European basis, and that some comparative evaluation is involved. Contributions range from a paper on attitudes to planning among senior civil servants based upon personal testimony to a paper which discusses grass-roots planning problems in Western and Eastern Europe. The main idea binding all the papers together is the attempt to inter-relate the problems on a national, international and inter-disciplinary basis. The implicit aim is to effect a systematic and gradual reform of attitudes to planning, at a time when 1960s optimism (pre-Oil Crisis) has given way to a sombre cast of mind that recalls the gloom of the depressed 1930s.

It only remains to the editors to express their thanks to the Social Science Research Council for providing funds for the meeting at Corpus Christi College, Oxford, in September 1976; to the College for the warm hospitality provided, and to all those who attended and contributed papers for their participation and co-operation.

INTRODUCTION: INERTIA AND IMPROVISATION: THE PLANNING PREDICAMENT

Jack Hayward

While the historian can turn his back upon the changes through which contemporary society is passing, the social scientist usually feels it incumbent upon him to seek to offer some explanation and even guidance in matters of public policy, even if scant attention is paid to his findings by those who precipitate or react to change. However humiliating it may be to confess that those who take decisions are unlikely to profit much from the work of social scientists, the fact is that the social scientist provides at best an explanation after the event of destabilising changes that often erupt unannounced onto the political scene. When the key variables frequently prove to be exogenous variables, beyond the control of those who endeavour to exert control over the process of change, the remedy for the decision-maker is either to moderate his ambitions to improvising interim solutions to intractable problems or to acquire the capacity to convert exogamous variables into endogenous ones. An undoubted attraction of comprehensive planning is that it appears to offer the means to satisfy this latter ambition, although it may simply internalise many of the destabilising changes and be compelled to repress their effects by an assertion of authoritarian powers. As for the attempt to offer intellectual guidance in a situation in which predictability is unattainable and adaptability represents surrender to circumstances, it seems to be foredoomed to failure, except where public power can ensure that reality will fit the plan. When the protagonists of intellectual guidance attempt to surpass an '*a posteriori* understanding' of a turbulent environment, experience suggests they are all too likely to discover that 'We are sorcerer's apprentices, but there is no sorcerer.'[1]

In the countries characterised by their political and economic pluralism, changes occurring within the 'wealth-producing system' (especially when it has been characterised by a traditional free enterprise market economy, as in Britain, rather than one with a pronounced statist emphasis, as in France) have threatened to overwhelm the regulatory capacity of public power to achieve piecemeal, gradual change through a process of partisan mutual adjustment of group interests through interaction. The resulting crises may take the form of paralysing conflicts or 'deadlock, where each of all the possible actions is unacceptable and can be frustrated by the group which would be most damaged by it.'[2] In societies which place an inestimable value upon the inter-action process as an end in itself, superior to any other collection of objectives, innovations that cannot be assimilated by this process are simply forgone until such time that they cannot be delayed any further. 'The kind of historical change captured by the image of the moving equilibrium has all the sedate and ordered pattern of the minuet, but history, minxlike, delights as well in the tarantella.'[3] (As the contrast we wish to draw is between East and West Europe, the *gopak* might be more accurately evocative than the tarantella!)

While the inexorable pressure of market competition was the trad-itional driving force in what Lindblom has dubbed the 'preference guided society', enabling it to 'muddle through' politically, backward economies required an 'institutional substitute . . . to overcome natural inertia' as Nove put it. In Soviet Russia the Leninist party devised a strategy of revolutionary mobilisation and tension calculated to galvan-ise the energies of the people to overcome the 'critical bottleneck' and 'interlocking vicious circles' that were underpinned by pre-revolutionary values.[4] The cultural contrast between the approach to policy-making hitherto adopted in West and East Europe emerges from a discussion by Sir Geoffrey Vickers of the type and rate of change that can be accom-modated in different societies.

> While some changes can be made slowly, others cannot be made so, because the self-preserving forces of the system are organised too strongly to admit their gradual entrance. Such changes can come, if at all, only by the sudden displacement of one set of dominant values by another . . . Whereas the process of peaceful change depends on continually exposing the appreciative systems of each of its mem-bers to the influence of his fellows through a process of dialogue, the revolutionary method is to build up new schemata of fact and value, insulated by every means from those which they are designed to replace; to accentuate their difference and to reject every invitat-ion to compromise.[5]

In the Soviet Union, the institution of a comprehensive, collectivist and centralised system of planning was part of a deliberate desire for intran-sigent polarisation to give the political leaders maximum support for the tasks of mass mobilisation for industrial modernisation.

I Planning and Planners

Planning by government is frequently confused with the economic technique of forecasting and the political technique of state intervention. However, while forecasting is a necessary part of planning, involving a prediction of what is likely to be happening 'other things being equal', it does not presuppose that there will be any action to modify what is anticipated will happen. Public intervention is also a concomitant of planning but isolated, *ad hoc* and improvised acts of intervention do not amount to planning. Nor does the existence of a formal document called a 'Plan', in which various planning activities are set out in print, establish the existence of planning, neither does its absence preclude the fact of planning. Planning as an implemented activity may bear little relationship to the formal descriptions of it, just as a constitution may be an exceedingly inaccurate guide to the working of a political system. If planning is not just a set of forecasts, interventions or documents, what is it? Planning goes beyond a rational calculation of what is collectively possible/probable, as revealed by projections or forecasts, to a governmental endeavour to reconcile such forecasts with what is politically preferred. This is attempted through the strategic use of the instruments of economic and social policy by the government, in concert with other economic and social organisations, to attain explicit quantitative and/or qualitative objectives in the short, medium and long term.

Such a broad definition covers a variety of planning systems, differing in the range, type and timespan of practices involved. At one end of the spectrum is a kind of planning close to case by case, day to day, routine decision-making, in which 'Planning concerns the fitting together of ongoing activities and only rarely involves inventing new ones. It has more the character of getting into step with the world than of changing it.'[6] Accepting the existing context of action as given, such planning is undertaken by the actors themselves. However, the increase in volume and the change in the character of state intervention necessitates a co-ordination of specific responses to particular problems, which may seek to approximate to an integrated comprehensive plan. The intellectual justification of this is the recognition of the complex interdependencies that are a concomitant of the proliferation of particular acts of public intervention, which appear to require harmonisation. At the heroic end of the planning spectrum explicit development objectives are fixed, backed by a government commitment to implement them. A comprehensive co-ordination of public policies is based upon an examination of a range of possible alternatives, with systematic revision of current public action in conformity with the policy objectives. Lastly, public power is used to secure the implementation of government priorities rather than acquiescence in a compromise with domestic or foreign interests.

To be able to sustain such a heroic view of planning, it is necessary to possess an ideological, political, administrative and societal system capable of surviving the strain of such an ambitious venture. Firstly, while no society is immune from the effects of an uncertain future, a 'closed society' can protect itself much more effectively from turbulences in its environment. Secondly, the publicity associated with choosing between alternative policies may provoke opposition from those whose preferences are not accepted by the official plan. This would be a serious problem in a liberal democratic polity, exposing latent conflicts between incompatible interests but it does not appear to have unduly incommoded countries where opposition is equated with subversion and dealt with accordingly. Thirdly, the preference of the mass public for the current satisfaction of their personal needs rather than sacrificing these for the benefit of future generations does not appear to have prevented the Soviet Union (and those countries who have modelled their planning systems upon it) from following a rigorous policy of capital accumulation and a sustained discrimination in favour of devoting resources to producer rather than consumer goods and to public rather than private consumption. Fourthly, whereas in pluralistic polities there is seldom any clear, overriding, collective purpose to which public action can be subordinated, in Communist polities it is taken for granted that the reverse will normally be true.

Nevertheless, Soviet-style planning suffers from some of the same bureaucratic difficulties that attempts at planning in Western Europe have encountered. The traditional state bureaucracy's line administration is primarily concerned with carrying out their routine work. The regular attainment of industrial growth is reduced to a bureaucratic routine. The bureaucrats' main purpose is simply preserving the organisation, which justifies their existence, rather than pursuing any grandiose societal objective or even fulfilling the ostensible functions for which the organisation exists.

Organisations . . . much prefer sterility to death. Given the supremacy of the end of organisational maintenance, opportunistic decision-making rather than planning is called for. Indeed, from the standpoint of maintenance the organisation may do well to make as few long-term commitments as possible. Advantage may lie in flexibility.[7]

While in non-Communist polities bureaucratic resistance may effectively preclude certain kinds of planning, in the Soviet system there is systematic violation of the formal norms of the state particularly at the middle and lower levels of the hierarchy. The objectives fixed from above are modified to suit the interests of their subordinates by informal primary groups who engage in semi-legal or illegal deals to attain the Plan's requirements. Thereby the needs of a rational-technical command structure are reconciled with bureaucratic problem-solving.

However, the pragmatic case for planning in the Soviet Union was based on the need to cope with the decision-making overload that resulted from the elimination of the market mechanism. The expertise of planners was supposed to consist in their capacity to reduce the uncertainties of an environment within which the government had to take its economic decisions. Party control ensured that interest aggregation at all levels took place in conformity with official ideology and objectives, with allocative decisions being mere detailed derivatives from the policy directives. 'The major cost is bureaucratic inertia and commitment to the status quo', which has to be corrected by recourse to the external yardstick of the market economies, so that 'it is debatable whether the Soviet model would continue to exist as it is if external stimulation were eliminated.'[8] So the Soviet planning system provides a paradoxical example of an inertia-prone organisation devoted to overcoming the traditional inertial tendencies of Russian society by pressuring producing units thanks to the example afforded by the capitalist economies.

Charles Lindblom has in fact argued that

> what distinguishes Communist systems from others is less that they plan the methods and sequences by which they intend to achieve their great goals than that they have great goals and act boldly to reach them ... They decided upon these goals, not in any planning process different from the processes that decision-makers who do not plan employ, but in the rough and tumble of politics, emboldened no doubt by their extraordinary power over the populace and guided perhaps by a more definite ideology than those that guide leaders in the market-oriented democracies. Boldness, however, is not planning.[9]

This point is well taken, de Gaulle having demonstrated that the French Plan could also be used in the service of grandiose goals in a mixed economy accustomed to state direction, with a self-assured elite to run both its public and private sectors. Furthermore, in so far as 'incremental-ism' can be given precise specification,[10] Lindblom is right to stress that Soviet planning starts from key decisions which are 'too important to be left to the ostensible planners', whose task is 'to reconcile all other resource allocation and production decisions with them'.[11]

However, it is even more difficult to separate politics from planning than it is to separate politics from administration. The planner, both in Communist and non-Communist societies, is a technocrat, whose expertise is adapted to suit political purposes. Any pretension to separate political ends from planning means is as illusory as the technocrat's claim to reduce partisan passions to the serene, scientific dimensions of a series of equations. The inability to depoliticise planning means that 'the planner loses his special status and legitimation'; it cannot be an 'antidote, correction, guide' to ordinary policy-making; with the result that 'Planning is swallowed up by its environment.'[12] Conceived as an agent of change, the planner paradoxically reinforces rather than reconstructs the status quo, because this is the price of achieving the policy object-ives of the plan. 'Orthodox planners cannot rationally and comprehensively govern the polity because they are not sufficiently able to change exist-ing power structures . . . Planning rationality cannot replace political rationality.'[13] The Saint-Simonian dream, in which the government of men would be replaced by the administration of things—which has so fascinated not only technocrats and their apologists in East and West Europe—has proved to be a pipe dream. It has seldom been the case that 'as the general standard of values is so commonly accepted, the functions of the state become so technical as to make politics appear as a kind of applied statistics.'[14] While planners have seldom risen above the subordinate status of being 'used' or 'employed', the resistance to their penetration as far as the exercise of political power has varied with the political regime. Their technocratic propensities have been curbed most completely in countries such as Britain, while to some extent in pre-1968 France and especially (with ups and downs) in the USSR, the exclusion of the planning process from the realm of political controversy facilitated encroachment by the planners into the policy-making sphere.

In pluralist polities, planners have found it less easy to appeal to the public interest represented by the government and have looked for allies amongst client interest groups. To escape from their undemocratic associations as so-called technocrats, the planners have developed a taste for public participation, not in terms of the mass public so much as special publics, who must be consulted in the course of plan prep-aration. This process, called *concertation* or consensus-building in the

French national economic planning process, where it is very much a window-dressing exercise, takes the form of 'advocacy planning' in more pluralist polities, where it has been particularly developed in the context of urban land-use planning. Recognising the capacity of interest groups to paralyse planning innovations, advocacy planning restructures the local decision-making process in the guise of redistributing power more widely.

> . . . It moves planning from postulating and pressuring goals of 'public interest' to a process of community dialogue, negotiation, and decision-making that produces an amalgam of 'private, or client interest'. It was thought that in advocacy planning, value premises would change from public interest espoused by a power elite to values based on compromise with specific client interests at various junctures of the urban policy process.[15]

What is evident is that public dissatisfaction with the way in which environmental planning has worked has increased and not diminished despite this attempt to give a sort of preference-guided procedural legitimacy to the activities of town planners.

II Institutional Dispositions and Ideological Predispositions

The ideological climate within which planning takes place necessarily has a pervasive effect upon its acceptability within the political and administrative system. Because centralised planning is regarded as an integral part of a Leninist decision-making system of democratic centralism, it has a legitimacy which planning in the non-Communist countries of Western Europe cannot hope to attain. By contrast with France, whose statist values make it less remote from the Soviet Union, in Britain the industrialising ideology was *laissez-faire* and the legitimacy of liberal political values was the main lesson of her historical experience. The presumption has therefore been—on the part of the government as well as of the governed—that the state should intervene reluctantly and with restraint.[16] The two halves of Germany provide an especially sharp contrast, with the Federal Republic deserting the statist tradition for the doctrinaire liberalism of the social market economy, while the GDR has embraced the Soviet-style planned economy without the marked variations developed by some other East European states, notably Hungary and Poland, even if we leave aside the heterodox case of Yugoslavia. When in the mid-1960s the Federal Republic resigned itself to incorporating partial elements of planning into its economic policy-making processes, the then Economics and Finance Minister expressed the consensus view, first enunciated in the SPD's Godesberg Programme of 1959, when he called for 'as much competition as possible, as much planning as necessary'.[17] The identification of the Federal Republic's postwar recovery with adherence to the social market economy meant that even modest indulgence in planning was akin to sin.

Because planning, as a new technique of public economic decision-making, had to strengthen the government's capacity to steer rather than merely react to change, it spawned new institutions and—insofar as it achieved any impact at all—modified the relative power of some existing institutions. It also raised problems of the public accountability of the new planning agencies. Institutional innovation is the easiest phenomenon to detect, with the birth of the Soviet *Gosplan* in 1921, the French General Planning Commissariat in 1946 and the British National Economic Development Office in 1962. One way to ascertain the extent to which the innovative ambitions associated with the introduction of planning met with success would be to trace the extent to which planning institutions were composed of new men with new attitudes, how far they were able to intervene in the processes of decision-making, ranging from policy conception through to implementation. It is important also to discover how far decision-making structures and processes were altered and adapted to accommodate planning, as well as to form an opinion of how significant these changes were in practice. Because of the close connections between annual budgeting and national economic planning, their relationship is a particularly good vantage point from which to observe the extent to which the budget is consistent with the plan. In Western Europe

> Criticisms of the traditional budgetary process have been a major factor behind the move to planning. As a result, planning efforts have tended to be resource rather than goal-oriented. The most pervasive form of planning is medium-term financial planning with its strong macro-economic orientation and its institutionalisation in finance ministeries. However, the end result of the attempt to relate planning to an already overburdened budgetary process has been to depress its analytical capacity and its innovative potential.[18]

It is a natural step from this to examine the relationship between bodies specifically concerned with planning and those concerned with day to day economic management, which brings us to the more general question of the administrative context of planning.

The relative organisational emphasis within the planning structure upon the functional, industrial/sectoral and territorial aspects of planning has changed over time. Both Soviet and French planning began with a strong industrial/sectoral emphasis, the verticalism of this approach being corrected to some extent by a central concern with key functional factors such as investment and manpower. However, despite the advantages of such a system for linking the planners with firms and transmitting pressure from above, the mid-1950s witnessed a switch to a territorial emphasis, which went much further in Soviet Russia than it did in France. Whilst France contented itself with a timid venture into regional planning, the draconian Khrushchev reforms of 1957 aimed at improving horizontal co-ordination at the regional level in the Soviet Union, based upon just over a hundred *sovnarkhozy*. However, administrative totalitarianism reasserted itself in the 1960s after Khrushchev's fall from power; the ministries retrieving many of their former functions; while in France a limited measure of regional deconcentration was aimed at increasing the effectiveness of central planning through regionalisation rather than attempting a genuine decentralisation of the planning process.[19] In both polities, centralised state control seemed to be indispensable if the drive for industrial modernisation was to be sustained.

While failures in plan implementation were to be a contributory factor to the 1960s economic reforms in Czechoslovakia, of which economic decentralisation was a notable feature, the centre-periphery model has remained relevant to the business of translating plans into achievement. A government concerned to retain control over the direction and pace of economic development, rather than responding to pressure from its environment, will persist with centralised planning. In the Soviet-style planning process

the conscious policy of putting pressure on all producing units is embodied in the control figures, the preliminary aggregate targets constructed by the state planning committee (*Gosplan*) after consultation with the political leaders and communicated by *Gosplan* down through the planning-control hierarchy to the producing units ... This pressure is undoubtedly relieved somewhat in the counter-planning and bargaining as the plan comes back up the planning-control hierarchy.

But 'a considerable amount of pressure is reinstated in the plan when it comes back into *Gosplan*,[20] so the plan is much more detailed rather than substantially different from the original draft. Adaptation to the need for iterative interaction in the planning process within a political system of predominantly public pressure upon the periphery yields very different results from those characteristic of a pluralistic political system of predominantly private pressure upon public decision-makers.

The answer to the pertinent question: 'just what is the steering capacity of the political system over its environment?'[21] is clearly different in East and West Europe. The political system possesses, in Communist societies, a much higher degree of autonomy from the constraints that operate in pluralist societies. It is more of a closed system in which planning is largely an intra-governmental activity. By contrast, in mixed economies where the private capitalist sector remains the senior partner and where the political system is the creature rather than the master of its environment, the propensity to inertia is very great unless the steering can be done by powerful and well-organised extra-governmental forces. A typical comment by a former British planner (after the planning euphoria of the early 1960s had waned) is that

> In economic policy, the influence government can in fact exert on the economy as a whole is in almost all cases marginal . . . so the objectives of government in economic policy are comparatively modest . . . the dice are normally loaded in favour of *immobilisme*.[22]

However, in Federal Germany, whose steering capacity has been compared unfavourably with that of Britain,[23] the banking system could fulfil some of the roles that the political system had abdicated. This further underlines the fact that economic success is not simply dependent upon the state's capacity to steer the economy. However, where a non-public agency does not in effect take over the state's overall co-ordinating and steering function, a more rather than less centralised planning process will be necessary to reduce the autonomy of sub-systems by a variable mixture of incentives and coercion, as French planning did in its heyday. Threatened by an institutional inertia derived from both the paralysing propensities of group pressures and the immobilisation of the ministries, it was thanks to a modernising elite, 'new men and new attitudes',[24] working to the policy directives of a heroic leader, that a new impetus was imparted to a country that, according to a French minister (Robert Boulin), accepts revolution provided vested interests are respected. Far from being a substitute for conflict resolution, the capacity to plan successfully presupposes that conflicts have already been resolved and leadership is provided through the political processes.

III Promethean and Sisyphean Planning

The Soviet model of Promethean planning, which deliberately abandoned the economic disciplines of the market economy for the political disciplines of state direction, was the result of long ideological and technical debate, as well as a decade's experience with, first, war communism and then the 'New Economic Policy'. It was a commitment to a teleological conception of economic development in which material and human resources would be mobilised for the most rapid industrialisation, aimed first at establishing a self-sufficient socialist system in one country and then achieving parity prior to overhauling the most advanced capitalist countries.[25] The purpose of economic activity was explicitly fixed and a breakneck pace was set—sometimes called 'planner's tension'[26]—the successive stages of the race to achieve a technologically advanced socialist society being marked by the five year plans, commencing with the first plan for 1928-32. Short-run annual plans, to fit in with the agricultural cycle of production, were also prepared but the priority for heavy industrial investment was reflected in the pre-eminence of the strategic plan over the annual tactics. Coming at a time when the capitalist economies were experiencing a cataclysmic economic crisis, this exercise in a state-controlled economy immensely impressed even those who intensely disliked the purposes to which it was being directed. Even though the ambitious targets were frequently not attained, Soviet planning offered hope where fatalism seemed to prevail, where the orthodoxy of market economies continued to govern the minds of the political, administrative and business leaders.

However, Keynesianism challenged the established orthodoxy and appeared to offer a remedy to chronic mass unemployment and the trade cycle without requiring the capitalist countries to adopt the political corollaries of Soviet-style planning. It would be enough to manage the economy intelligently by using the instruments of state intervention in hitherto inconceivable ways and to an unprecedented extent. This was the approach accepted by the inheritors of the Fabian tradition in Britain, although the Webbs themselves favoured the substitution of a comprehensive, detailed, techno-bureaucratic planning which they discerned in the USSR and which inspired them to write their eulogy of *Soviet Communism*. The mainstream of Labourite socialism in Britain and Continental Social Democracy relied at most upon extending state interventionism into *ad hoc* exercises in partial planning of public services such as education and health, as well as defence policy and transport policy. However, the key assumption of the Keynesian approach was that public intervention was auxiliary and subsidiary to the market economy. It was utilised to counteract the undesirable effects of the market economy, notably in the case of the trade cycle, the public sector stepping in to boost investment and consumption when the private sector was depressed. However, if fluctuations in public sector investment were not themselves to become destabilising in their effects, it would have to be planned in conjunction with private sector investment. This minimal type of planning was accepted generally by many of the less doctrinaire liberal conservatives and by the German Social Democrats, while the more radical Social Democrats in Sweden wanted to make the public sector the senior element in the partnership.

While public ownership might be regarded as a vital factor in determining the relative weight within the planning process of the public compared to the private sector, the Keynesian focus upon public control rather than upon public ownership sought to bypass this issue which was controversial in Britain but not (until the 1970s) in France. The evidence within the mixed economies of Western Europe seems to indicate that public ownership has not, as such, necessarily facilitated the planning process. Where public corporations have attained a large measure of managerial autonomy, as they have in Italy, they may regard themselves as committed to fit their activities to national planning requirements. However, they are just as likely to be used by the state for dealing with emergencies, on a case by case and *ad hoc* basis, which amounts to 'trouble-shooting' rather than planning. A leading proponent of planning in Italy, the former Minister Ugo La Malfa, could argue

> that State Holdings have respected all the objectives assigned to them under the Five Year National Plan for 1966-70; I believe that, unfortunately, this represented a unique exception to the general neglect with which the plan has been treated, starting with the State itself.[27]

However, with the onset of the crises of the late 1960s and early 1970s, the entrepreneurial state corporations like IRI and ENI tended to be forced by politicians to cope with immediate difficulties by improvising expedients of dubious economic soundness. The Saraceno philosophy that the public sector should, on the basis of its financial self-sufficiency, be in a position to substitute for the ineffectiveness of Keynesian macroeconomic techniques the structural reorganisation of Italian industry as the spearhead of economic growth and elimination of unemployment, was a victim of the new environment of the 1970s.[28] Belated mid-1970s attempts in Britain to imitate the Italian approach through the establishment of a National Enterprise Board and planning agreements seem foredoomed to as complete a failure as the early 1960s attempts to adopt French-style planning. The key to economic success both in Italy and in the Soviet Union seems to be the existence of a group of public sector managers who have been able to force through a policy of industrialisation. In both countries they have faced opposition; from a feeble state and incompetent bureaucracy in Italy, from the 'military-heavy industry establishment' in the USSR.[29] In both countries comprehensive planning has suffered as a consequence.

Whilst for ideological and emotional reasons it is difficult for the Soviet Union in particular to accept the view that East and West Europe are converging towards an intermediate or mixed type of planning and market economy, there has been a great deal of evidence that such convergence has occurred in a piecemeal way. While the gap between the extremes still indicates a persistent polarisation, it can be argued that 'The French government surely plans more than the Yugoslav, and only a little less than the Hungarian.'[30] Although it is true that France is not typical of advanced capitalist societies, it has served as a model to be imitated, although few have been able to emulate its achievements. The post-1968 reforms introduced in Hungary were based upon the reconciliation of continued central planning and macro-economic management with market forces. To achieve this, it was argued,

> Planning should take into account market relations, in general not directly opposing market tendencies but guiding and influencing their development by means and methods which are in harmony with the nature of market relations ... Intervention should occur only where the national interest or basic allocations made by the plans are threatened.[31]

The main aims of the reforms were to give greater managerial autonomy to state enterprises (although this had led to problems, particularly over-investment) and some scope to supply and demand factors in price fixing. In Poland, since 1971, some large industrial and trading enterprises have been given greater scope for initiative, with incentives being changed from the percentage of plan fulfilment to performance measured by the increase in value added as the basis for awarding wage increases and in profit as the criterion for determining managerial bonuses. While Czechoslovakia's attempt at economic reforms pointing in the direction of the Western-style economy came to a disastrous halt with Soviet military intervention, the Hungarian and Polish reforms, more strictly circumscribed to matters of economic management, have been allowed to proceed and may point the way for developments in other East European countries. In Western Europe the 'Eurocommunist' attempts at disassociation from the Soviet Union by the Communist Parties of Spain, Italy and France, have significantly been located more in the cultural and political fields than in that of economic policy.

It may be that the mixed economies of Western Europe, where the task of planning is seen as more akin to the endless and ineffective heroism of Sisyphus than to the self-sacrificing, once-for-all heroism of Prometheus, are closer to political and economic reality than the collectivised economies of Eastern Europe. The pretentious assumption of omnicompetence involves immense dangers for the polity because every controversial issue places in jeopardy the authority of the state. While the vicissitudes of prices and incomes policies in capitalist systems have provided the occasion for much scorn and derision, communist systems have experienced severe strains in their attempt to allow the price mechanism to balance the supply and demand of basic commodities. 'In Poland, one government (that of Gomułka in 1970) has been toppled and another (Gierek's in 1976) has been seriously shaken in the process of trying to make prices once again perform their traditional function . . .'[32] For contrasting evidence, one may consider the case of Britain where—unlike France—the deeply-rooted ideological reluctance to accept statutory regulation of prices and wages has meant that great efforts have been made to secure voluntary agreement by peak business and labour organisations to restrain prices (1971-2 by the Confederation of British Industry) and wages (successive post-1974 'social contracts' between the Government and the Trades Union Congress). Whereas in Poland the attempted reintroduction of market principles has provoked riotous resistance, in Britain the attempt to restrain market power by public intervention has led to investment and labour strikes. Both governments have been compelled to yield. Convergence towards a mixed or intermediate type of planning clearly has its negative as well as its positive aspects.

IV Interrogations

In the light of the heavy human and economic costs of planning and the frequency with which it has proved impossible to implement plans effectively, especially in pluralist-capitalist societies, we must ask the question: should governments resign themselves to improvising reactions to external circumstances? Should they accept the severe limitations upon the public capacity to steer development? It has been penetratingly observed that 'The experience of regulating a national economy or a business corporation is sometimes more analogous to shooting rapids than to steering a great circle course',[33] so that planning is often just a public relations exercise to lend a spurious air of rationality to a series of political expedients. Sometimes the best arguments in favour of of planning are the unintended side-effects that it produces but this is a paradoxical basis for justifying a plan. It may therefore be that the general area of state intervention rather than the special case of planning is the more appropriate one to study.

Dror has ventured the view that 'a certain utopian element may be essential for gaining the necessary support and may be fully compatible with a realistic approach to planning and with successful plan realisation.'[34] Insofar as the 'necessary support' is not simply that of select elites, the price of public support may be very high. Altshuler has argued that

> Government never moves slowly enough or poses issues clearly enough to give everyone his say. It is fair to say that only when government moves at a snail's pace and deals with issues of rather direct and immediate impact can a significant proportion of the great multitude of interests express themselves. Therefore, democratic planning of a highly general nature is virtually impossible.[35]

Such a pessimistic conclusion will undermine the position of those who seek to develop a more comprehensive type of national economic planning, not simply to increase efficiency in decision-making but to make it more democratic. However, this does not entail succumbing to the inevitability of inertia. It means that at a time when the capitalist economies are reverting to chronic unemployment and the communist economies are failing to sustain their past growth rates, governments might be well advised to content themselves with admittedly imperfect partial forms of planning. In the absence of an overriding public purpose, governments can be expected to rely upon expeditious solutions that do not disturb existing power relationships and therefore adapt to rather than overcome the situational constraints.

Notes

1. Herman R. van Gunsteren, *The Quest for Control. A critique of the rational-central-rule approach in public affairs* (London, J. Wiley & Sons, 1976), p. 16; cf.

12. See also L.J. Sharpe, 'The Social Scientist and policy-making', *Policy and Politics*, IV, No. 2, December 1975, p. 7 ff.

2. Sir Geoffrey Vickers, *Freedom in a Rocking Boat. Changing Values in an Unstable Society* (Harmondsworth, 1970, Penguin edn, 1972), p. 60.

3. C.E. Russett, *The Concept of Equilibrium in American Social Thought* (1966), p. 169.

4. Alec Nove, *The Soviet Economy* (London, G. Allen & Unwin, 1961, 3rd edn, 1968), pp. 109-10; cf. pp. 326-7. See also Sidney and Beatrice Webb, *Soviet Communism: A New Civilisation* (London, V. Gollancz, 2nd edn, 1937), ch. 8 *passim.*

5. Sir Geoffrey Vickers, *The Art of Judgement. A study of policy making* (London, Chapman & Hall, 1965), pp. 212-13.

6. Van Gunsteren, op.cit. p. 2; cf. 9. See also numerous publications by Aaron Wildavsky, notably 'If planning is everything, maybe it's nothing', *Policy Sciences*, IV, 1973, pp. 127-53.

7. Edward C. Banfield, 'Ends and Means in Planning', *International Social Science Journal*, XI, No. 3, 1959, reprinted in Andreas Faludi (ed.), *A Reader in Planning Theory* (Oxford, Pergamon Press, 1973), pp. 146-7; cf. pp. 145-8.

8. Guy Benveniste, *The Politics of Expertise* (London, Croom Helm, 1973), p. 195; cf. pp. 24-6, 194. See also Gregory Grossman, 'Soviet Growth: routines, inertia, and pressure', *The American Economic Review*, May 1960, L, No. 2, pp. 62-4.

9. Charles E. Lindblom, 'The Sociology of Planning: thought and social interaction' in Morris Bornstein (ed.), *Economic Planning, East and West* (Cambridge, Mass., Ballinger, 1975), p. 57.

10. John J. Bailey and Robert J. O'Connor, 'Operationalising Incrementalism: Measuring the Muddles', *Public Administration Review*, XXXV, January-February 1975, pp. 60-66.

11. Lindblom, p. 54.

12. Van Gunsteren, p. 10.

13. Ibid. See also the introduction and conclusion to Jack Hayward and Michael Watson (eds.), *Planning, Politics and Public Policy. The British, French and Italian Experience* (London, Cambridge University Press, 1975).

14. Comment by the Swedish economist Herbert Tingsten, quoted by E. Haas in S. Graubard (ed.), *The New Europe* (Boston, Mass., Houghton Mifflin, 1964), p. 70. More generally, see various works by Jean Meynaud: *Technocratie et Politique* (Lausanne, Meynaud, 1960); *Planification et Politique* (Lausanne, Meynaud, 1963); *La Technocratie, mythe ou réalité* (Paris, Payot, 1964), English translation Faber, 1968. For a more idiosyncratic view see P.J.D. Wiles, *Economic Institutions Compared* (Oxford, Basil Blackwell, 1977), pp. 215-16, 285-7.

15. Earl M. Blecher, *Advocacy Planning for Urban Development* (New York, Praeger, 1971), p. 13; cf. chs. 2 and 7 *passim.* See also Paul Davidoff, 'Advocacy and Pluralism in Planning', *Journal of the American Institute of Planners*, XXXI, November 1965, reprinted in Faludi, pp. 277-96. On the British manifestation of participatory planning, see the Skeffington Report, *People and Planning*, HMSO, 1969, and comments by L.J. Sharpe in Hayward and Watson, pp. 333-6.

16. Jack Hayward, 'National aptitudes for planning in Britain, France and Italy', *Government and Opposition*, IX, No. 4, Autumn 1974, pp. 400-10.

17. Karl Schiller quoted in K.H.F. Dyson, 'Planning and the Federal Chancellor's Office in the West German Federal Government', *Political Studies*, XXI, No. 3, September 1973, p. 348. See also Nevil Johnson, *Government in the Federal Republic of Germany* (Oxford, Pergamon Press, 1973), p. 197.

18. K.H.F. Dyson, 'The World of the West European Planner: A view from the inside', *Government and Opposition*, XIX, No. 3, Summer 1974, p. 323. On the French case, see below ch. 2.

19. On the Soviet experience, see Alec Nove, *The Soviet Economic System* (London, Allen & Unwin, 1977), pp. 70-5. On the French, British and Italian regional developments in the 1960s, see Hayward and Watson, op. cit. Part IV.

20. Herbert S. Levine, 'Pressure and planning in the Soviet Economy' in Henry Rosovsky (ed.), *Industrialization in two systems* (New York, J. Wiley, 1966), p. 271.

21. K.H.F. Dyson in *Government and Opposition*, op.cit. p. 329; cf. pp. 324 ff.

22. Michael Shanks, 'The "irregular" in Whitehall' in Paul Streeten (ed.), *Unfashionable Economics* (London, Weidenfeld and Nicolson, 1970), p. 255. Shanks' book *The Stagnant Society* (Penguin, 1961) was a major formative influence on the pro-planning climate of opinion in Britain during the early 1960s.

23. K.H.F. Dyson, 'Improving policy-making in Bonn: why the Central Planners failed', *The Journal of Management Studies*, XII, No. 2, May 1975, p. 170. See also Andrew Shonfield, *Modern Capitalism* (London, O.U.P., 1965), chs. 11 and 12.

24. Stanley Hoffmann, *Decline or Renewal? France since the 1930s* (New York, The Viking Press, 1974), p. 450.

25. See E.H. Carr and R.W. Davies, *Foundations of a Planned Economy, 1926-1929*, chs. 32 and 37 in *The History of Soviet Russia* by E.H. Carr (1969, Penguin edn, 1974); cf. Sidney and Beatrice Webb, *Soviet Communism*, op.cit. ch. 8.

26. Wiles, op.cit. pp. 290-3.

27. Quoted in Stuart Holland (ed.), *The State as Entrepreneur* (London, Weidenfeld and Nicolson, 1972), p. 218; cf. pp. 39-42, 81-91, 312-14.

28. Romano Prodi in Raymond Vernon (ed.), *Big Business and the State. Changing Relations in Western Europe* (Cambridge, Mass., Harvard University Press, 1974), pp. 56-8 and ch. 3 *passim*.

29. J.P. Hardt and T. Frankel, 'The Industrial Managers' in H.G. Skilling and F. Griffiths (eds.), *Interest Groups in Soviet Politics* (New Jersey, Princeton University Press, 1971), p. 207; cf. pp. 171, 174-5.

30. Wiles, op.cit. p. 544.

31. Tamas Morva, 'Planning in Hungary' in Bornstein, op.cit. p. 278.

32. Andrew Shonfield, 'Can Capitalism Survive till 1999?', *Encounter*, January 1977, pp. 14-15.

33. Vickers, *The Art of Judgement*, op.cit. p. 106.

34. Yezekhel Dror, 'The Planning Process: a facet design', *International Review of Administrative Sciences*, XXIX, 1963, reprinted in Faludi, op.cit. p. 341.

35. Alan Altshuler, 'The goals of comprehensive planning', *Journal of the American Institute of Planners*, XXXI, August 1975, reprinted in Faludi, op.cit. p. 201.

1 MACRO-ECONOMIC PLANNING IN MIXED ECONOMIES: THE FRENCH AND BRITISH EXPERIENCE

Jacques Leruez

Historical Background

Cross-channel cultural fertilisation has always been intense. Yet in the economic field, the influence of British liberalism was considerably tempered by the French administrative and business traditions which combined to encroach upon *laissez-faire* inside and free trade outside. After the Second World War, the impact of Keynesian economics was by no means negligible; yet France began to evolve an original system of medium-term planning which came to be known as indicative planning and exerted in the early sixties a strange fascination on the British political and economic establishment. This 'new technique of ruling'[1] which proved that the country of Champagne and *articles de Paris* could at last be taken seriously to the point of becoming even more pragmatic than its North-Western neighbour, was born from the conjunction, in the early post-war period, of two favourable elements. The first was the experimental approach of the new Fourth Republic despite its long series of short-lived weak governments that were content to live on piecemeal measures and rely for medium-term thinking and action on others and especially on an efficient administration. The second element was the presence in a number of key posts—not only in the Civil Service but also in the new public sector and even in private industry—of men whose training, background and attitude during the war (many of them had been active in the Resistance movement, whose political programme advocated the creation of a planning organisation) made them intellectually akin to each other and ready for pragmatic action.

Jean Monnet, Francois Bloch-Laîné, Pierre Massé, Claude Gruson were such men, but there were many other 'neo-realists'[2] as they were later called by Duroselle. They were sometimes described as apolitical but although they had no taste for ideological wrangling and stayed aloof from day-to-day party politics, it did not mean that they had no long-term political views. Indeed they were not content with restoring the French economy such as it was before the war; that seemed to them a very unambitious objective. What they wanted was to transform and

26

strengthen a country with a tradition of cowardly protectionism, to get it ready for European integration and later for world-wide competition. This certainly explains why, in the late forties and early fifties, the European lobby was very much the same as the planning lobby; this was symbolised by the very person of Jean Monnet—he not only launched the First Plan in 1946 but was a few years later the initiator of the Schuman plan which was to give birth to the European Coal and Steel Community whose first chairman he became. All these are well-known facts now. At the time, the planners were happy to work in relative obscurity; their work was so obscure indeed that, as late as 1956, a whole book could be published on the state of the French economy (at a time when the reconstruction period was finished) and could describe what were in fact the results of the First Plan, and hardly mention the existence of the planning commissariat although it claimed on its jacket that the last ten years had given France a new future![3] This obscurity was not to last and the political status of planning was much enhanced during the preparation of the Fourth Plan. That was the time when Pierre Massé (planning commissioner from 1959 to 1966) found that he could sit back and expound to keen publics (in France and the EEC) the general philosophy behind the Plan;[4] that was also the time when General de Gaulle tried to give some grandeur to what, in former days, he called *'l'intendance'* by talking of *'l'ardente obligation du Plan'*. This publicity was of course mainly intended for domestic consumption; yet it must also be understood within a European context. In many French planners' minds, European economic integration meant among other things, the adoption of the French planning methods by their European partners. Now, Germany—and notably its Minister of Finance and Economic Affairs, Ludwig Erhard—was passionately opposed to anything that smacked of state intervention. So French planners had to look elsewhere for allies.

Precisely at the same time, British opinion was in a receptive mood. For several years past, the notion had dawned upon many observers that Britain's economic performance was not as good as its immediate neighbours', especially as far as growth was concerned. (It is around 1960 that output *per capita* started to be higher in France than in Britain.)[5] For this state of affairs, most observers and many businessmen held responsible the Keynesian management of the economy by governments of both parties that had prevailed since the demise of the war controls, i.e. largely a regulation of demand by monetary and fiscal means which was to originate the stop-go cycle. The stop-go cycle was accused of putting a brake on growth, especially by holding back

productive investment in future growth: during the 'stop' phase, high
rates of interest and poor demand were no incentives to invest; during
the 'go' phase, the fear of a new deflation and consequent over-capacity
was supposed to restrain the more enterprising. Subsequent studies[6]
have shown that stop-go was not so detrimental to the smooth working
of the economy as was believed at the time. It remains that this belief
prevailed in the early sixties and played a considerable part in the con-
version of British industry to the idea of planning.

This is not to say that planning was an entirely new idea in the British context. Indeed the post-war Labour government had toyed with
the notion but to no avail. Having inherited the apparatus of controls
of the war economy which they called a planning structure, when it was
at best a rather cumbersome machine for the allocation of scarce resources, they were unwilling—or unable—to remodel it so that it could
be used as a framework for modernising the economy and paving the
way for future development. Some institutional attempts at comprehensive planning were made (creation of a Central Economic Planning
Staff headed by a Chief Planning Officer assisted by an Economic Planning Board inside the government machine) but what the Labour government meant by 'planning' was hardly more than general co-ordination;
in any case the new institutions had very little impact on future
economic policy and were very soon forgotten. Moreover, some more
modest experiments in sectoral planning (such as Stafford Cripps's
development councils) which could have become the equivalent of the
modernisation commissions in France were virtually still-born. Besides,
when the Conservatives came back to power in 1951, the notion of
planning was associated in public opinion with 'socialist' intervention
and could thus be discarded in total indifference.

Consequently, the first thing the advocates of planning in the early
sixties had to do, was to persuade the business community that planning like the French was totally different from the British experiment
of the forties and did not increase state intervention. This demonstration
was all the easier as the most important coherent group advocating planning consisted of industrialists, gathered round the chairman of the
Federation of British Industries' economic policy committee.[7] In fact,
these businessmen were persuaded that planning would do the reverse
and increase the influence of business on the government. This is what
happened in France, in the event, but was not bound to happen in
Britain owing to the unions' much bigger say in policy-making. In any
case, by November 1960 the group had persuaded the FBI not only to
accept the idea of planning but to suggest that government and industry

might meet to consider 'whether it would be possible to agree on an assessment of expectations and intentions which should be before the country for the next five years.'[8] It took more than a year before the government and the TUC gave their formal approval to the scheme (January 1962). The National Economic Development Council was born. Meanwhile, the French planners had come to London to give an account of their methods at a conference (Easter 1961) sponsored by the NIESR (National Institute for Economic and Social Research) and PEP (Political and Economic Planning, the editors of *Planning*). It gave Pierre Massé another opportunity to expound the philosophy under-lying French planning.

The Philosophy of French Planning: Ideal and Realities

What Masse calls the 'spirit of the plan' is the 'concert' of all economic and social forces in the nation. This concept of 'concertation' or *économie concertée* introduced by Jean Monnet has been best defined by Bloch-Lainé as

> a system in which representatives of the state (or other public bodies) and those of companies (public or private) meet in an organised way to exchange information, to compare their forecasts and either to reach decisions or to make recommendations for consideration by the government.[9]

So the plan is not the work of the government alone but the common child of the 'partners' of the mixed economy: government, employers, workers; hence, the tripartite structure of planning which has allowed the old French tradition of piecemeal intervention (that, according to some observers, dates back to Colbertism in the seventeenth century) to lapse in many ways. That was at least Monnet's intention. But this point deserves further discussion.

How does the plan get implemented then? Massé insists that the consensus achieved at the time of its preparation is in fact projected forward into the execution; this is what he also calls the 'spontaneous execution' of the plan. Another factor favouring the plan's implement-ation is the coherence and the accuracy of the projections, especially in the basic industries, which avoid costly upheavals in investment program-mes. For Massé the plan is 'a reducer of uncertainty'. Then if it is the best market-research exercise possible on a national scale, why should it not be trusted by industrialists? Of course, Massé admits that there are other means of implementation. The first element resides in the direct control the government machine has (through the *Fonds de Développement Economique et Social* on which the planning commission is represented) over the investments in the public sector but also in that part of the private sector where it controls the level of investment through its financial assistance: house-building or the steel industry for instance. Altogether, state-controlled investment has represented 50 per cent of overall investment from the sixties. (The same proportion is to be found in Britain; this is the best measure of the mixed character of the two economies.) The second source of influence is of course the whole apparatus of selective measures, more often indirect financial controls (such as tax rebates, extended credit, reduced interest rates, refundable subsidies, equipment premiums) than direct administrative restraint (such as building permits and office-building restrictions in Paris). Massé prefers to call them incentives. Others might be more inclined to call them coercive methods. Consequently, planning can be said to be anti-*dirigiste* to the extent that it gives more cohesion to state intervention whose selectivity is justified and rationalised by the plan strategy, but it does not prevent the government and especially the Ministry of Finance from keeping at hand *dirigiste* instruments which it can use, plan or no plan, in a discretionary way. This explains why Giscard d'Estaing in his last years as Minister of Finance could be accused by the opposition of being both a *dirigiste* and an anti-planner, because of his case-by-case intervention which was not always in accordance with the Sixth Plan's basic strategy (of which the opposition did not approve anyway). All the same, the French plan may be said 'to have teeth in it somewhere', a privilege the former Secretary of State for Economic Affairs (1964-6) George Brown desperately wanted (and did not get) for the British plan; here again not so much because the government lacked any means of intervention but because they were at the disposal of other ministers more concerned with short-term action than with medium-term planning.

Something more must be said to correct Masse's picture of French planning. In the very early sixties, it is a fact that 'concertation' and public adherence to planning were rather impressive. Only the CGT (*Confédération Générale du Travail*), the Communist-led and largest of French unions (2.5 million members), remained reticent at all times, mainly for doctrinal reasons (the necessity of upholding the class-struggle) although it took an active part in the modernisation commissions. Conversely, the other unions, notably the CFDT (*Confédération Française Démocratique du Travail*) with approximately one million members now, were rather enthusiastic and enjoyed their participation in the commissions. But the mood changed. First de Gaulle declared that the plan was part of his grand design for France. Planning, to which Monnet had tried to give a technical, corporatist and, as much as possible, non-controversial image, thus took on a political dimension. The opposition took up the argument, urged more 'democratic' planning (by which term it meant that it should propose more radical reforms) and the small PSU (*Parti Socialiste Unifié*), the conscience of the non-Communist left at the time, went as far as proposing a 'counter-plan'.[10] Yet there were more practical reasons for the unions' change of mood. First, there was the 'stabilisation plan' introduced in 1963 after a period of overheating that followed the end of the Algerian war. This series of piecemeal deflationary measures (which had nothing to do with a plan as it is understood here) were hastily taken by the Minister of Finance (Giscard d'Estaing) and the cuts in public spending were bound to affect the public investment targets of the Fourth Plan. The general impression was that *'l'ardente obligation'* of the plan did not apply to the government. A second step in the decline in the confidence in planning took place when the Fifth Plan was started in 1966; then the unions were shocked to discover that the planners officially forecast for the last year of the plan (1970) a small but significant pool of unemployed. While the government declared it was inevitable, the unionists considered instead that it was intended to play in the private sector the same restrictive role as the wage policy that was being tentatively applied in the public sector. The third step was taken in 1968 which marked the real death (although it was not always appreciated at the time) of 'concertation' (which proved to be—to say the least—a misunderstanding between the social partners) and also because it started a radicalisation process in the CFDT and led the two larger unions to refuse more insistently than before all 'class collaboration'. In 1969, when the Sixth Plan was being prepared, the CFDT left the commissions because it did not approve of the draft guidelines, while the CGT stayed but only as an observer. They both boycotted the latter part of the preparation of the Seventh Plan in February 1976 before the final draft was written. The government was then left negotiating with smaller unions which represent hardly more than one million members, the representatives of the employers and particularly the CNPF (*Conseil National du Patronat Français*), the French equivalent of the CBI. As an acute British observer of French planning has put it,[11] the Sixth and Seventh Plans can hardly be considered as national plans but as 'plans of the government', because the consensus-building phase is no longer devoted to looking for an understanding but 'to testing the reaction of different social groups to the government's intended medium-term economic policy'.[12] True, but besides the fact that national plans were bound to be government plans as well, in order to be credible, the emphasis on industrialisation in the Sixth Plan and on creating as many jobs as possible in the Seventh Plan, together with the absence of a coherent workers' attitude to counterbalance the employers' view, forced the government to rely much more than before on the *patronat*'s goodwill to have a fair chance of achieving its aims; so the plan is as much the child of the industrial establishment as that of the government alone.

When planning was introduced to the British, it was still in its optimistic phase. Moreover, Massé gave them a still rosier picture by insisting on the 'powerful psychological factors' that help implement the plan and on the climate of confidence in growth it produces, notably by 'reducing uncertainty'. This is how he put it:

> The logic of 'indicative planning' consists in . . . extending to a nationwide scale the market surveys made by each single firm . . . The Plan . . . is not binding on anybody. Firms are not relieved from making their calculations and forming their own assessments of the risks. But because of the Plan they are better informed when making their own plans.[13]

Of course, Massé did not entirely overlook all governmental means of intervention but he considerably minimised them. This presentation might explain the sequel; the British prepared two fine full-scale plans that make easy literature to read but that rely too much on the 'spontaneous implementation' Massé had led them to expect.

The Structures of Planning

France

The planning process clearly derives from the conception of the plan. It is divided into four stages: the information (or analysis) stage, the dialogue (or consensus-building) stage, the guide to action stage (or drawing up of the plan proper), the implementation stage. The CGP (*Commissariat Général au Plan*) intervenes at all stages either as a coordinator or as an adviser to the three partners of planning: government, employers, workers. Although it does not have direct powers of decision, its influence is considerable. It is an autonomous body strategically well-placed inside the government machine. Attached to the office of the *Président du Conseil* at first, it was later transferred to the Ministry of

Finance and Economic Affairs without being integrated into its structure; now it comes directly under the Prime Minister. According to one of its former members, Yves Ullmo, ' . . . with ups and downs, the CGP enjoys a fairly large measure of independence necessary to enable it to carry on its tasks of promoting consensus-building, yet without being excluded from the governmental and administrative apparatus.'[14] As it has only sixty senior officials at its disposal (most of them senior civil servants called *chargés de mission*) it does very little research and has to rely for its statistical information and general projections on the work of other bodies, mainly INSEE (*Institut National de la Statistique et des Etudes Economiques*) and the Forecasting Division of the Ministry of Finance and also on private studies prepared by the employers' association and the trade unions.

Hence the importance of the modernisation commissions whose number, structure and object have varied in the course of time but whose work has been from the very beginning essential. The network of commissions, though gaining in sophistication, has become less cumbersome with the Seventh Plan. For the Fifth Plan there were twenty-five commissions (twenty 'vertical', i.e. sectoral, five 'horizontal', i.e. covering one particular aspect of the co-ordination of all sectoral activities) involving about 3,500 persons. Approximately the same number of persons was involved in the preparation of the Sixth Plan for which two types of vertical commissions were set up: those corresponding as before to the main sectors of economic activity and those concerned with collective services outside the market (or partially outside the market) like education, health, social welfare, cultural affairs. With the Sixth Plan a new body appeared: the committee which is smaller in membership than the commission but has very similar terms of reference; unlike the working-party which prepares a special report for one particular commission to which it is attached, the committee works independently. The commissions bring together between twenty and fifty people, the committees still fewer members and the working-parties only around ten. For the Seventh Plan, the number of commissions and committees was cut to nineteen (among which there were seven horizontal commissions or committees), the industry commission involving the highest number of working-groups.

Although simply consultative, the commissions take part in the entire planning process. The information stage is very important for their non-official members, especially for the unions. They come to state their demands and learn the intentions of the government. For the government, of course, the preparation does not really start then. There is indeed a non-public pre-preparation stage inside government departments which, since the Fifth Plan, has become an essential part of the plan. It would be wrong though to infer from this remark that the important decisions have already been reached before the public preparation starts. For instance, in early 1975, the government started the consultations for the Seventh Plan with, in mind, a smaller growth target than the one finally adopted; it was so frightened by the unemployment projections for 1980 prepared by the employment and labour committee that it decided to go for the same rhythm of growth as before the crisis. It remains however that the consensus-building stage has tended to become less important nowadays since, in most cases, consensus cannot be reached, the radical unions abstaining from the preparation of the detailed recommendations since they do not approve the main targets. As to the last stage (implementation) it is obviously the task of the various spending departments concerned, with the help (and under the supervision) of the Ministry of Finance; and although the CGP itself plays an important part as an adviser and gad-fly in the various interdepartmental committees of which it is a member, the role of the commissions has so far been hardly more than purely formal despite the fact that they meet once or twice a year to supervise the implementation of their recommendations and contribute to the yearly report of the CGP to the government on the implementation of the plan.

Thus the planning process in France is both comprehensive and coherent and even among its detractors it is generally admitted that its structure is the best possible. Compared to it, the planning structure in Britain is partial and its elements appear badly connected with each other. It is partial in two ways: first, it has never been concerned with implementation even when there were full-scale plans; second, it has been generally restricted to industrial planning.

Britain

The first step in the introduction of indicative planning in Britain was the setting up of a central planning agency: the Neddy organisation. It was and is made up of strongly inter-related bodies: the National Economic Development Council assisted by the National Economic Development Office and the Economic Development Committees.

The NEDC is a small top-level assembly which has had a high turnover since its first creation in 1962, but its membership has remained around twenty: six employers, six trade unionists, two chairmen of the nationalised industries. Only the ministers (from 3 to 7) and the independent members (from 2 to 4) have fluctuated in number. Its chairman has been the Chancellor of the Exchequer (except between October 1964 and June 1970 when it was chaired by the First Secretary of State for Economic Affairs (1964-8) and later by the Prime Minister himself (1968-70)). The director-general of NEDO sits on the council among the independent members. The NEDC meets once a month for a whole day and sometimes for a whole week-end at Chequers (when the Prime Minister is in the chair).

Together with NEDC, NEDO was created as an independent agency attached to it. Its legal status is unclear, as it is not a statutory body, but its staff of around 220 and its working expenses are paid out of the state budget. Its director-general is appointed by the government after consultation with the council. From the beginning, about three-quarters of the staff (economists, statisticians, industrial experts) were drawn from industry, mainly the management side (the unions having very few such experts to provide), the remainder coming from the universities and the Civil Service. Following his appointment as director-general, Sir Ronald McIntosh tried to recruit junior officials from the unions. In September 1975, John Cousins (son of Frank Cousins, a well-known retired union leader and former minister) accepted the post of manpower and industrial relations director after 12 years as a full-time official in the Transport and General Workers Union. Recruited on fairly long-term contracts, NEDO officials are not technically civil servants, though the rules affecting their jobs on the whole are quite similar to those of the Civil Service. As Joan Mitchell has put it, they are 'public servants in a general way. But they are not the servants of the government.'[15]

Then came the birth of the 'little Neddies' or EDCs (Economic Development Committees). The first EDCs appeared early in 1964 (when the Conservatives were still in office) but most of them were created by Labour in the period 1965-6. They came to be as many as twenty-four in the late sixties but some were demoted during the Heath government. They have revived since 1974. At the end of 1975, there were nineteen of them (including the process plant working party, a smaller more specialised group). In their heyday (the period 1966-9), they gathered more than 400 people, among them top representatives from the industries concerned. Generally they are smaller than the French modernisation commissions (from eight to twenty-three persons), their approximate structure being the following: 45 per cent management (including public enterprise management), 20 per cent unions, 15 per cent independent experts, 10 per cent NEDO staff (senior as well as junior members), 10 per cent state representatives (mainly Departments of Industry, Trade, Energy).

A word should be said of the planning structure between 1964 and 1969 when there existed, separate from the Treasury, a planning ministry, the DEA (Department of Economic Affairs), which was in charge of medium-term national and regional planning, and incomes and prices policy, while the Treasury was supposed to deal with day-to-day economic management and financial questions. In practice, the division of work was not so easy to achieve and after the failure of the National Plan put forward by the DEA, the Treasury regained its traditional ascendancy. The DEA was finally abolished in October 1969, and the Treasury was again in charge (with the Cabinet Office) of the general sponsorship of the NEDDY organisation.

Comparative Discussion

Looking only at the institutions, one is struck by the similarities between them. This is scarcely surprising since the British attempt at planning deliberately took the French experience as a model. Indeed the British organisation constitutes the nearest institutional imitation that could be imagined in a country whose administrative traditions are so different. Even NEDC itself had its counterpart in France (at the time it was created) in the *Conseil Supérieur du Plan* which fell rapidly into abeyance (despite a few attempts to revive it), partly because it was too big (around fifty people), hence rather cumbersome; partly because in its advisory role on the plan's guidelines, it could be replaced by the *Conseil Economique et Social* (CES), a third chamber, representing economic and social interests, created by the Fourth Republic constitution, which survived the constitutional change of 1958.[16] Now a new council (although mainly political) could be compared to NEDC. It is the *Conseil de Planification* created by President Giscard d'Estaing in 1974. It meets monthly with the President in the chair. Its other members are the Prime Minister, the ministers of Finance, Industry and Labour (and other ministers according to the subject matter of the meeting), the planning commissioner and two economic advisers from the President's private staff. Yet it is a planning body only in the sense that it tries to co-ordinate the different departments' medium-term programmes (which they used to negotiate directly with the Ministry of Finance) and to decide the long-term orientations of economic and social policy, inside or outside the plan's framework.

If we look a little deeper though, the differences appear. The Neddy organisation differs from the CGP in both its basic nature and the source of its authority; from the start, the British government has wanted to be no more than one among three equal partners. By so doing, it made sure that the planning agency should be outside the conventional machinery of Whitehall and would remain the 'neutral ground' that is so important both to the CBI and the TUC. This position however was more a liability than an asset in the event. It is surely an asset by allowing Neddy a measure of freedom to express and publish its views, if necessary in opposition to the Treasury. But it is a liability in at least three ways. First, it means that NEDO has very little influence over the council and does not possess the freedom of initiative enjoyed by the CGP. Behaving more as the head office staff of a private firm towards its board of directors, NEDO's prime function is to prepare working documents for the council; even in the EDCs, NEDO representatives tend to act more as secretaries and intermediaries than as a source of leadership or positive guidance as the *chargés de mission* do. The second liability is that NEDO has no statutory working relations with the Treasury and the other economic departments, nothing comparable anyway to the special relationship which the CGP enjoys with the Ministry of Finance (mainly its forecasting section and INSEE; this relationship seems to have improved recently, especially with the budget directorate). Furthermore—still more important—NEDO has no close link with the Prime Minister's private office. At a lower level, in the EDCs, one finds representatives of the government, but the civil servants occupy junior grades in their departments. Consequently they are rarely heavy-weights compared to some high-ranking industrialists with whom they deal. Besides, they do not remain long in the same job and avoid committing their departments too much. This absence of strong formal links has two consequences in practice. First, NEDO is cut off from all confidential governmental information. According to Andrew Shonfield, it was so even in 1962 when NEDO was in charge of preparing a five-year medium-term plan: 'The planning officials had no right of access to official documents or to the government's discussions about its own plans.'[17] Things surely were less clear-cut than that and anyway they changed when the planners were transferred to a government department in 1964. Yet, not very long ago, the clothing EDC was refused by the Department of Trade confidential information supplied by importers to the government. The reason given was that it would constitute a serious breach of the principle of confidentiality in government-industry relations. (As if the EDC was not the best medium for these relations!) The EDC wanted regular access to import surveillance licences to establish in full knowledge if some high cost imported garments could be supplied instead by domestic manufacturers.[18] The second consequence is that the planning organisation is in no way associated with the implementation of its recommendations, whereas, as we have seen, the advantage of having the CGP as part of the French government machine enables it to have well-placed representatives in the departmental and inter-departmental committees concerned with the implementation of the plan. Nevertheless, even in France, 'planning is only very partially a decision-making process. The Plan is a guidelines document, whatever its commitment value may be. Every decision stated in the Plan needs to be confirmed by a later decision.'[19] This is bound to be so, since the plan being theoretically at least the result of consensus-building and containing always an element of interest group demands, the government cannot be automatically committed to implement all the 'pre-decisions' taken; the same is true consequently of the other partners in the consensus-building process. Despite this reservation, the watch-dog role of the CGP is very important in practice and hardly exists in the case of NEDO.

On the other hand, we have already pointed out that the part played by the modernisation commissions in the implementation of the plan was hardly more than formal. As to the EDCs, they were intended as planning bodies only in a vague way.[20] In any case, at the time of the NEDC plan (1963) they did not exist; when the National Plan was prepared, they were hardly in full working order. The only time when the EDCs were used in a relatively similar way as their French counterparts was after the publication of *The Task Ahead* (February 1969) which was meant to be no more than the draft of a plan. Then NEDO and DEA organised a full consultation of all the 'little neddies' to examine whether the proposed growth-targets could be met, but this planning exercise came to no really practical conclusion. Thus, failing any national economic strategy, the EDCs had to be content with trying to improve industry's competitive power and efficiency. It is no wonder then if their existence was terribly undramatic for several years; those that did survive at all the Heath government's first months of neo-liberal enthusiasm, were only given a new lease of life when Labour came back to power in 1974.

It would be tempting therefore to conclude—as many observers have done—that, because it has very rarely had the opportunity to undertake real planning, the Neddy organisation is not an effective body and has survived only because subsequent governments did not want to incur the discontent of the CBI and the TUC which, every time its suppression was mooted, declared their prompt support. Is not this attachment precisely the sign of a certain degree of success? This is what Berry, Metcalfe and McQuillan have suggested in a survey, which shows rather convincingly that Neddy should not be judged according to 'criteria which are no longer appropriate to the range of activities in which Neddy is engaged'.[21] For them, when Neddy was created, the emphasis was more on the technical aspect of the planning process (preparation of a medium-term plan, search for more expert economic advice) than on the political and organisational factors (tripartite participation, consensus-building). Although a minor theme at the beginning, this latter aspect was essential in preventing the disappearance of Neddy when the DEA was created in 1964 mainly out of its economic division. This transfer of substance and the subsequent failure of the plans not only did not destroy Neddy but transformed it into what Berry, Metcalfe and McQuillan call a 'network organisation' whose 'effectiveness depends on its utilising, influencing and developing the organisational networks with which it is concerned, to increase their capacity for co-operative, collective action and improve industrial performance.'[22] Yet it is easier said than done. Insisting on the low level of organisational capabilities of the groups concerned and the low level of interorganisational integration,[23] the authors conclude:

> The lack of effective day-to-day collaboration between government and industry and between management and unions is not just a matter of ideology. In many industries, collective institutions have neither the resources nor the organisation required to allow them to co-operate in areas of mutual interest.[24]

Allowing for these weaknesses, Neddy has gradually been metamorphosed from an institution for indicative planning into an instrument for bringing about slow but significant change. This is certainly a very fascinating demonstration. Yet, besides the fact that there does not seem to be any inconsistency between having indicative planning and bringing about change by consent (one thinks of Professor Hayward's formula: 'change and choice: the agenda of planning'[25]), we are not happy either with the authors' conclusions when they seem to imply that Neddy's capacity to bring about change derives entirely from its present structure as a network organisation. After all, although it has always been and still remains a governmental organisation, the CGP has been an effective instrument for dramatic change, since it did no less than transform—or at least help to transform—France into a modern industrial society which it was definitely not before the Second World War.

Achievements and Limitations of Planning

One of Jack Hayward's first remarks in *Planning, Politics and Public Policy* is the following:

> Before attempting to characterise more precisely what type of political and administrative policy-making process is involved in the enterprise called planning, it should be made clear that we are interested in a process that cannot be identified with a particular document called a plan. The existence of a formal plan is not a prerequisite of planning . . .[26]

Indeed, if planning is broadly considered as the opposite of the 'muddling through' process which has too often been typical of British politics and economics, one can easily conceive that an overall plan is not a prerequisite of planning. The fact that since the early sixties, the British government has published regularly a five-year programme of public expenditure, can be considered as a partial planning exercise. The same is true of the experiments in manpower planning attempted along two lines: an incomes policy (voluntary nor not, with or without administrative controls), first for six years (1964-70), then for two years (1972-4), finally from August 1975 to at least August 1977; a national industrial training system that has become more and more sophisticated since its creation (1964). Let us mention also the efforts at co-ordinated modernisation undertaken first by the Industrial Reorganisation Corporation (IRC) between 1966 and 1971 and the Industrial Development Executive (from 1972 onwards), not to mention the search for a new industrial strategy.[27] Conversely, the existence of a thick, comprehensive and consistent document called a plan is no proof of the existence of planning, if this document, as was the case with the 1965 National Plan, has no influence whatsoever on the government's short-term economic policy. In spite of these qualifications, it remains that the existence of a formal plan makes planning easier to detect. This has of course been the case in France at all times since 1946.

The First Plan (1947-53) was essentially a reconstruction plan and concentrated upon the strengthening of the basic industries. It was mainly financed through Marshall aid. The Second Plan (1954-7) successfully tried to convince the business establishment that expansion could be continued though reconstruction was finished. The Third Plan (1958-61), while pursuing economic growth, sought to get a hitherto highly-protected French economy ready for trade competition inside the EEC. With the Fourth Plan (1962-5) and under the influence of Pierre Massé, a new dimension was added: the plan's basic aim was to resist 'american-isation' by sparing France the 'civilisation of the gadget' (it went as far as not caring about the under-development of the telephone system) and to achieve a 'less partial idea of man'; consequently, the emphasis was put on the qualitative aspects of an expansion now taken for granted. Practically, it meant that public infrastructure (mainly schools, hospitals, roads) was to be privileged without 'productive' investment being sacrificed; private consumption was then to be discouraged. The Fifth Plan (1966-70) was on much the same lines; a regional dimension was introduced. Besides, a tentative incomes policy was attempted in the public sector, but it foundered on the shoals of the 1968 'events'. For the Sixth Plan (1971-5), President Pompidou had asked the planners to concentrate on a new effort at industrialisation in order to resist international competition and keep up with the Germans—the French Joneses. Meanwhile, as far as public investment was concerned, the stress was put on those developments that might be directly useful to industrialisation (telephone, roads, technical education). As for the Seventh Plan (which started from 1 January 1976 although it was published in April and definitely approved by Parliament in July), its main ambition was to adapt the French economy to a post-oil crisis world.

The history of British 'plans' is comparatively shorter and sadder. After its creation in 1962, Neddy produced a five-year plan covering the years 1962-6. When the DEA was created in 1964, the NEDC plan was abandoned and replaced in September 1965 by the National Plan, a six-year forecasting exercise which was intended to last until 1970. In July 1966, the harsh restrictive measures decided by the Labour government were to spell the death of the plan. One can then consider that these two 'plans' were no more than mere exercises in public relations meant to persuade the 'social partners' to adopt more flexible attitudes in the field of state intervention as far as the employers were concerned, in the field of incomes policy in the case of the unions. After a period of disillusionment, the DEA made a second attempt at comprehensive planning by publishing, in February 1969, a 'planning document' as it was called by its initiators who had then learnt to be prudent: *The Task Ahead.* It was meant to provide 'a basis for a further stage in the continuing process of consultation between government and both sides of industry about major issues of economic policy'.[28] So it constituted only one of the stages in the planning process whereas both its predecessors had been the culmination. Consequently it outlined procedures for consulting industry through the 'little Neddies', the boards of the nationalised industries and the trade associations for the private sector, when there was no EDC available. This consultation lasted about nine months; to our knowledge, this was the first time something akin to the French planning process took place in Britain. But when the consultation came to an end, the DEA had disappeared and its responsibility for medium-term policy had returned to the Treasury which, as a department, had no vested interest in the success of the new process. Yet a fresh document was duly published[29] by the then Chancellor, Roy Jenkins, early in 1970. It contained a modest 23 pages (compared with the 400 odd pages of the National Plan), revised the earlier estimates of the *Task Ahead* and was soon forgotten. At least one of NEDO's subsequent reports might be considered as a planning document,[30] but the change of government in February 1974 meant new priorities in government thinking.

It is useless to search British 'plans' for a different priority each time—they are not sufficiently sophisticated. Besides, they are obsessed with the highest possible growth-rate. The NEDC was built around a 4 per cent yearly growth-rate. Seeing that the NEDC target was too optimistic, the team of economists that prepared the National Plan (which was not really different from the first one)[31] opted for a 25 per cent growth-rate over six years (or about 3.8 per cent a year), thus saving the Labour ministers—who had claimed on the opposition front bench that the Conservative growth-target was too modest—an embarrassment. Again *The Task Ahead* proposed to fix a precise growth-target, yet it offered a choice between three models: a pessimistic one of a little less than 3 per cent, an optimistic one of nearly 4 per cent, a medium model of 3.25 per cent which the planners favoured. Once the consultation was finished, two possible growth-targets were retained for the period 1969-72, an optimistic one of 3.75 per cent, a pessimistic one of 3 per cent. In the event, not even the pessimistic target was achieved. The result of this obsession with growth was that the 'plan' appeared as an instrument of conservatism. Since progress was seen not as an opportunity to eliminate deficiencies and injustices, but as the current structure of production writ larger, anything that could produce greater efficiency and improved productivity was considered as satisfactory *per se*. It remains that, even if judged by the only criterion by which it is fair to judge it (the capacity of achieving sustained and faster growth), British planning is a failure, as Figure 1.1 shows.

The basic cause of this failure is easy to detect: planning has never been taken seriously by successive governments, keener to find a political expedient by which they could show domestic and foreign public opinion that they were trying hard to solve British problems. Once a new crisis

Figure 1.1: Targets and Achievements of the Policy of Stimulating Growth in Britain.

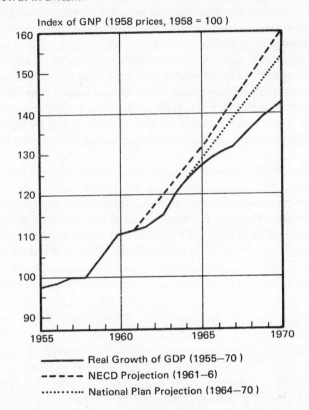

Index of GNP (1958 prices, 1958 = 100)

———— Real Growth of GDP (1955–70)

– – – – NECD Projection (1961–6)

············ National Plan Projection (1964–70)

arose (generally a run on the pound stimulated by an external payments deficit) the plan was cast aside instead of being used as a means to overcome the crisis. Conversely, the final test of the reality of French planning seems to be its capacity to survive a crisis, whether purely economic (like the runaway inflation of the periods 1948-51 and 1956-8, the deflation plan of 1963) or political (Pinay's short-sighted liberalism in 1951, de Gaulle's return to power in 1958, Pompidou's succession in 1974). We do not mean only that it survived as an institution (after all so many institutions survive, especially in Britain, for no other reason than that they do exist) but as a real force in policy-making.

One must not infer from these remarks that the profound transformations which the French economy has experienced since the Second World War can be attributed to planning alone. According to Carré,

Dubois and Malinvaud, who have attempted to analyse the causes of post-war French growth,[32] one cannot isolate as more decisive than the others any of the factors favourable to growth (whether physical, cult-ural or institutional) that have benefitted the French economy. For them, planning has played an essential part undoubtedly, not so much by itself but as part of a dynamic economic policy which, nearly every time it has had to choose between a stable currency and expansion, chose expansion (while the British—until 1972 at least—made exactly the opposite choice) which is not, of course, the most glorious feature of French post-war expansion. It remains that the general growth-targets contained in the plans have to a remarkable extent been achieved:

Table 1.1: GDP Growth-rates: Targets and Achievements in France

	Second plan (1952-7)	Third plan (1957-61)	Fourth plan (1959-65)	Fifth plan (1965-70)	Sixth plan (1971-5)
Forecast	4.4	4.7	5.5	5.7	5.9
Achievement	5.4	3.8	5.8	5.9	3.7

Sources: Carré, Dubois and Malinvaud, op.cit. p. 238 and *Le Monde,* 3 January 1976.

Of course, the achievement of the overall growth-target did not mean that sectoral targets were all achieved (indeed they were not, sometimes in essential sectors) but it meant that most sectors grew in relative har-mony with a sufficient knowledge of what was expected of them. Accord-ing to a survey by INSEE in 1967 (with a sample of 2,000) and quoted by Carré, Dubois and Malinvaud, 80 per cent of industrial firms were aware of the Fifth Plan's overall growth-target whereas two-thirds knew what growth-rate was expected in their sector. In the same survey 24 per cent of industrialists declared that the plan targets had had con-siderable influence on their investment decisions, 37 per cent little influence, 39 per cent none at all. The answers varied very much accord-ing to the size of the firms; the smaller firms (less than 100 employees) attaching little importance to the plan (8 per cent great influence, 28 per cent little influence, 64 per cent none at all) and the bigger firms (more than 5,000 employees) attaching great importance to the targets (51 per cent great influence, 42 per cent little influence, 7 per cent none at all).* The French plan could then be said to create a general 'climate

*A similar enquiry by NIESR in 1963 about the NEDC plan showed that 17 per cent of British firms reported that they had been somehow influenced by the target of 4 per cent, 9 per cent adding that they had taken it into account when preparing their own investment and production programmes. That was a modest beginning, but given the inertia in such fields not at all negligible.

of expansion' that had a real impact on the behaviour of industry. This impact was still bigger in practice owing to the multiplier effect that the decisions of bigger firms had on medium and small businesses. Yet it played only a small part in the detailed allocation of resources which was still accomplished through the market, because planning was done by industrial sectors, not by firms, however big they were. As for public investment (about half of gross fixed capital formation is controlled by public authorities, if one includes public building aid) the influence of planning was not negligible, especially during the first two plans. From then on public firms and local authorities have known that if they wanted a good chance of getting a new venture started they had to have it 'written in the plan'. In the event, the real influence of the planners was revealed by the way they rescued their essential investment programmes at a time when the government wanted to make cuts in public spending, in 1959 and 1963 for instance. Most public infrastructure targets in the Fifth and Sixth plans were not quite achieved, the government insisting at least until 1974 on having a balanced budget (this was M. Giscard d'Estaing's golden rule, when Minister of Finance); but obviously the cuts would have been easier to make if the plan had not been there to point—for all to see and especially the political opposition—to what had been considered from the start, as the minimum needs.

The trouble with France is that this virtuous circle seems to be at an end; the Sixth Plan came dramatically short of its growth-target when, in 1975, the first regression in output since the war happened in the non-agricultural sector (0.3 per cent of GDP). This bad result was of course due to the world economic crisis (which the planners had not foreseen) but it was made worse by Finance Minister Fourcade's deflationary package of June 1974 which came too late (after the Spring presidential election) and proved too restrictive (on account of the deflationary effect on Western economies of the quadrupling of oil prices). After the Fourcade deflation came the Fourcade reflation (September 1975) which achieved a modest recovery in output and cut unemployment by a small amount, yet unleashed inflation again and by combining with the Summer 1976 drought generated an increased balance of payments deficit. Then there was the Barre 'plan' of September 1976 which had nothing to do with planning proper and was in fact a series of budgetary and monetary measures combined with a three months' price-freeze and tentative incomes policy. One cannot help feeling therefore that the French Ministry of Finance has adopted methods of crisis management that are very similar to those of the British Treasury in so far as 'the urgent' will have 'triumphed over the important'.[33] These methods brought to France the stop-go cycle that has affected Britain for so long. This explains why the Seventh Plan has inspired many cynical comments. For one thing, the chosen growth-target (between 5.5 per cent and 5 per cent of GDP per annum) did not look too realistic, not so much when compared to past trends but in relation to the new economic environment. Many observers felt that it had been chosen for the highly political reason that the government could not countenance the unemployment projections provided half-way through the preparations of the plan by the Employment Committee. On top of that, the Barre measures, more concerned with fighting inflation and achieving a more balanced development 'by preparing the foundation for sounder growth' inevitably meant that a brake would be put on private consumption and thus on domestic output. Thus official forecasts published for the Spring meeting (June 1977) of the *Commission des Comptes de la Nation* showed that much catching up would be necessary in the last years of the plan if the overall growth-target was to be achieved, yet this was unlikely to occur. Should we derive from this analysis that the Seventh Plan is 'a castle in the air' like the British National Plan of the sixties? We should not go as far as that, if only because of the twenty-five 'priority action programmes' which constitute the hard core of the plan to which the government is committed 'whatever happens'. Nevertheless one cannot avoid the impression that, contrary to what was the common assumption in the sixties—that planning made growth possible—the reverse—that after all it was growth that made planning possible—might be more true.[34] Perhaps this evolution was inevitable in our economies that are still dominated, however partially, by the market mechanism.

In an important study published as a supplement to its monthly magazine *Patronat Français*[35] in 1968, at the time of the preparation of the Seventh Plan, the CNPF emphasised the drawbacks of the French system of planning, as it saw them through the experience of the Fourth and Fifth plans. They could be summed up under four main headings. Firstly, many of the plan's methods, most of them twenty years old, were better adapted to an economy of scarcity than to the present conditions of growth among which competitiveness was the key formula. In other words, it was more important to sell more than to produce more. One form of competitiveness particularly seemed to be overlooked in the plans: international competitiveness. Secondly, the apparatus of the plan had become very cumbersome; despite the amount of work that went into their reports, the output of the commissions was often questionable and some of the commissions could easily be dispensed with. Thirdly, there is a distortion between the aims of the plans and actual economic policy. Of course, Massé had said: 'the plan expresses not only what is possible but also what should be done', yet, if both aspects are too far apart and if the means to achieve the aims are not put forward in full detail, the plan can hardly be taken seriously. What the *Patronat* had precisely in mind here was the fact that most French plans (and especially the Fifth Plan) aimed at reducing the share of private consumption for the benefit of fixed capital formation and never achieved it, because of the political difficulty of introducing a restrictive incomes policy. Fourthly, the 'myth' of the plan, i.e. the conviction in most quarters that the plan achieved a lot, was a cause of rigidity. By reducing the uncertainty of economic life, it had blunted many industrialists' sense of enterprise and in many ways perpetuated attitudes inherited from the time of protectionism. Consequently, the CNPF recommended not the demise of the plan but its adaptation.

Two main issues emerged; the second duly paid the usual lip-service to the plan as a consensus-building instrument for the information and education of men. The first point was essential. It went a long way to describe the ideal plan as imagined by the employers. It agreed that the government should provide the nation from time to time with a full-scale report on its economic strategy; accordingly this planning exercise (which the CNPF would prefer to call 'overall programming') should include all public activities and its contents should be defined in relation to the needs of the market economy and yet be considered by all public servants as guiding their actions. Above all the plan should not go into detailed forecasts as far as individual private firms were concerned and be content with a market survey of the main sectors: farming, energy, engineering, building, transport for instance. However, 'growth being dependent on private enterprise initiative, on the risks run that cannot be planned and that planning cannot forecast', it is important that 'firms and employers' associations should be encouraged to develop their own forecasting services which, owing to a better adaptation to their needs, will be both more useful and more necessary to them.'[36] In other words, what the CNPF was demanding was a complete reversal of priorities inside the mixed economy; not only should planning not interfere with the market while becoming more compelling for the public sector; it should also provide a congenial environment for private enterprise. Of course, that was what the *Patronat* had always felt. What was new at the time of the Sixth Plan was the way in which that feeling had become the orthodoxy in many quarters. It partly explains why the

Sixth Plan and still more the Seventh Plan remained so vague as to what was expected of the private sector, while emphasising the need to reduce the squeeze on profits; why they insisted so much on the government commitments as far as public expenditure was concerned and also on the evaluation of the international environment, especially the average growth-rate of the GDPs of France's main trade partners.

Planning in France has, then, been affected by two developments: one that the planners tried hard to achieve, the emergence of an open economy affected by international competition; the other that the planners could not foresee, the fact that steady growth can no longer be taken for granted, although it is partially the consequence of the first development. Thus the national plan has been more or less replaced by a government plan that receives full publicity and appears to some observers as a smoke-screen for semi-confidential corporate planning with an outward-looking strategy.

In conclusion, three questions come to mind. Will the British economy not become more capable of a fast and regular growth when it gets the full benefit of North Sea oil, making macro-economic planning easier through an improved government control of the sources of energy? Conversely, has not the French economy, since the early seventies, entered a circle of stop-go that will be aggravated by its lack of energy at home and will eventually destroy its much admired dynamism? Finally, can national planning survive in countries which are part of an open economic system affected by floating exchange rates and multinational companies and dominated by the US economy which remains the most powerful but also the most unplanned of all?

Appendix I: Essential Land-marks in Comparative Planning, 1945-76

FRANCE	*BRITAIN*
1946 — Creation of the *Conseil Economique et Social* (CES). — Birth of the *Commissariat Général au Plan* (CGP) and the first *commissions de modernisation*.	Sir Stafford Cripps, President 1946 of the Board of Trade, sets up working parties to prepare the reorganisation of industry.
1947 — *First plan of modernisation and equipment* (1947-53) also called 'Monnet Plan'.	Industrial Organisation and 1947 Development Act. Town and Country Planning Act. — First *Economic Survey* published.

FRANCE	BRITAIN	
1948 — Birth of OEEC. First Plan updated to take Marshall aid into account	— The *Long-Term Programme* published with Marshall aid in view.	1948
1954 — *Second plan* (1954-7).		
1955 — Creation of FDES (*Fonds de Développement Economique et Social*).		
	— Appointment of the Council on Prices, Productivity and Incomes by Harold Macmillan.	1957
1958 — *Third plan* (1958-61).		
1961 — Creation of regional prefects and interdepartmental regional conferences.	— Treasury reorganised following the *Plowden report*.	1961
1962 — *Fourth plan* (1962-5).	— Creation of NEDC and NEDO in January.	1962
1963 — Stabilisation plan.	— The NEDC 'plan': *Growth of the UK Economy to 1966.*	1963
1964 — Birth of DATAR (*Delegation à l'Aménagement du Territoire*) separate from the CGP. — Birth of CODER (*Commissions de Développement Economique Régional*).	— First 'little Neddies' set up by NEDO. — Industrial Training Act. — Creation of the DEA and of Mintech (Ministry of Technology). — Joint Statement of Intent on Productivity, Prices and Incomes signed at the DEA. — Creation of ten economic regions.	1964
	— Creation of REPBs (Regional Economic Planning Boards) & REPCs (Regional Economic Planning Councils). — National Board for Prices and Incomes created. — National Plan published in September.	1965
1966 — *Fifth Plan* (1966-70).	— Enactment of a statutory prices and incomes policy (1966-70). — Creation of the IRC (Industrial Reorganisation Corp.).	1966

FRANCE	BRITAIN	
	— Industrial Expansion Act.	1968
1969 — Creation of a Ministry for Industrial and Scientific Development. — Creation of IDI (*Institut de Développement Industriel*).	— Publication of *The Task Ahead*. — Abolition of the DEA. Medium-term planning transferred to the Treasury.	1969
1970 — *Sixth Plan* (1971-5).	— Creation of DTI (Department of Trade and Industry), DOE (Department of Environment) and CPRS (Central Policy Review Staff or 'think-tank').	1970
	— Abolition of IRC and NBPI. — Industrial Relations Act.	1971
1972 — Regional Reform Act. Setting up in each region of a political body, the Regional Council, and of an Economic and Social Committee.	— Creation of a National Industrial Relations Court. — New statutory prices and incomes policy (1972-4) — Industry Act. Creation of a Ministry for Industrial Development and an Industrial Development Executive assisted by Regional Industrial Development Boards.	1972
	— Creation of Employment Services Agency and Training Services Agency. — Creation of Ministry for Consumer Affairs and Office of Fair Trading.	1973
1974 — Creation of a Central Planning Council chaired by the President of the Republic.	— Abolition of Pay Board, NIRC and Industrial Relations Act. — Creation of DOI (Department of Industry) and DOT (Department of Trade). — Voluntary incomes policy (social contract).	1974
1975-1976 — Preparation of the *Seventh Plan* (1976-80).	— Creation of the NEB (National Enterprise Board).	1975
1976 — Creation of a Ministry for Consumer Affairs. — Publication of the *Seventh Plan*.	— New industrial strategy discussed.	1976

Notes

1. A. Shonfield, *British Economic Policy since the War* (London, 1958), p. 163.
2. S. Hoffmann *et al.*, *France: Change and Tradition* (London, 1963).
3. J.M. Jeanneney, *Forces et faiblesses de l'économie française* (Paris, 1956).
4. His book *Le Plan ou l'Anti-Hasard* published in 1965 was a collection of essays mostly written in the early sixties.
5. See J. Hayward in J. Hayward & M. Watson (eds.), *Planning, Politics and Public Policy. The British, French and Italian Experience* (London, 1975), Table I, p. 10. This very useful book, the only really comparative work in the field, will be quoted several times in the course of this chapter. For other comparative data about France, Britain and the EEC, see J. Leruez, *Economic Planning and Politics in Britain* (London, 1975), Tables 12.1, p. 196 and 13.1 (a) and (b), p. 204.
6. For recent investigations see NEDO *Discussion Paper No. 3,* January 1976. Also A. Whiting 'Is Britain's poor growth performance due to government stop-go induced fluctuations?', *The Three Banks Review,* no. 109, March 1976, pp. 26-46.
7. The FBI became the CBI (Confederation of British Industry) in 1965 by merging with two smaller bodies, the British Employers Confederation and the National Association of British Manufacturers.
8. FBI, *The Next Five Years, Report of the Brighton Conference* (1960).
9. F. Bloch-Laîné, *A la recherche d'une économie concertée* (Paris, 1961), pp. 5-6.
10. A book suggesting an alternative plan was actually published in 1965 by a group of left-wing politicians, unionists and economists (Julien Ensemble, *Le Contreplan,* Paris, 1965) but it was not quite what the PSU had suggested.
11. D. Liggins in 'What can we learn from French planning?', *Lloyds Bank Review,* April 1976, no. 120, pp. 1-12.
12. Ibid. pp. 4-5.
13. 'Economic Planning in France', *Planning* 454 (14 August 1961), pp. 219-20. For a more detailed analysis of the way French planning was introduced to the British, see the above report and also Leruez, op.cit. pp. 87-9.
14. Hayward & Watson (eds.), op.cit.; see the chapter in Part I on France by Y. Ullmo, p. 47.
15. 'The Function of the NEDC', *Political Quarterly* 34 (4), 1963, pp. 354-65.
16. See J.E.S. Hayward, *Private Interests and Public Policy. The experience of the French Economic and Social Council* (London, 1966).
17. A. Shonfield, *Modern Capitalism* (London, 1965), p. 152.
18. See *The Financial Times,* 11 December 1975.
19. Hayward & Watson (eds.), op.cit. See the comments on France by Y. Ullmo, p. 47.
20. The terms of reference when the committees were first established were the following: 'each committee will: 1. examine the economic performance and plans of the industry and assess from time to time the industry's progress in relation to the national growth objectives, and provide information and forecasts to the Council on these matters; 2. consider ways of improving the industry's economic performance, competitive power and efficiency and formulate reports and recommendations of these matters as appropriate.' (NEDO, *Activity Report,* HMSO, 1964).
21. D.F. Berry, L. Metcalfe & W. McQuillan, 'Neddy. An organisational metamorphosis', *The Journal of Management Studies,* vol. II, no. 1, February 1974, p. 4.
22. Ibid. p. 15.
23. See ibid. table III, p. 17 and table IV, p. 18.
24. Ibid. p. 18.
25. Hayward & Watson (eds.), op.cit. Introduction, p. 1.
26. Ibid. p. 2.
27. See ch. 4 below. The same endeavours have taken place in France. The main

difference—and it is substantial—is that they are generally integrated in the plan.

28. *The Task Ahead*, p. 1.

29. *Economic Prospects to 1972. A revised document.*

30. *Industrial Review to 1977*, October 1973.

31. In each case, it was headed by Sir Donald MacDougall, first as economic director of NEDO, then as director-general and head of the economic planning division at the DEA.

32. J.J. Carré, P. Dubois, E. Malinvaud, *Abrégé de la croissance française. Un essai d'analyse économique causale de l'après-guerre* (Paris, 1973), p. 269. (Shortened from *La Croissance française*, Paris, 1972).

33. Quoted from Roger Opie in 'Planning in the United Kingdom' in M. Faber and D. Seers (eds.), *The Crisis of Planning*, vol. 2, pp. 208-16.

34. For a full evaluation of the Seventh Plan see *Economie et Humanisme* (October 1976), pp. 2-73: 'Planification française et rédeploiement industriel'.

35. Supplement to no. 280 *Patronat Français*, January 1968. 'De la forme et des méthodes d'un plan national dans un système d'économie de marché', p. 24.

36. Ibid. p. 19.

2 THE BUDGET AND THE PLAN IN FRANCE

Jean Carassus

The French experience in planning a market economy is well known for its originality. How has it evolved over the last few years, at a time when the international and national context was particularly unfavourable to the planned development of an economy? One can throw some light on this question by relating the recent evolution of national planning to the modernisation of the regular instruments of economic activity used by the state, known as the 'rationalisation of budget options' (RBO).

I propose to deal with this question in four stages. Firstly, reference to the events of the late sixties will allow us to describe certain optimistic schemes aimed at integrating the planning process with the management of French administration. This was the period, both in the United States and in many European states, at which operations of the 'planning-programming-budgeting system' (PPBS) type were launched and applied. Secondly, an examination of the practical application of RBO in France will demonstrate what the results of this action were in fact. Thirdly, the application of the Sixth Plan (1971-5) and the preparation of the Seventh Plan (1976-80) provide evidence of considerable modifications in the process of French national planning. Fourthly, by establishing a connection between the Plan and RBO processes we shall be in a position to formulate some hypotheses about the recent evolution of planning and of the conduct of state activity.

A Late Sixties Vision

By the end of the sixties, French planners had acquired more than twenty years' experience. Since the period of *dirigisme* in the First Plan (1947-53), national planning had undergone considerable change. 'Generalised market research' during the Fifth Plan (1966-70) produced a general framework for state economic policy on the basis of detailed, exhaustive and consistent forecasts of production and consumption in each branch of the economy. The procedures of 'concertation' were developed, the methodology used was gradually perfected: sectoral programming frameworks, prospective economic budgets, national accounting; all these produced an independent development of national planning under the direction of the Planning Commissariat, but without any formal links with the work of the ministries, particularly in the

53

budgetary field.

While this progress was achieved in the field of planning, the programming and management of the ministries had developed very little since 1945. The Costs and Output Committee, established in 1946, still existed but its real impact was limited. The 'functional budget' used since 1959 was only a new presentation of the budget after the event. 'Organisation and methods', started in the same year, was confined to the improvement of practical aspects of administrative work. It seemed essential to challenge in a much more radical way methods of choosing between policies, budgetary procedures and the administration of the ministries. After a trial period at the Ministry of Defence, RBO was introduced in certain other ministries (such as the Ministry of Finance, Public Works and Housing [*Equipement*]). It was generally adopted in 1970, at the beginning of the Sixth Plan, with the setting up of the RBO Interdepartmental Committee, composed of the representatives of all the ministries, some private interests and academics, responsible to the Minister of Finance. The main problem was that of the productivity of the French economy, in the context of international competition. Now that the role of the state had become directly involved in the economic processes, with productivity at their centre, it was impossible to evade its duties. The state could no longer be satisfied with an indicative National Plan, establishing medium-term objectives; it became in part an economic apparatus whose day-to-day intervention determined the very economic process itself. Another reason for this was the growth of public needs; it was necessary to make a choice between increasingly indispensable infrastructures, in order to be able to respond to the socialisation of life-styles. The major options in this matter were defined by the Plan; the choice between particular infrastructures was not established within its framework.

RBO sought to respond to these two problems in so far as it

carried out research methodically; applied it to public action and used all the available techniques of analysis and accounting, of forecasting, of organisation and management, aiming at a coherent and orderly definition, before putting such policy into effective and precise operation.[1]

We shall consider later what is meant by this rather abstract and generalised definition.

The RBO system originated in particular with the 'planning-programming-budgeting system' applied from 1961 by McNamara at the US

Department of Defence, which was in 1965 applied generally to the whole federal administration by President Johnson.[2] Its origin was, in fact, more micro-economic than macro-economic. The changes in the programming and management of the large American private enterprises have had a great influence on these new methods. RBO should achieve great progress in the management of the budget; it uses the newest methods of computation and management and makes good by this the backwardness of the techniques of economic policy compared with those of planning.

One must now ask if there is any connection between planning and RBO. Are not these two approaches radically different? Initially, optimism was general. Bernard Cazes saw these two processes as mutually cross-fertilising.[3] The detail and the precision of the overall policies of the Plan were to guide the short- and medium-term RBO programmes of each ministry. Likewise, the political debate every five years, at the time of working out the Plan, ought to put the annual budget debates on the RBO framework in better perspective. Conversely, revising policies in order to adapt them to circumstances ought to influence the Plan, which would only be revised in exceptional circumstances. The classification by objectives of all the results of the work carried out by RBO would complete the programming of the infrastructure guidelines of the Five-year Plan.

At that time, a prominent official of the Planning Commissariat considered that the introduction of RBO methods had a very positive influence.[4] He thought they would make the Plan more flexible and bring it closer to the problems of current economic policy. They also ought to help secure the decentralisation of responsibility 'in order to allow a more sensitive adaptability of micro-decisions, within the framework of the objectives set out at the national level.' Even more ambitious, it was hoped that the shared views held at the Planning Commissariat and the Ministry of Finance (responsible for carrying out RBO) would 'gradually produce a structure of objectives applicable to the whole of economic and social development'. Additionally, the 'structure of objectives' ought to provide a connection in various areas between national planning and the day-to-day work of the ministries. This would happen at three levels: (a) the 'goals' of the state's activity; (b) the 'efficiency' of public services; (c) the 'basic functioning' of those services.

Thus the idea of a system of planning and administration, in which every action of the state would be integrated, was defined. In order to analyse how these schemes were put into practice, it is necessary to describe briefly the French experience of the seventies, in so far as it concerns the operation of RBO, as well as the more recent developments of the Sixth and the Seventh Plan.

Rationalisation of Budget Options in Practice

The RBO scheme was very ambitious from the outset: it aspired to give a new interpretation to the very role of the state; to introduce, on a large scale, methods of economic computation to guide ministerial decisions; to modify the system of programming and working of the administration by using the experience of the private sector. From 1970 onwards, this experience was defined as a transformation of the administration along three lines:

(1) the preparation of investigative studies of options, using economic computation and cost-benefit analysis;
(2) the transformation of the traditional budget into a 'programmed budget' with a multi-annual forward look and reclassification of public services according to the objectives they had to attain;
(3) the introduction of modern methods of management (management by objectives and monitoring of performance) particularly into the field services of the ministries.

Together, these three changes should lead to an integrated system of decision-making/programming/administration of all public activity. Let us now see what we can say about the nature and development since 1970 of each of the three dimensions of RBO.

Since the beginning of its operation, the definition of an RBO study was very fluid. At the start, the Ministry of Finance made very simple recommendations: an RBO study should be linked with the budgetary cycle in order to elucidate financial options; it should be rigorous in evaluating the costs and benefits of policies; it should not be used as a pretext to support demands for exceptionally large funds; and it ought to outline the ways of pursuing a new policy within the sectors studied.[5] In fact, these recommendations were seldom followed; the 1975 summing up of six years' work acknowledged that some of them had helped in decision-making and that a number had used techniques which were little known before the RBO operation.[6] These included a cost-benefit approach, which took into account not only the measurable costs and receipts but also the non-commercial effects of policies; economic accounting on the basis of updated budgets and multi-criteria analyses, weighting various criteria in assessing policies. However, the Ministry of Finance recognised that out of the first seventy RBO studies carried out,

the majority enquired into marginal subjects, and the great majority
were not used to guide decision-making.

In 1975 it was decided to recast the guidelines of RBO operations, by
starting a dozen priority studies. An RBO study was not to be determined as much by its administrative location as by the type of methods
used. One person would be appointed by a ministerial or, if necessary,
an interministerial committee, to take responsibility for the formation
of an *ad hoc* working group, and to remain in permanent contact with
the ministry or ministries concerned. Such a study, supervised by the
Ministry of Finance, should not take longer than a year and it ought to
result in realistic improvements of budgetary decision-making and the
information system. It was hoped to obtain short-term studies, essentially
of an economic or financial character, centred on the most urgent
problems of the government's economic policy, dealt with by highly-
placed officials, with direct access to the ministers. A January 1977
assessment enables us to make a rather severe preliminary assessment
of this operation. In 1975 and 1976, thirteen studies were undertaken
on the most essential subjects: the future of the motorcar, the improvement of old housing, immigration policy and so on. Their fault lay in in-
sufficiently practical conclusions, in the non-interministerial character
of the studies, in not using RBO techniques.

The second line of attack by the RBO operation was the transformation of the normal budget (which was presented essentially in terms of
the state's resources) into a 'programmed budget', which would rearrange
the resources of different branches of the state according to its objectives,
in the light of multi-annual forecasts. Four features characterise the
'programmed budget': the presentation of all the activities of a ministry
in terms of a programme (with objectives to be attained, financial
resources, allocated personnel, expected results); the inclusion of these
programmes into the budgetary classification; the discussion of the
budget in programme terms; and the use of indicators allowing one to
measure costs and results of the programmes.

The assessment produced by the Ministry of Finance in 1975 was as
follows: eight ministries had worked out a structure of programmes; four
had included it in the budgetary classification; but only two had attempted a discussion in terms of a programme. As to the indicators which
existed in practice, they were more discursive and statistical, than in the
form of an assessment of the results and costs.[7] We have not yet had
sufficient experience but a methodological framework has been drawn
up, which, in particular, associates the notion of a 'programme' with
the definition and objectives of a specific policy and with budgetary

resources, and which is followed henceforth with a specific aim, which varies according to the sectoral intervention of the state concerned. At any rate, the experiment of 'programmed budgets' was continued, with the whole 1978 budget being presented in programme terms.

Furthermore, the government has thought it necessary to reinforce the role of such budgets by using them in three fields: the re-evaluation of the ministries' expenditure, normally conducted from year to year ('revision of approved services'); the presentation of the budget to Parliament in programme terms; and fixing the government priorities as from the 1979 budget—something which goes beyond the normal role of the budget.[8]

We can only touch briefly on the third aspect of the RBO operation, the modernisation of the functioning of the ministries, because of the differences between their practical problems and those of national planning. This modernisation has several aspects: it concerns simultaneously personnel management (the system of 'management by objectives'); control of management, based on accounting data (introduction of analytical accountability); the extra-accountable matters (indexing and so on), which are often computerised. This last concern, having been given priority in certain ministries (Ministry of Public Works and Housing, and Ministry of Postal and Telecommunication Services), nowadays appears to be secondary, compared with the first two. One must also point out the importance of creating or of improving the system of communications, particularly in the field of accounting, as part of the modernisation of management methods.

An assessment of RBO in practice shows that the results fall far short of the initial objectives. There is no integrated system of studies/budget/control in the French administration. This having been said, it must be admitted that there has been some partial progress; particularly improvements in the link between studies and the process of decision-making, and in the case of programmes which were actually put into practice. Meanwhile, how was national planning proceeding?

The Sixth Plan and the Preparation of the Seventh Plan

From 1968 onwards the dominant theme of 'growth policy' was replaced by that of 'industrialisation', which became the central objective of the Sixth Plan. While according to the Fifth Plan industrial policy was no more than a part of economic policy, with some specific means of action, in the Sixth Plan it became the mainstay of the state's economic policy.

Special priorities were established favouring certain specific sectors, particularly with regard to their competitiveness in the international markets ('protected' sectors and 'exposed' sectors). Simultaneously, the growth of public needs in terms of infrastructures, amenities and so on, led to the definition of 'collective functions'. Five-year programming dealt with investment credits, grouped under headings, each corresponding to a 'collective function' (such as transport), and the state undertook to cover some 60 per cent of the investment credits of the Sixth Plan.

As far as methodology went, the principal innovation of the Sixth Plan was the elaboration and utilisation of a macro-economic physical-financial model (model FIFI). This allowed the projection of national accounting up to the final year of the Plan.[9]

As Figure 2.1 shows, the Plan's structure had five main inter-related components: (1) supply (national production and imports); (2) nominal rates of pay (depending on the level of unemployment and prices); (3) prices and incomes; (4) investment capacity, bearing in mind the amount of self-financing available; (5) demand (home and export).

Figure 2.1: Structure of the Sixth Plan

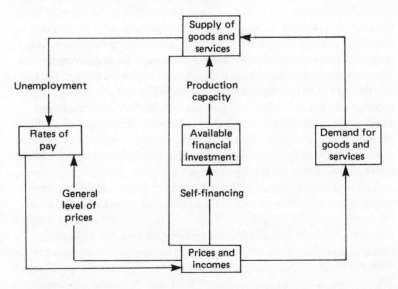

The model took the international environment into account, singling out the 'protected' sectors, where the balance between supply and demand is secured by price:

```
┌──────────┐              ┌──────────────┐              ┌────────┐
│  Demand  ├─────────────▶│  Production  ├─────────────▶│ Prices │
└──────────┘              └──────────────┘              └────────┘
     ▲                                                       │
     └───────────────────────────────────────────────────────┘
```

as against the 'exposed' sectors, where prices are imposed by foreign
competition:

This model can be used in three possible ways:

(a) to prepare simulated projections of the economy;
(b) to study economic policy variants;
(c) to synthesise the work of the various commissions.

Among other innovations of the Sixth Plan, apart from beginning to
regionalise the national plan, the 'examination at half-course' would
allow the revision of objectives, according to circumstances. As a matter
of fact, the recession of 1974-5, not envisaged even partially by the planners, severely undermined the realisation of the Sixth Plan.

Another experiment was the working out of 'finalised programmes'
defining objectives to be attained in certain sectors, with corresponding
financial means (capital and current expenditure separately) and attainment indicators, and of an official responsible for each programme.
This was one of the main links between the Plan and RBO but there were
no real links between programmes and the RBO sectoral studies except
in two sectors: road safety and prenatal policy.[10] In any case, these
finalised programmes were only concerned with relatively marginal
subjects and with very small amounts of money. In fact, the preparation
and implementation of the Sixth Plan and the launching of the RBO
operation were two separate processes.

The severe recession of 1975 had a powerful influence upon the
preparation of the Seventh Plan. Despite the circumstances, the Plan
forecast a sustained growth (5.5-6 per cent per annum for gross national
product, 7.2 per cent for industrial growth), attempting to limit the
rate of unemployment and inflation, which remained the main problems.
With the Seventh Plan, the process of French planning underwent significant modifications, as much from the point of view of its preparation,
and the bodies concerned in it, as in its presentation and the methodology used. The creation, at the end of 1974, of a Central Planning
Council showed simultaneously the importance of a sectoral emphasis
and the wish to link planning with the short-term economic policy. The

Council consisted of the President of the Republic, the Prime Minister, the Minister of Finance, the Minister of Labour and the General Commissioner of the Plan. It met once a month to define the orientation and resources to be made available to the various sectors (energy, agriculture, housing). This body had very extensive powers, and sought to ensure the consistency and the eventual reorientation of the Seventh Plan. A less important role was given to the commissions, whose number was cut down drastically. On the other hand, the Ministries took a much greater part in planning, either through the work of the Central Council or through administrative groups in the preparation of the Plan. Regional bodies were consulted in order to find out their preferences concerning the programming of public infrastructures.

The final version of the Plan contained a first report, devoted to strategy and giving only general directions, aimed at guiding budgetary options from 1976 to 1980. The five-year budgetary headings covering 'collective functions' in the Sixth Plan were eliminated. A second report outlined twenty-five priorities programmes (PAP), to be financed by the state, costing 200 milliards of 1975 francs over five years (this being 12 per cent of the 1975 budget multiplied by five). More precisely, these funds covered 21 per cent of investment credits and about 4 per cent of current credits.[11]

Each programme was made the responsibility of one minister, fixing precise objectives, necessary resources, expected results and the indicators by which to measure the results. The cost of each programme varied between 0.5 milliards and 12 milliards of 1975 francs, apart from education (21 milliards), and the improvement of the telephone system (94 milliards, which was more than 45 per cent of the whole). Apart from these national programmes, 170 regional programmes of lesser importance were actually proposed (100 milliards of 1975 francs in all with the state supplying 20 milliards).

The FIFI model, despite some revisions,[12] was used less for the Seventh Plan than for the Sixth Plan. It was used more in the preparation of the simulated projections of the economy for 1980, and for the study of variants within overall economic policies, than as a framework for synthesising the work of the commissions.

Despite a certain revival of RBO at the beginning of 1975, there was no genuine co-ordination between it and the preparation of the Seventh Plan. The RBO priority studies, for example, did not correspond to the programmed priorities of the Plan, and these themselves were not integrated in the programmed budgets of the ministries. There was no direct link whatsoever.

Some Precepts

Nevertheless, relating changes made in the Seventh Plan (already anticipated in the Sixth Plan) with the partial revival of RBO allows one to
advance hypotheses about new forms of planning and administration of
state action in France. We are still far from an integrated plan and budget, such as was envisaged by certain officials of the Planning Commissariat at the end of the sixties. In fact, there is no formal link between
the Plan and RBO. There is no intermediate formula, like the one which
appears to exist in the British system with the Public Expenditure Survey
Committee (PESC), which supervises the multi-annual programming of
public spending.

All the same, one can offer two conclusions: on the one hand, RBO,
even though it had not fulfilled the early hopes, did produce a series of
partial experiments which can serve as examples; on the other, the
process of planning has undergone remarkable modifications during the
Sixth and the Seventh Plans (see Figure 2.2). It is possible to formulate
a hypothesis, according to which there is a closer link than would appear
at first sight between planning and RBO: a new conception of planning
has developed, by taking up in an implicit fashion certain RBO principles.

It may even be possible to pursue this paradox further and to state
that it is because of the difficulties encountered by RBO—even though
smaller than those of the American PPBS[13]—that the Plan, in some
respects, has been more influenced by RBO than the budget. Let us
now examine briefly these closer links from the point of view of the
conception and functioning of the Plan, of the role of institutions, and
of the methodology used.

From the point of view of its conception, the comprehensive character of the Plan appears only in the form of general indications and not
as a relatively precise framework. The practical aspect of the Plan is to
be found primarily in the priority programmes (PAP) for which the
state assumes responsibility. Now those priority programmes (according to the Seventh Plan experiment with 'finalised programmes') adopt
the principles of the RBO programmes: the sectoral or intersectoral
field; the definition of objectives; the inclusion of all necessary resources,
divided into investment and non-investment credits; a clearly designated
official responsible for the programme; the definition of indicators
measuring the results. The obvious multi-annual character of the programmes also involves one of the principles of RBO, even though this
has been hardly applied in practice.

From the viewpoint of the working of the Plan, its 'rolling' character
is established: in collaboration with the Planning Commissariat each

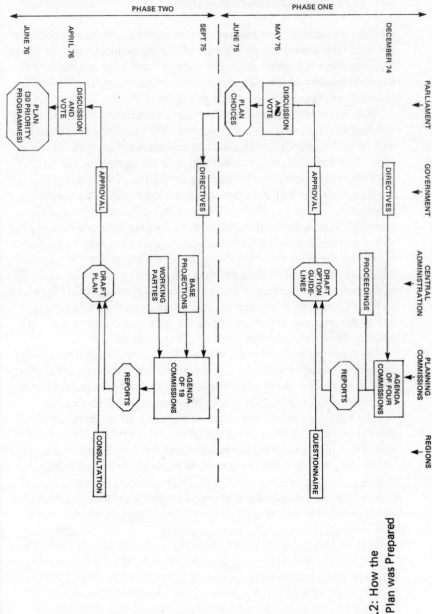

Figure 2.2: How the
Seventh Plan was Prepared

minister responsible for a programme can undertake corrective action at
the time each annual budget is prepared. At the national level, the Central
Planning Council makes certain that there is continuity and carries out
any re-evaluation of the Plan that may prove necessary. This 'rolling'
character of planning is one of the principles of RBO.

Does this mean that the closer linking of conception and functioning
will lead to a fusion of the two processes? The Planning Commissariat
wishes, for instance, to bring about an integration of separate elements
of the PAP into the programme budgets of the ministries. For its part,
the Ministry of Finance underlines the difficulties of such integration. In
the first place, the PAP are often interministerial, unlike the budget
programmes. Secondly, they only bear upon one partial aspect of the
ministry's action, unlike the structures of the programmes which overlap
all the actions of each department. Thirdly, they have only a provisional
character (the duration of the Plan), unlike the budgetary programmes
which are permanent.[14] This problem was studied particularly carefully
in the case of the Ministry of Public Works and Housing. There appeared
to be a contradiction between the PAP based upon the administrative
will of the ministry, concentrating all the necessary resources for implementing an operation in the hands of a single official.

From the institutional point of view, RBO is essentially a movement
centred on the administration and the ministries. The Seventh Plan also
reinforces the role of the administration, both during its preparation and
its implementation (the role of administrative working parties, the
Central Planning Council bringing together the main ministries, each
priority programme being the responsibility of a minister, financing discussed as a function of the priorities of each ministry). This concentration on the administration tends to limit the impact of its reforms, as the
state apparatus is unitary, admittedly heterogeneous, but composed of
inter-related elements (central government, Parliament, local authorities,
public bodies). It is difficult to improve one element, without taking
into account its relationship with the others.[15]

From the standpoint of the techniques used, it is impossible to talk
of closer links. Some economic computation which is at the centre of
RBO work has already been employed by the Plan (since the Fifth Plan,
as in the case of road investments). All the same, there seems to be a
contradiction between the essentially macro-economic approach of
planning and a micro-economic conception of RBO. But one can conclude in both cases that the use of certain techniques has diminished
(this is true both of the FIFI model which was used less frequently in
the Seventh than in the Sixth Plan, and in the cases of cost-benefit

analysis, multi-criteria analysis, and so on—all of which are very little used by RBO).

The implicitly closer linking of planning and RBO is not surprising. A centralised five-year plan, inflexible and applied without collaboration with the administration, cannot be effective. Coming together can bring about genuine improvements. But is this not a retreat from planning? Could one go so far as to speak of 'unplanning'? In effect, the global, macro-economic character of the Plan seems to have disappeared. The five-year perspective with a 'rolling' plan is less constraining than formerly. Does not the management of the Plan by the ministries mean a fusion of the medium-term Plan and short-term economic policy, to the detriment of the former? Is this tendency inevitable, seen in the new context of national and international market economies? Is planning itself still possible? Should one not be satisfied, at best, with a multi-annual programming of public expenditure without a medium-term perspective?

I think it would be more correct to talk of new forms of planning, less formalised and using fewer of the usual techniques to clarify options than formerly, rather than of 'unplanning'. Despite the fact that the uncertainties of economic prediction have increased, comprehensive management of the economy according to a Plan is as indispensable as diversified functioning of the RBO type. Both types of management of the economy co-exist, and will continue to co-exist, even if the forms may vary considerably. There is not so much a risk of 'unplanning' as of using rational methods less often, for both planning and the rationalisation of options, and of favouring decision-making without much scientific investigation. Difficult economic circumstances should rather provide the stimulus to develop and improve rational methods of planning and administration of state activity.

Notes

1. P. Huet and J. Bravo, *L'expérience française de RCB* (Paris, 1973), p. 55.
2. In the United Kingdom similar experiments were attempted at the same time: analyses of costs and outputs, output budget and later the PAR system (programme analysis review). See Hugo Heclo and Aaron Wildavsky, *The Private Government of Public Money* (Berkeley, University of California Press, 1974), ch. 6.
3. B. Cazès, 'Les rapports entre RCB et planification nationale', *Analyse et Prévision*, July-August 1970.
4. M. Rousselot, 'La RCB et le Plan', *Objectif, Revue RCB du Ministère de l'Equipement*, October 1969.
5. Cf. statement by M. Taittinger, Secretary of State for the Budget, *Commission Interministérielle de RCB*, 19 January 1971.
6. Cf. statement by M. Cortesse, Director of Forecasting at the Ministry of Finance, *Commission Interministérielle de RCB*, 31 January 1975.
7. Cf. statement by M. Deroche, Director of Budget at the Ministry of Finance,

Commission Interministérielle de RCB, 31 January 1975.

8. Cf. statement by M. Durafour, Minister of the Economy and of Finance, *Commission RCB,* 27 January 1977.

9. Cf. Aglietta-Courbis, 'Un outil du Plan: le modèle FIFI', *Economie et Statistiques,* no. 1, May 1969.

10. Statements at the *Commission Interministerielle de RCB,* 18-19 January 1971.

11. J. Bravo, 'Le lien entre le VIIe Plan et le Budget', *Cahiers français,* no. 182, 1977.

12. Rossignol, 'La nouvelle donne économique mondiale et le modèle FIFI', *Economie et Statistiques,* no. 64, February 1975.

13. Cf. Allen Schick, 'A Death in the Bureaucracy: The Demise of Federal PPB', *Public Administration Review,* March-April 1973; and R.L. Harlow, 'On the Decline and Possible Fall of PPBS', *Public Finance Quarterly,* January 1973.

14. Cf. statement by M. Deroche, Director of Budget, *Commission RCB,* 27 January 1977.

15. The report on the reform of local authorities (*Vivre Ensemble,* known as the Guichard Report, 1976) takes into account, for the first time, all the state apparatus.

3 FINANCIAL PLANNING IN EASTERN EUROPE

Michael Kaser

The Classic Soviet-type Model

Phrases such as 'finance is the handmaiden of the planner' or 'the budget follows the plan' have rightly characterised Soviet-type planning since its prototype was founded in the USSR during its First Five-year Plan. The Soviet credit and fiscal reform of 1930 effected two major transformations to previous financial flows: it forbade mercantile credit and introduced turnover tax and profit deduction as the channel of 'forced saving'. With a subservient Ministry of Finance and a 'Monobank' state banking system, the central planning office (*Gosplan*) would in principle determine the structural dynamism of the economy and ensure the consistency of current factor allocations. By the first measure, enterprises were no longer allowed to offer any other command over resources greater than that set by current real transactions. Two preconditions had already been established: enterprises had to break even and could not derogate from centrally-set prices in their mutual transactions. The first, which was the essence of *khozraschet* (cost-accounting), ensured that each enterprise clear its accounts with all others; if profits were earned, the credit and fiscal reform provided that they could only be disposed by authority. The second allowed that authority to forecast what profits (if any) would be earned and what aggregates of goods and services were available to meet final demand in money. It so happened that, at the mid-point of the First Five-year Plan, the world depression made Stalin's choice of autarky more logical (though it was not the sole rationale) and these financial flows were constrained to a virtually closed economy. Such self-sufficiency was not a necessary concomitant, but the isolation of the national financial mechanism simplified the operations of planning and management. The communication of exogenous changes—as was *par excellence* foreign demand for Soviet goods and hence the power of the USSR to import—was minimised by an ambitious programme of import-substitution and the mechanism whereby home transactions adapted to foreign trading conditions was removed.

The principal exogenous variables in domestic demand—first, the size of the annual harvest and hence of farmers' incomes and, second, the pattern of consumer tastes—could be matched to the authority's preferences as exhibited in the plans it communicated by adjustment of the relevant sets of prices, viz. procurement prices to farmers (which were rightly described as a 'tax in kind') and retail prices to households (through turnover tax).

The term usually applied to the function of prices under such a financial system was 'passive' as opposed to the 'active' price mechanism of a market. The active set of mensurations was of quantities in a system of 'material balances'.

The classic Soviet-type model could have gone further towards complete quantity-planning than the Soviet Union did. The mirror image of a Walrasian price mechanism is the 'Marshallian planned economy'.[1] Walras, in his *Elements of Pure Economics,* conceived Adam Smith's 'invisible hand' as the voice of a hypothetical auctioneer who informs economic agents (i.e. enterprises and households) of the prices of goods and services. The agents reply by stating how much of each good or service they would sell or buy at that price. The auctioneer evaluates those messages, assesses whether demand exceeds supply or supply demand and communicates a target for a given quantity of production or consumption to each enterprise.

The symmetric version for the planned economy cannot realistically embrace households: even War Communism in early Soviet Russia, the campaign for moral incentives in mid-period Castroism in Cuba and the Cultural Revolution in late Maoist China, could not tally changes in rations precisely to work motivation. But it is meaningful for enterprises. The central authority despatches draft plans of inputs and outputs to enterprises as a question: 'What would you do if these were incorporated into the national plan?' The enterprises reply, 'Given your draft, the quantities I would make are such and such and those I use would be so and so.' On co-ordinating these replies, the authority decides whether to enact the plan or to circulate a new draft. The interaction between enterprises and authority is the 'method of successive approximations' employed in the classic Soviet model.

As Ames has pointed out,

> The two processes—one for a competitive, the other for a planned economy—have several features in common: they determine an outcome for the entire economy in one fell swoop [so they are truly general equilibrium models]. Moreover, they are at least potentially anonymous and operational and therefore decentralised [in the sense that] ... the price messages, the plan messages and the response-to-plan messages could all be formulated in such a way that no message-

receiver need know the name of a message-sender; no message-sender need write an address on his message; and so that the numbers . . . describe real actions such as outputs, consumptions, money payments etc.[2]

It is not relevant to the present exposition to pursue Ames's analogies with the Marshallian firm in a competitive economy, save that, although some valuation procedure has to exist so that enterprise incomes and expenditures can be defined, there is no need for prices. But in his more limited case where prices are used, the money flow corresponding to his plan messages are an illuminating presentation of financial planning in the classic Soviet-type model. There are four sets of monetary aggregates for enterprises:[3]

(1) the total money payments that each enterprise plans to make (i.e. the money value of the goods and services it plans to buy);
(2) the total money receipts of other enterprises from each enterprise (i.e. the money value of goods and services to be sold by other enterprises);
(3) the total money payments that other enterprises plan to make to each enterprise (i.e. the money value of goods and services to be bought by other enterprises);
(4) the total money payments that each enterprise plans to receive (i.e. the money value of the goods and services it plans to sell).

If an enterprise can neither carry over balances nor extend or receive credit, it cannot wish to obtain revenue above (or below) the plan without simultaneously desiring expenditure above (or below) plan. For each enterprise, the money valuations of any deviation of its activities from plan must be zero. The state may pursue a 'neutral' monetary policy, redistributing funds in accordance with the physical requirements of its plans. Thus the budget would deduct from some enterprises as taxes or profit surrender as much as it added to other enterprises in subsidies and the banking system would operate a revolving fund, granting credits to some enterprises as it received repayments of past loans from others or lending out interest payments as they came in. It is often asserted that a 'real bills doctrine' is followed in a Soviet-type economy, such that an excess supply of money is impossible.

The Monetarist Version of Soviet-type Practice

Two features of empirical experience, as represented by inflationary pressures for consumers and for capital goods, suggest, however, a monetarist version, viz. that the money supply is not neutral: it can exceed that planned and the excess directly determines the rate of inflation. Under strict price control for both consumers' and producers' goods, the inflation is repressed and is manifest in failure of quantities of goods to equal those implicit for the controlled prices (which are ostensibly fixed at market-clearing levels). In considering how such divergencies from the financial plan can arise, emphasis must be placed on the absence of any Keynesian budget-deficit financing and on the supply-determined nature of the economy. The Soviet-type model cannot as readily be brought within Keynesian macro-economics as it has just been shown to be tractable to Marshallian micro-economics.

The Soviet Ministry of Finance (save during the Second World War) has not incurred a budget deficit since 1926. Revenue has always exceeded expenditure in the public accounts and the surplus allocated to the expansion of bank money.[4] Gosbank both holds the government's account and is the ultimate in banker's banking by administering the monopoly of a monobank system. The term 'monobank' was introduced by Garvy because

> The particular form of banking organisation developed originally in the Soviet Union combines in the State Bank most of the attributes of a central bank with those functions of commercial banking that are relevant in the communist economy and also with a wide range of activities related specifically to the characteristics of such economies ... The monobank is supplemented by a small number of banks that serve special functions, including an Investment Bank, which is the key institution for channelling funds into fixed capital.[5]

Wiles has distinguished the latter groups as funds. Linking them with corresponding financial institutions in market economies, he considers that

> Investment banks, merchant banks, discount houses, finance houses and the like are funds, not banks: they do not normally create money. Their essential tasks are to manage the investment affairs of the clients ... It borrows only to lend ... it only lends what it has borrowed.[6]

In the Marshallian terms described above, the subsidiary banks (considered further below) are just another group of enterprises receiving as much money from others (including the monobank) as they pay. The mono-bank is funded by the budget surplus, but supplements those funds solely by administrative decision, whether for bank money or for cash.

The supply determination of planned economic performance is the justification for so limitless a role in money creation. A system, such as a capitalist market economy, the activity of which is demand deter-mined, has to relate constraints on bank money to the behaviour of depositors. A monobank on the other hand has only to adapt its money issue to the behaviour of the authorities.

The authorities may not require that issue of money at an anticipated velocity of circulation precisely to match the transactions which the planned supply of goods and services should evoke. Two cases of dis-parity between the volume of money and transaction demand may be cited.

The first relates to that part of the money issue termed 'active'. Wages and salaries in the Soviet-type model are paid in cash (banknotes and coin) and households spend cash in state shops or with suppliers of services, which bank their takings. The monobank provides from these takings the currency required for a further round of wage and salary payments. Collective farmers receive dividends from their farms in cash and in kind: the cash element is paid into shops and the like as they buy goods and services, supplemented by some share of the wage and salary receipts of those households who buy foodstuffs from collective farmers' income-in-kind or the produce of their private plots. The same circuit can be applied to privately-produced goods and services (artisan products, 'side-line' taxi drivers or painters etc.). The monobank estimates when and where households will spend their disposable cash, after deduct-ing such non-spent flows as direct taxes, payments to non-*khozraschet* institutions,[7] net deposits in the savings bank (a fund of the monobank) and household's precautionary demand for liquidity (one of the factors in currency hoarding). The bank relates these sums to planned supplies of goods and services at planned retail prices as the 'balance of money incomes and expenditures of the population'.

That balance was deliberately set in disequilibrium in the USSR between the First and the Fifth Five-year Plans, i.e. those drafted while Stalin was General Secretary of the Communist Party. Stalin had declared his promotion of allowing aggregate cash incomes to exceed the value of the goods and services put on offer by contending at a Party Congress in 1930 that 'as a result of the advantages of socialism, the increment in effective demand of the masses in the Soviet Union always exceeds the increment in production, pushing it forward.'[8] The unspent

purchasing power in the period 1930-56, when the principle was re-
tracted, was demonetised by compulsory subscription to state bonds
(a sort of obligatory 'open market operation' practised on the household rather than on the banking sector), by a major currency reform in
1947 which decimated all but the equivalent of cash in private hands
above a month's average wage and by penal confiscation at every
opportunity (from kulaks, from those detained, imprisoned or executed
for political reasons, from 'speculators', etc.). When some of Stalin's
political excesses were condemned at the 1956 Party Congress, Mikoyan,
then in charge of consumer affairs, declared the repeal of the policy,
and the Party Congress of 1961 implicitly called for market-clearing
retail prices and money supply in stating that 'the output of consumers'
goods must meet the growing consumer demand in full and must conform to its charges.'[9] Since that date, however, household incomes
have increasingly been deposited in the state Savings Banks and the
'overhang' of unspent purchasing power has evoked much western
comment.[10] Publications of Soviet consumer incomes and expenditures
are not, however, sufficiently comprehensive to allow estimation of the
balance as drawn up in Gosbank: the documented sources in fact show
an excess of expenditure over income in the sixties and early seventies.[11]
The excess of cash creation is indisputable and has been demonstrated in
the familiar manner of retail shortages, shopping queues, and waiting
lists, preferential supply for favoured or privileged customers and
parallel markets.

A source of disparity between monetary supply and transaction
demand lies, secondly, in 'passive' money. Virtually all bank money is
comprised within the 'passive' category, though some 'active' money
appears in the private deposits made in the state Savings Bank just
mentioned. 'Passive' money, as Wiles has pointed out, has some equiv-
alents in market economies; he cites imprest or earmarked accounts
and divisions of authority for disbursing on current or on capital
account.[12] The monobank authorises the investment bank (i.e. 'fund')
to open such accounts for capital formation as is required to supplement retained profits to meet the capital investment envisaged in
the authorities' annual plan (and checked for consistency with the
allocation of resources for current requirements by material balances).
It is particularly on capital expenditure that excess bank money seems
to have been created, but a general policy of taut planning meant that
the automaticity of settlements for current transactions has not always
ensured that micro-economic financial plans were met both as to payments and receipts.

The Western literature commenting on capital finance abounds with examples of excess bank money. For Wiles, when passive money becomes active, 'the great case was always the construction industry even during the classical period.'[13] The proliferation of building starts, the inconsistency of quantity surveys and 'estimate-prices' with actual quantities and prices, the unplanned dispersion of investment projects and inflation of costs have contributed to excess monetary supply in investment finance.

The Divestment of Physical Planning

The devolution of management in the course of the economic reforms of the mid-sixties exaggerated the disparities between money supply and planned transactions and led to a substitution of monetary for physical controls, which widened the area open to disparities. Even as early as 1958-9 the tentative experiments in decentralisation in Czechoslovakia and Poland

> greatly complicated financial planning, just at a time when stability appeared to be an essential condition for the success of these innovations. Enterprises, keeping larger liquid balances, can more easily shift their funds from working capital accounts to investments or capital repairs, and are generally less predictable in their financial decisions than they were before they received their new prerogatives.[14]

The 'overinvestment crisis' in Czechoslovakia that ensued (and, with other factors, caused industrial growth to stop and turn into decline) was a prime cause in inducing the government to accept some measures of economic reform in 1965. Because that acceptance was grudging, conflict emerged within the political leadership (Antonin Novotny as Party First Secretary preferring maximum retention of central controls and Ota Šik urging further devolution) and was temporarily resolved by the victory of the 'reformers' between January and August 1968, when the government of the USSR forcibly intervened.

The three features of financial planning for investment which all countries of East Europe adopted as part of the reforms—to a lesser degree in the USSR than elsewhere—were a reduction of budget finance in favour of funding from retained profits and depreciation charges; the provision of proportionately more investment credit by the banking system (the 'fund' banks); and the introduction of interest charges on capital assets not bearing interest as part of a bank provision. Table 3.1

shows how rapidly the shares of investment funding in passive money changed in the second half of the sixties.

Table 3.1: Sources of Finance of Gross Fixed Investment in State Sector

	Percentages					
	Budgetary Subsidies		Enterprise Financing		Bank Credits	
	1965	1969	1965	1969	1965	1969
Bulgaria	63	32	30	38	7	30
Czechoslovakia	69	35	23	42	8	21
GDR	40	27	35	50	25	23
Hungary	86	51	13	37	1	12
Poland	46	28	45	36	9	36
Romania	61	44	37	41	2	15
USSR	61	50	39	49.5	0	0.5

Source: H.F. Buck in Laulan, op.cit. p. 136.

The political factors which accompanied economic reform also required changes in financial planning for active money. Generally the full-employment constraint which all governments had embraced could not be abandoned.

> Any relaxation of a rigid job-maintenance policy would doubtless be perceived by many workers as an abandonment of socialism ... The job maintenance policy is consistent with reliance on a market mechanism only if conditions of a sellers' market exist throughout the economy.[15]

Hungary since its reform retains a market relationship between enterprises, though under strict limitations on price setting; Poland has adopted some elements of such relationships and Czechoslovakia has them under suspension, but available for reapplication if conditions should prove appropriate. An excess of the money supply over planned transaction need remains.

Industrial Financial Planning in Poland

The Polish enterprise is here taken to exemplify a contemporary practice of financial planning at the micro-economic level; practice as adopted after 1971, i.e. following the change of administration from Władysław

Gomułka to Edward Gierek as Party First Secretary at the beginning of that year. Pricing practices were altered with the wholesale-price reform of 1 January 1971. Uniform price formation was abandoned in favour of foreign-trade pricing for products imported, leaving the traditional cost-pricing for those largely domestically-manufactured. Foreign trade organisation was reformed at the same time to integrate—though by no means fully—decision-making in domestic and external transactions.

The principal domestic organisational change was the formation of 'large economic organisations' (*Wielkie Organizacje Gospodarcze*), abbreviated below to WOG. Finance for a WOG could be drawn from its development funds (from the retained profits of its constituent production enterprises), from bank credits and from budget grants.[16] The development fund is that part of net profit (gross profit less repayment of bank credits and appropriations to the reserve fund) left after deduction of the bonus fund. The authorities determine the formula for allocations between the two funds, but the bonus fund is taxed on a sharply progressive scale.

The gross profit itself is, in summary, computed as the value of sales less the costs incurred in production, turnover tax and any other levies, a charge of 5 per cent on the net value of capital assets and a 20 per cent tax on the wage bill.[17] The precise financial flows are more fully set out in Table 3.2, which distinguishes transfers to and from the state budget (and other quasi-budget funds) and those with the credit system. The diversity of determinants of transfers with the budget contrasts with the simplicity of the classic Soviet-type model, wherein turnover tax and deductions from profits were both *ad hoc* to the enterprise concerned and the year of assessment and the overwhelming source of enterprise outlays from gross profit. The two outlays which were *ad valorem* and relatively small were surrender of depreciation charges (*pro rata* to capital stock), and social insurance premia. The post-1971 practice allows the enterprise or WOG to forecast its liabilities to the state (and hence replace concern with negotiating low transfers from profit by determination to increase profit). By the same token, central financial planning became more difficult: forecasting errors cannot be arbitrarily filled by higher imposts on other enterprises.

Outlays may be classified into three groups. The first is sales tax. This group predominantly includes the turnover tax, introduced in 1944 partly as a tax on 'high-profit products' such as alcohol or petrol, partly to adjust wholesale ('transfer') prices to retail prices which will clear the market for the quantity of the consumer goods planned to be produced in the given year. It also includes tax on raw materials, almost

Table 3.2: Flows between the Fiscal-Financial System (State Budget and Banks) and the Industrial Enterprise in Poland

---

OUTLAYS

1. Payments to the state budget and to para-budgetary funds such as social insurance:
   1.1   taxes and levies on the wage-bill:
       1.1.1. tax of 20 per cent on the wage-bill and on bonuses paid to management;
       1.1.2 tax on other net remuneration for work;
       1.1.3 social insurance premia amounting to 15.5 per cent of the wage and pension-fund contributions;
   1.2   levy of 5 per cent on the enterprise's own financial assets ('own permanent financial means');
   1.3   turnover tax and other indirect taxes;
   1.4   share of depreciation charges due to the state budget;
   1.5   levy on export profits (introduced w.e.f. 1 January 1975);
   1.6   tax on the development fund, as constituted from retained profits;
   1.7   tax on the managerial bonus fund.
2. Transfers to the credit system:
   2.1   interest at 8 per cent on credits for investment or working capital;
   2.2   repayments of investment credits.

RECEIPTS

3. Receipts from the state budget:
   3.1   reimbursement of investments with respect to export products;
   3.2   payment of differential between domestic transfer prices and import and export prices;
   3.3   subsidies to cover operating losses;
   3.4   investment grants.
4. Bank credits for investment.

Source: Gliński, Kierczynski and Topiński, op.cit. pp. 68-9.

only on building materials. The second group represents taxes on factors of production. This group includes charges on capital (the 8 per cent interest charge on bank credit, the 5 per cent levy on enterprise own funds, the state's share of depreciation allowances, and other bank interest at 3-4 per cent). It also comprises wage taxes such as that of 20 per cent on the wage-bill and premia for social insurance and the pension fund. The third group comprises taxes on enterprise income. This includes the tax on export profits and the tax on the two funds constituted from profits, the development fund and the bonus fund.

Flows of funds within the industrial system are represented by profit transfers within the WOG or *zjednoczenie* (industrial association), either to cover operating losses or to supplement capital formation in enterprises where profits are less than planned investment. Three levels of investment funds created by these flows and by profit retention may be distinguished: centrally-run development funds, enterprise development funds and reserve funds. In this considerable affinity may be found with the practice of Hungarian financial planning from 1 January 1968, when the same three sources of capital finance were constituted. The difference with the Hungarian system lies in the former's renunciation of physical planning, such that financial planning became the sole means of control over enterprise performance. Poland has retained some physical planning, directives issued by the authorities to the WOG, which must ensure that the performance of its enterprises execute those requirements (though by which enterprise is at its discretion). But the tendency is for the authorities to divest themselves of these, substituting the array of financial obligations of which the structure has already been built.

The survival of the Hungarian reform, little changed for nearly a decade, is both a testimony that its authorities made a competent (though by no means an ideal) choice and an incentive for Poland to adopt a similar practice.

Notes

1. The term and the first exposition of a Marshallian scheme is due to Edward Ames in *Jahrbuch der Wirtschaft Osteuropas*, Band 5, 1974, pp. 11-40.
2. Ibid. p. 14.
3. Ames, in *Jahrbuch der Wirtschaft Osteuropas*, Band 1, 1970, p. 39.
4. See standard texts such as G. Garvy, *Money, Banking and Credit in Eastern Europe* (New York, 1966), p. 21, and T.M. Podolski, *Socialist Banking and Monetary Control* (Cambridge, 1972).
5. Garvy, op.cit. p. 19.
6. P.J.D. Wiles, *Economic Institutions Compared* (Oxford, 1977), pp. 313-14.
7. Soviet usage distinguishes between 'enterprises', which operate on *khozraschet*, and 'institutions', which are paid for by public or social budgets (central or local government, trade unions, the Party etc.).
8. Cited, in the context of a fuller discussion of this policy, by the present writer, *Soviet Economics* (London and New York, 1970), p. 120.
9. Ibid. p. 121.
10. See among others Norton T. Dodge, 'Inflation in the Soviet Economies' in *The Roots of Inflation: The International Crisis* (London, 1975), pp. 218-23.
11. Individual series of aggregates compiled by the present writer in A.H. Brown and M.C. Kaser (eds.), *The Soviet Union since the Fall of Khrushchev* (London and New York, 1975), pp. 212-13.
12. Wiles, op.cit. pp. 324-5.
13. Ibid. p. 325. Among the principal commentaries (in order of publication) are D. Hodgman, 'Soviet Monetary Controls through the Banking System' in G. Grossman (ed.), *Value and Plan* (Berkeley and Los Angeles, 1960); M. Lavigne, *The Socialist Economies of the Soviet Union and Eastern Europe* (London, 1974), ch. 6; G. Grossman (ed.), *Money and Plan* (Berkeley and Los Angeles, 1968); Gertraud

Seidenstecher, 'Capital Finance' in H.H. Höhmann, M.C. Kaser and K.C. Thalheim (eds.), *The New Economic Systems of Eastern Europe* (London and Berkeley, 1975); and Yves Laulan (ed.), *Banking, Money and Credit in Eastern Europe: Colloquium* (Brussels, 1973).
14. John M. Montias, 'Inflation and Growth: The Experience of Eastern Europe' in W. Baer and I. Kerstenetzky (eds.), *Inflation and Growth in Latin America* (Homewood, Illinois, 1964), p. 247.
15. David Granick, *Enterprise Guidance in Eastern Europe* (Princeton, NJ, 1975), p. 24.
16. B. Gliński, T. Kierczyński and A. Topiński, *Zmiany w systemie zarzdzania przemysłem* (Warsaw, 1975), p. 121.
17. For a slightly fuller summary, see H. Machowski, 'Poland' in Höhmann, Kaser and Thalheim, op.cit. pp. 95-9.

4 INDUSTRIAL POLICY IN BRITAIN, 1972-77

Stephen Young

Introduction

This analysis of aspects of British industrial policy since the 1972
Industry Act cannot attempt a comprehensive treatment of the subject.
After some definitions and a brief survey of industrial policy in the preceding decade, we discuss selected aspects of industrial policy between
1972 and 1977: the 1972 Industry Act; the role of the National Economic
Development Office; the importance of the British Overseas Trade Board;
the Regional Development Agencies; the 1975 Industry Act, the National
Enterprise Board and planning agreements. We conclude with an analysis
of certain features of the evolving relationship between government and
industry; the extent to which there has been industrial planning during
the period under review; and problems of implementation.[1]

Features of Planning

The overall relationship between government and manufacturing industry
has many separate component parts. From the government's side it comprises areas where government exerts controls, as for example over compulsory prices and incomes policies, and other fields where government
seeks to promote changes in existing industrial practices. Examples of
the latter include investment and the promotion of mergers. Policies
for industry in this paper will be taken to mean government policies in
specific fields like training or export promotion.

By contrast industrial planning is a much broader concept as it
necessitates the welding together of policies in specific fields of industrial
policy like those mentioned above.[2] Industrial planning can be the manufacturing input into a broader planning exercise for the whole economy,
or it can take place at the level of a specific sector like shipbuilding. In
abstract terms the existence of planning implies government standing
back from its day-to-day relationship with industry, analysing the existing position, establishing aims, and producing and then implementing
solutions to achieve the aims. A crucial factor is whether the implementation of policy becomes an end in itself, or is a means to an end, a
means towards implementing a wider plan. These and other related
issues will be discussed at the end of this chapter.

The British Experience 1962-71

The background of the development of planning in Britain since the 'dash for planning' in 1962 has been ably summarised by Jacques Leruez in chapter 1 and there is no need to repeat it here. Associated with the development of planning in the mid-1960s was the development of detailed policies in such areas as research, training and merger promotion. Initially at any rate, these were partially devised to implement the plans. However, after the collapse of the National Plan in 1966, the application of these detailed industrial policies became an end in itself, as there was no framework with which to link it. The most important feature of the late 1960s was the way in which government policy began to concentrate not on specific sectors of industry but on individual firms. In the mid-1960s emphasis was laid on advice and persuasion. It was assumed that a letter to individual machine tool firms from the Chairman of its Economic Development Committee (EDC) would lead to action in the sense that the firm would respond positively by investing in new equipment, by increasing productivity and exports, or by merging with another company. Yet this did not happen because the individual firm was in practice free to ignore all such attempts by government via agencies like the National Economic Development Office (NEDO) to persuade it to act in new ways.

The result is summarised in the adjacent diagram.[3] Whitehall hoped to be able to change industrial practices at the level of the firm by 'filtering' advice and ideas to the firm via government agencies with no executive powers like the Government Research Establishments and NEDO. When it became clear that this approach was having little impact and a bottleneck was building up, the Labour Government changed its strategy. It sought to by-pass the bottleneck by developing direct links with individual firms. Government departments like the Ministry of Technology and executive agencies like the Industrial Reorganisation Corporation (IRC) with their own finance began to concentrate on improving Britain's industrial performance by channelling selective financial aid to chosen firms. In 1970 when the Conservative Government returned to power, its initial industrial policy was based on an attempt to scale down both aid to industry and government involvement in the running of industry.[4] Although some advisory services were eliminated and the government refused to support some industrial projects, the approach met with little overall success. The government found that in the long run it could not refuse aid to Upper Clyde Shipbuilders, Rolls Royce, the Mersey Docks and Harbours Board and the motorcycle company Birmingham Small Arms. The retreat from the 'disengagement' policy was symbolised by the 1972 Industry Act.

Figure 4.1: How Government tried to Influence The Individual Firm

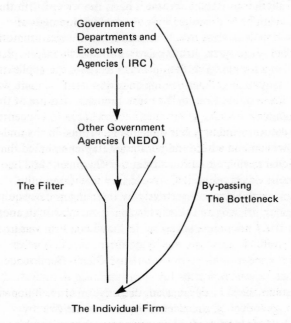

Significant Developments between 1972 and 1977

The 1972 Industry Act

The 1972 Industry Act brought regional and industrial policy together into one Act.[5] Many of the measures—cash grants towards new plants for example—had been tried before, but some new ideas, like cash grants for the expansion of factories already in the assisted areas, were brought forward. Other ideas were applied more widely by the Act. Financial support to maintain jobs had been applied to Scottish shipbuilding companies in the 1960s for example. That principle was now made available throughout the assisted areas. These were substantially expanded, with Special Development Areas (SDAs), Development Areas (DAs) and Intermediate Areas receiving differing levels of assistance. Some aspects of regional policy continued to be applied outside the Act. Advance factories are built under the 1972 Local Employment Act for example.

The Act made a variety of financial inducements available to companies to encourage them to act in new ways. Regional Development Grants were made available at varying percentages of the total cost of buildings and plant and machinery (according to the type of assisted area), incurred by firms already in the assisted areas as well as those moving in. Under Section 7 of the Act two categories of selective financial assistance were available. Under Category A, various types of financial assistance were provided for projects creating new jobs. Under Category B, finance was available for modernisation projects which safeguarded existing employment. In some cases companies with acute liquidity problems were helped under Section 7(b) even though it was outside the normal guidelines.[6]

Section 8 of the Act made it possible for the Government to provide assistance to individual sectors of industry for general schemes to promote structural change through rationalisation, re-equipment and rebuilding.[7] Examples of industries that have since been helped in this way include wool, clothing, machine tools, ferrous foundries, paper, offshore oil supplies, printing and textile machinery and poultry-processing equipment. The same principle applied to the shipbuilding industry (although it was available under a separate section of the Act). Most money was initially spent on the ferrous foundry scheme. Section 8 also gave Whitehall power to provide financial assistance to individual companies or outside the assisted areas on a selective and discriminatory basis.[8] Despite a great deal of attention and speculation in the press, this part of the Act was little used. There were two schemes to help machine tool companies, two schemes to help motor vehicle producers (Chrysler and British Leyland), two to support motorcycle firms (including a workers' co-operative), one to help finance an instrument company and one scheme to help construct tug/supply vessels to assist with oil extraction in the North Sea. These ranged from £1.725 million for the last project to £162.5 million for Chrysler. British Leyland will cost hundreds of millions but most schemes have been under £5 million.

There does seem to have been some industrial planning in the case of Section 8. In the first couple of years after the start of the Act there was a conscious attempt by the Industrial Development Unit (discussed below) to stand back, examine large parts of manufacturing industry sector by sector, and to produce a short list of those where financial inducements would be likely to trigger off extensive modernisation schemes.[9] In the case of wool, for example, £18 million of state money seduced the woolmen into putting up £65 million of their own money in an industry with bright export growth prospects. Other industries that were attractive to the planners, as in the 1960s, were those—like machine tools and textile machinery—producing capital equipment which others buy to improve their own productivity and output. There has been an element of planning in these cases but the process of implementing each scheme has amounted to an attempt to improve the performance of a sector in a rather vague way without reference to a framework of aims set out in a sectoral plan. This has been very much a case of successive governments focusing on individual firms. Regional Offices of the Department of Industry (DoI) have been active in encouraging companies to put in applications.

On the other hand, it is true that successive governments have also used Section 8 in an *ad hoc* way, without a plan, as cases have arisen. With British Leyland and Chrysler the DoI found it had no option but to provide substantial funds to companies that were allowed to run into a crisis situation. In these cases, as in shipbuilding, motorcycles and with two machine tool companies, successive governments have been involved with the problems of each industry since the mid and the late 1960s (1971 with motorcycles). In theory at least it could have been possible to apply some sort of planned reaction to these crises. Yet it must be stressed that successive governments have not readily given in to all applications under Section 8. Half of the fourteen applications received in 1975-6 were refused. One of the most interesting developments during that year was the publication in January 1976 of a paper entitled *Criteria for Assistance to Industry*. It is the most detailed statement of its kind produced by any British government on this difficult problem since the onset of the new-style interventionism in the 1960s. It emphasised repeatedly the need to back viable firms and increase the international competitiveness of British industry, but it accepted the need to support some companies to prevent the social cost of massive redundancies.[10]

The machinery to implement the 1972 Act was notable for the way in which new organisations were established within government departments. An Industrial Development Unit (IDU), manned by businessmen and people from the City, was created within the Department of Trade and Industry (DTI). Similar outside experts went into the regional offices in the assisted area, with Regional Industrial Directors being appointed from outside the civil service to work alongside the senior civil servant in the region. An Industrial Development Advisory Board was established to advise ministers on decisions under Section 8 of the Act. Equivalent Industrial Development Boards (IDBs) were created to advise on the applications under Section 7 at the regional level. To begin with applications of under £500,000 could be dealt with at the regional level, but this was later raised to £2 million. Successive governments spent about a quarter of the total assistance they have provided to private industry through the Act.[11] In 1974-5, for example, £486 million out of a total of £2,075 million was covered by the Act. Other major items included Regional Employment Premium (£191 million); assistance to advance sectors like aerospace (£291 million); re-financing of fixed rate export credits (£528 million); and functioning of the labour market, principally industrial training (£202 million).

The Role of the National Economic Development Office (NEDO)

NEDO's role has evolved since 1972. There has been very little attempt at planning in any form, apart from the attempt in 1973 which collapsed in the face of the oil crisis and the three-day week occasioned by the Conservative Government's confrontation with the coalminers in 1973-4. During the period being reviewed it concentrated on the identification of industrial problems through the EDCs. The Machine Tool EDC, for example, pressed the government for various changes in policy, as over the counter-cyclical investment scheme based on the Swedish model.[12] The Wool Textile EDC has been more influential in helping to launch, and then extend, the Section 8 scheme referred to earlier. More general work has also been done on assessing the position and performance of British manufacturing industry as compared with other advanced economies. It has built on the fact that this type of work continued quietly right through the 'disengagement' period after the 1969 planning exercise.

This has put NEDO in a position to become more involved in the short-term day-to-day issues because it is in close and continuing touch with industry. It has thus been able to articulate some of industry's objections to the policies of successive governments, on such issues as inflation, price control, profitability and the impact of taxation and other factors on company liquidity. In 1975 it was there, ready to push the concept of planning when political decisions were made to explore the possibilities. In November 1975 the National Economic Development Council (NEDC) met under the Prime Minister's chairmanship in his country residence at Chequers to consider a document entitled *An Approach to Industrial Strategy*. This formally ushered in a new attempt to come to terms with the problems posed by industrial planning. The factors lying behind the renewed interest in planning help to explain the form it took. NEDO itself is certainly partly responsible for the existence of the Chequers industrial strategy. Over the years it has gone on and on arguing the case for a more rational and

integrated approach based on the prospects for individual industries
and sectors, with less emphasis on the stop-go methods of running the
economy, and an *ad hoc* approach to industrial crises dealing with them
as they arose. Another source of the revived emphasis on planning was
a new interest in the French approach amongst senior civil servants
from the Treasury and the DoI. They continued to visit Paris on a
regular basis in the 1970s. Yet another long-standing factor dated
back to the days of the Heath administration. The work of the IDU in
examining the prospects and problems facing a series of industrial sectors in 1973-4 has been mentioned above. There was also the compilat-
ion of a detailed list of industrial sectors sponsored by the DoI, with
an analysis of their problem. Related to this point, there was a desire
to avoid the chronic bottlenecks and shortages that emerged, in foundries, for example, as the economy began to expand rapidly in 1973.
Whitehall was looking for ways of avoiding the rise in imports that had
always accompanied a boom.

One of the reasons why the CBI did not like the concept of planning
agreements as it was put forward in 1974-5 was its emphasis on a direct
link between government and the individual firm. One means of water-
ing this down was to suggest that instead of emphasising the approach
to individual firms, government should look in a more detailed way
than it had before at specific industrial sectors. Although this can be
seen as an attempt to broaden the context of planning agreements (see
below), it also, in effect, suggested a more detailed approach to the problems facing individual industrial sectors than the EDCs had previously
undertaken.

The final cementing factor was Britain's deteriorating economic position in 1974-5. It was the fear of what *might* happen if the British economy carried on reeling from crisis to crisis that provided the source of
political support for the Chequers strategy. The Governments of Wilson
and Callaghan were faced with the prospects of a collapsing pound and
the fear of what the Director-General of NEDO called an 'irreversible
decline' in British manufacturing industry. Together with the pressures
from the other factors mentioned above, a renewed attempt at planning
in some way or other appeared to offer a route away from the edge of
the precipice.

The origins of the revival of interest in planning in the mid-1970s go
a long way towards explaining the nature of the Chequers industrial
strategy. In two important ways it differed from previous attempts at
indicative planning in Britain. Firstly, in the past, governments had fixed
on a rate of growth they would like to see in the GNP over the next

five years. They had then imposed this approach from the top, and asked the EDCs to work out the implications of, say, a 4 per cent rate of growth for their industries in terms of investment, productivity, manpower and so on. The details had been added together and a plan had been published. With the Chequers strategy, the emphasis was on starting with the industries that were there and analysing what they could do in the light of the constraints on them. The approach was thus reversed. The government and NEDC were seeking to build up from the bottom on the basis of what was possible and not impose targets from above. Secondly, this 'bottom-up' approach created the need to examine the various problems facing the individual sectors. At first sight, this appeared to be what happened before. It could be argued that this is exactly what the Little Neddies were doing in the late 1960s after the collapse of the National Plan in July 1966. Their attention was then focused on the non-planning function they had all been given of examining the structural and other problems facing the industry, in order to improve its economic efficiency. The central difference between the series of *EDC Activity Reports* published in the mid and late 1960s and the approach of a decade later was that the emphasis was now on much more detailed sectors.

This approach appears to have two advantages. First it can be argued that it has much more chance of successfully identifying the constraints to growth than previous attempts, precisely because it is much more detailed. Secondly, by examining more detailed sectors, it is possible to involve a far greater proportion of senior executives from industry. There are representatives of almost all the companies involved on the Industrial Trucks Sector Working Party. The people who are making the decisions at the level of the firm in industry are thus involved in the process of making policy. This goes some way to getting round the argument that in the past the EDCs could only speak for part of an industry.

The main characteristic feature of the Chequers strategy was its flexibility. The White Paper was critical of previous attempts at planning and advocated a much more open-ended approach with a readiness to adapt to changing circumstances: 'The government views the development of an industrial strategy not as a single finite operation but as a continuing and existing process.'[13]

The first stage was a systematic statistical study of different sectors of manufacturing industry. This led on to the establishment of the thirty-nine sector working parties (SWPs) mentioned above. 'The aim will be to identify those sectors most important for achieving our economic objectives, both for the government's purposes and for those of private industry.'[14] The job of each SWP was to analyse the problems facing companies wanting to expand in that sector. Their reports were considered by NEDC and the government.

The next stage came in January 1977 when five sectors were picked out for priority treatment: industrial engines, construction equipment, office machinery, electronic components and domestic electrical appliances. It was felt that some companies in these sectors were world leaders in their markets. Ministers met the five SWPs and companies were then invited to suggest how the government could help them through crash programmes designed to reinforce and extend their production and exporting successes. The other SWPs continued with their work, moving towards the formulation of medium-term strategies for their industries.

The summer of 1977 thus appeared to be a watershed. The period of the approach to an industrial strategy of finding out whether it was possible, appeared to be complete. The work of emphasising the problems and possible growth of specific sectors had led to five being picked out. The issue then became whether the analysis could lead onto the development of an industrial strategy, with different programmes for individual sectors, and to their implementation.

The Importance of the British Overseas Trade Board (BOTB)

In 1964 the British National Export Council (BNEC) was established as a purely advisory body. Its financial resources of £1 million were basically only sufficient to cover its administration. The Board of Trade retained executive control, taking the decisions about spending money on export promotion itself. In May 1971, as part of its wider review of the organisation of Whitehall, the Conservative Government decided to rationalise the official trade services, and to replace the BNEC with a board of businessmen, bankers and civil servants to direct the range of official trade services from within the DTI. The absence of any trade unionists stressed the importance attached to recruiting expertise from the boards of major firms.[15]

The BOTB was established late in 1971, and began work in January 1972. The Board's first action was to appoint a Task Force, with instructions to review the government's aims in export promotion. The Task Force and its working party were made up of industrialists and civil servants, with representatives from the British Electrical and Allied Manufacturers Association, and the London Chamber of Commerce. Its findings were based on a survey of 70 companies, 15 trade associations, some Chambers of Commerce and the CBI. The Board retained a low profile for most of 1972 while it exam-

ined its potential role. It became more active after the publication of
the Task Force Report, and of a report outlining the Board's own reaction to it. The Board defined the situation in which it began work as
'a nation devoting more of its resources than most others to exports . . .
but failing to maintain its share of world trade.'[16] In responding to this
challenge the Task Force Report clearly influenced the Board's priorities, especially within the areas of activity outlined below.

Establishing a sound working relationship with industry and convincing industrialists that the Board can help them is a task that the
BOTB constantly faces. A lot of energy has been spent on publicising
the Board, and addressing audiences brought together by Export Clubs,
trade associations, Chambers of Commerce, and other similar organisations. Seventy thousand copies of the 1972 edition of the *Export
Handbook*, listing services for exporters, were distributed in 1972 and
1973, for example. The government weekly journal *Trade and Industry*
provides a readily available means of publicity for the Board. If the
BOTB is to reach potential new exporters it has to concentrate on such
activities.

The BOTB is responsible for the government commercial intelligence
services which cover a wide range of activities. It took direct responsibility
for the Export Intelligence Service, which had previously been part of
the Board of Trade/DTI. The BOTB took steps to sharpen the provision
of information on such things as export opportunities, markets and
potential agency cases. A temporary three-month free trial offer scheme
became permanent in 1975. By mid-1975, about 6,500 firms, accounting for about 80 per cent of British exports, had become subscribers.
In response to the Task Force Report, the Board expanded the Export
Marketing Research Scheme to cater more effectively for industries'
needs. It covers research commissioned by trade associations and in-
house projects for firms with no export marketing research capability.
The direct promotional activities of the Board are much more selective
than the commercial intelligence services. The organisation of trade
fairs overseas and of inward missions, for example, involves the chan-
nelling of resources to specially chosen industries and even to picked
firms, and discriminating in their favour against others. In 1973, the
Board supported 6,521 firms at 318 overseas trade fairs. The biggest
British machine tool exhibition ever held abroad, for example, was at
Stuttgart in April 1973, and resulted from a BOTB initiative. The
Board provides help for trade associations that organise inward missions.
These are groups of overseas buyers of a particular product on a tour
of Britain to visit the factories of interest to them. Seven hundred such

visits were arranged in 1973 and representatives from fifty-two overseas governments able to exert influence over the placing of orders in Britain came in 1974.

The Board also promotes in a selective way by trying to match up overseas demand with domestic producers. The European Components Service, for example, identifies potential overseas customers in the automative, aerospace, engineering, electronics, and offshore oil supplies industries, and tries to alert potential British suppliers. Another example is the work of the Overseas Projects Group which provides assistance towards the cost of activities of firms trying to sign contracts for building airports or other large projects overseas.

One of the Board's most important initiatives was to establish and run a marketing centre in Tokyo at a cost of about half-a-million pounds a year. Between eight and ten exhibitions are organised each year, the subject being chosen as a result of market research work in Japan. A fee of £100 gives a firm information, help with shipment of exhibits for an exhibition, a free exhibition stand and £400 towards the travel and accommodation costs of two representatives per firm. The Exports to Japan Unit has been established in London to alert firms to opportunities in Japan.

The BOTB has tried to concentrate not just on promoting exports, but on generating new ones. The Board has taken the initiative and tried to boost exports by working directly with industry on its Product Selection Exercise. The Board's Special Planning Unit worked out a list of twenty countries with the fastest growing markets in the world and, for each, a list of fifty-eight products most likely to do well in the next decade. There had been discussions with seventy-two trade associations and 180 companies by June 1973 on how official resources could best complement the firms' own efforts to find the world's fastest-growing markets. Further talks were held with the trade associations and 1,200 firms in 1974-5. Similar planning work was done to pick out advance technology products that have high export potential for the late 1970s and early 1980s. The Overseas Project Group attempted to identify major projects overseas for which tenders might be submitted by British concerns. It helped British firms win contracts for large projects abroad worth £250 million during 1973 and the first nine months of 1974. Of the 155 projects in which it became involved during that period, 120 were in countries picked out as markets with major potential growth. Similar direct talks have also been used with regard to the public sector.

With commercial intelligence services and direct promotional activities, the BOTB has basically been responsible for running export services operated by the Department of Trade, albeit in some cases in new ways. The generation of new exports is a completely new government function in the sphere of export promotion in Britain. An attempt has actually been made to stand back and take a comprehensive view of Britain's whole export promotion strategy, with a view to adapting policies and concentrating resources on particular markets and specially picked industries. This can be clearly seen in the case of Japan, which has been picked out as one of the fastest-growing markets in the world. The BOTB itself has done some extensive market research and drawn up a list of the products that are likely to do best in the country. Products selected from this list have been the subject of exhibitions for British companies at the British Marketing Centre in Tokyo. The experience of the machine tool industry shows that this approach clearly pays off. Three outward missions went to Japan in 1973-4. Firms in the industry subsequently took part in a major exhibition there. Sales in Japan rose from £269,000 in the first four months of 1973 to £1.04 million in the same period in 1974.

In this short account of the Board it has not been possible to cover the whole range of the BOTB's approach, or all aspects of its work within each of the areas of activity outlined above. However, the feature that stands out is that, although the Board has connections with other organisations like the Export Credit Guarantees Department and the DoI, it appears to have been doing its planning in a vacuum. The connection between its work and other areas of industrial policy is discussed further below.

Regional Development Agencies

In 1975 the Labour Government established a Scottish Development Agency and a Welsh Development Agency. They have the job of improving the performance of manufacturing industry in their areas and have access to financial resources for the task. Experience from the early 1970s shows that there is considerable scope for planning by such regional development agencies. The Northern Ireland Finance Corporation (NIFC) was established with a fund of £50 million in 1972 with the aim of preserving the essential fabric of the regional economy and helping to improve its structure. To begin with, it concentrated on helping companies suffering from liquidity problems or other difficulties resulting from the civil strife there. It later moved into a new phase of trying to diversify Northern Ireland's industrial base away from linen, shipbuilding and agriculture. In July 1973, for example, it took a 50 per cent equity holding in a steel stockholding company. The aim was to assist the regional economy by providing steel users with a cheaper and more readily available supply of steel.

The Yorkshire and Humberside Regional Office of the DTI sought to use the 1972 Industry Act in a similar way. It analysed the regional economy and decided to aim not just at protecting existing jobs, but at diversifying the industrial base away from its traditional reliance on coal, wool and steel. It tried to use the Industry Act to attract headquarters of manufacturing companies and service industries on the grounds that headquarters, unlike branch factories, do not close during a recession. Such decision centres attract other service industries in their wake. The Regional Office, working with the Yorkshire and Humberside Development Association, the Regional Economic Planning Council and the newly established Industrial Development Board, also set out to attract fast-growing industries that were not strongly represented in the region. Examples include electronics and plastics processing.[17]

The Highlands and Islands Development Board (HIDB), established in 1965, is also an example of an industrial development agency on a regional basis. Between 1965 and 1974 it spent £21.8 million in grants, loans and the acquisition of equity holdings in supporting 3,069 projects. It also analysed the structure of the region's industry and then proceeded to support mainly indigenous firms like the Harris Tweed companies. This, it judged, would have more long-term value than the attraction of outside industry. Yet the importance of the HIDB is that it has a wider role. It is an example of an organisation that uses its funds on non-industrial projects in order to develop the overall regional infrastructure and social fabric. In 1974, for example, it spent £102,504 on sixty-two non-economic projects, including sports and recreational facilities for workers attracted by North Sea Oil Developments, a TV relay, village halls and touring theatres. It also advises local authorities on community matters like the provision of schools. The impact of its non-economic activity is thus wider than its expenditure suggests.[18] At a different level the Development Commission (DC) has a similar role to play in England. It promotes small-scale rural industry and is active in preserving the fabric of the rural community.[19]

All these organisations, but particularly the HIDB, have been responsible for some measure of industrial planning. They have proceeded on the basis of trying systematically to solve the problem they have analysed. The HIDB experience has been particularly significant because it has tackled not just the industrial problem but important related aspects. By going outside the straightforward preservation and creation of jobs, it has played a pioneering role in the British experience of such agencies. Many have argued that it has important lessons for the Scottish and Welsh Development Agencies.

The 1975 Industry Act, the National Enterprise Board (NEB), and Planning Agreements

The 1975 Industry Act put the proposals contained in the Labour Government's 1974 White Paper, *The Regeneration of British Industry*, on the statute book.[20] The NEB was established with extensive powers to make grants and loans to, and take equity holdings in, private enterprise firms. The NEB is an executive agency set up, like the IRC but in contrast with the IDU, outside any government department. It broke new ground when compared to the IRC by establishing regional offices in Liverpool and Newcastle to try and create new jobs in areas of high unemployment. The NEB's offices are staffed mainly from the City and industry and it is run by a Board which consists of industrialists and trade unionists.[21]

Lord Ryder, the NEB's first Chairman, identified four roles for the NEB. The first two were providing funds to individual companies for industrial investment and, like the old IRC, promoting the rationalisation and restructuring of firms, or groups of firms, within particular industrial sectors. The NEB's third role was as a state-holding company for shares in individual companies. Some, like British Leyland, were inherited from the government; others were acquired on the NEB's initiative. Finally Lord Ryder argued that the NEB was a central instrument of industrial policy and, as such, had a crucial role to play in solving problems highlighted by the industrial strategy being worked out under the auspices of NEDC.[22]

During the period of Lord Ryder's Chairmanship, from November 1975 to July 1977, the NEB quietly avoided controversy. It was clear from the first Report that the emphasis was on the deskwork and discussion with industrialists and other government organisations. These were an essential part of the process of establishing the Board's priorities. By April 1977 the NEB had acquired interests in 23 companies.[23] These ranged from large-scale investments in wholly-owned companies like Rolls Royce down to relatively tiny investments in small firms. During this period the NEB laid great emphasis on acquiring equity in individual companies. There were very few examples of it providing loan facilities without buying shares.

The key issue is whether the NEB can be genuinely independent of the government, assessing projects on commercial rather than political criteria. The NEB Guidelines Direction of 1976 makes clear that while the DoI has considerable scope informally to shape the NEB's investment programme, the Secretary of State for Industry's permission is needed before the Board can act in some vital matters. For example, his consent is needed if the cost of acquiring share capital exceeds £10 million or where the acquisition would give the NEB 30 per cent or more of the voting rights. The extent to which the Board is allowed to act upon its commercial judgement rather than under political pressure is revealed in part by the corporate plan that the NEB is required to submit annually to the government.

A second proposal in the Department of Industry's White Paper of 1974 was the concept of planning agreements between government and major firms.[24] The aim was to provide a framework within which decision-making within government and industry could be improved by a mutual sharing of information about future plans. The substance of a planning agreement was to be agreement about the company's future strategic planning. The government could help through the provision of finance for research or export promotion. The intention was that planning agreements would be voluntary. The theory was that by concluding a series of planning agreements with major companies, the government could have a substantial impact on the economy as a whole because it would be influencing the decisions made by these big companies, and by implication their suppliers, contractors and other trading partners. The government felt that 'planning agreement discussions should in due course provide a valuable means of influencing a significant proportion of the UK's manufacturing industry.'[25]

Although the government argued forcefully that it attached considerable importance to planning agreements,[26] little progress was made in the period following the passage of the 1975 Industry Act. In 1976 most interest came from companies (like the process plant producers) that depended on government for orders. Other companies remained suspicious, partly because of the danger of trades unionists having access to confidential commercial information through their involvement in the discussion. Although there were discussions with a dozen or so companies, the planning agreement concluded with Chrysler early in 1977 remained a solitary success. Despite extensive discussions, it became clear that it would be a question of years before planning agreements would have time to have any substantial impact. In theory the concept of such agreements was important because it was the ultimate expression of the idea, mentioned at the start of this paper, of bypassing the bottleneck and developing direct links between govern-

ment and its agent on the one hand, and individual firms on the other.
In practice, however, given the unwillingness of ministers to use the
powers in the 1975 Industry Act to compel companies to negotiate
planning agreements, the idea made no positive contribution to the
development of industrial planning in the period under examination.

Features of Industrial Policy in Practice

The Evolving Relationship between Government and Industry

One of the most important features of this period has been the way in
which industrial policies have become more and more detailed. The
1972 Industry Act, for example, has been used by successive governments in an ever widening variety of ways. Interest relief grants were
one innovation introduced by the Act. These have been widely used.
The Chequers strategy represented a new approach in the sense that it
was more detailed than any previous NEDC exercise. The trade pro-
motions services represented a clear example of the way in which existing services were amended, in fact tailored, to meet the needs of industry.
The Export Marketing Research Scheme, introduced in 1969, and pro-
gressively refined, was a typical case in point.

This willingness by successive governments to meet the needs of
industry reflects a central problem that constantly faces Whitehall. The
disappointing performance of British manufacturing industry leads
some to suggest that means must be found to change management practices to improve the average performance of industry. It is argued that
it is only by improving the performance of management that manufacturing industry can move away from 'irreversible decline'. The theme of
the late 1960s, whereby the firm increasingly became the main focus of
government policies, has continued. More and more attempts have been
made to reach the decision-makers in industry, either by using the filter
in an attempt to provide a service of practical use to the firm or through
by-passing it.

The increasingly detailed and complex nature of industrial policies
has altered the nature of the relationship between government and
industry. Without an immense amount of detail it is impossible to con-
vey the tremendous variety of ways in which government seeks to
regulate, encourage, advise, cajole, and even bully individual firms into
new practices. The expansion of industrial policy has had four important consequences for the overall relationship between government and
industry.

The first arises from the need to formulate and implement these policies. The result has been an increase in the number of agencies involved in the overall relationship between government and industry. Examples of new advisory and executive organisations have already been mentioned. Other more long-standing ones have been adapted to meet new circumstances. There are more than a thousand people, for example, involved in NEDO and on the sector working parties.

The second consequence results from the first: these new organisations have to be staffed. By contrast with France, where civil servants often go out into industry on a regular basis, the practice in Britain has increasingly been to invite industrialists and trade unionists to serve in government itself or on advisory committees. Examples include the IDU and the IDBs created under the 1972 Industry Act. The emphasis throughout has been on the contribution of management, especially in an executive capacity.

The third consequence follows from the previous one. Governments now draw up such detailed policies that they have actually to *rely* on the special knowledge of outsiders working in government organisations, trade unions, or trade associations. The Task Force recommendations to the BOTB amounted to a survey of what industry thought of the policies that had previously been in operation. They were amended largely because of the Task Force Report. The Section 8 schemes for the wool textile and machine tool industries have had very erratic take-up rates. Whereas the former has been extended because it was over-subscribed, the latter met initially with very little response. One of the reasons for this may have been that the Wool Textile EDC was much more extensively involved than the Machine Tool EDC in formulating the details of the scheme that was offered to firms. Whitehall relied more effectively on the wool men than on the machine tool industrialists.

The fourth consequence has been the acceptance of the need to implement on an increasingly wide scale policies that discriminate between industries and between firms within an industry, giving some different and thus preferential treatment. The Treasury and the DoI appear far more ready to accept this as normal than they did a decade ago. There was no equivalent in the 1950s or even the 1960s to the series of industries that received preferential treatment under Section 8 of the Industry Act and the Chancellor's Accelerated Projects Scheme, designed to bring forward capital investment projects that had been postponed.[27] Such industries have in fact had preferential treatment over others with regard to new investment. It does not appear beyond the bounds of possibility now that there might be, for example, different price control codes operating for manufacturing industry to allow it to achieve greater profitability, as compared with the food and drinks industries where prices are more politically sensitive.

Industrial Planning?

We have already demonstrated that industrial planning exists in various ways in a variety of places within the government machine. The BOTB has been attempting to plan British overseas trade services in the sense that it has stood back and analysed the problem and constructed a solution before seeking to implement policies designed to achieve the aims. This attempt appears to have foundered in the sense that the Product Selection Exercise is now receiving less priority because its implementation created problems.[28] It could be argued for example that there was no point in trying to concentrate attempts to generate new exports of machine tools on, for example, the Swedish and Brazilian markets, if the machine tool manufacturers wanted to tackle the Eastern European markets which were outside the twenty selected countries. It can also be seen that if you concentrate on only a few products in, for example, Canada, you prevent producers of other equipment from attempting to break into that market.

There has been some attempt at planning on a limited scale in some individual sectors. An attempt has been made to analyse the capacity that will be needed in the steel industry in the next decade.[29] Plans have been drawn up, but they have not been implemented for political reasons. Attempts have been made in a less precise way under Section 8 to rationalise and modernise the wool and ferrous foundry industries, to increase productivity and exports. Here the technique has been to analyse the future problems of the sector in a less detailed way than in the steel industry and make money available for those industries. The initiative over implementation has been left to the individual firms. It can be argued that there has been some limited sectoral planning, but the process of giving aid has often been an end in itself, and not a means of implementing a wider economic plan. Within small geographical areas like the Highlands and Islands and Northern Ireland there have also been attempts to plan. Here the analysis has indicated the need to broaden the base of the local economy by diversifying into new sectors. The implementation has consisted of the attraction of different types of incoming industry and the creation of new ventures. What stands out from this analysis is that there is little integration of such planning activities as there are in different policy areas. It has been proceeding in an *ad hoc*, compartmentalised fashion. The progressive refining of industrial policies through the detailed provision of advisory services or selective financial aid often becomes an end in itself.

However there is some evidence that the reports of the SWPs have
led to a greater integration of the planning activities in the different
policy areas. The NEB appeared to be basing its investment strategy at
least partly on the SWP reports.[30] Early in 1977 its regional offices
began to have some success in creating new jobs in areas of high unemployment. Several of the SWP reports highlighted the need for new
attempts to enable British companies fully to exploit overseas marketing
opportunities. The NEB appears to have been working closely with the
BOTB. A good example has been the creation, largely as a result of
the NEB taking the initiative, of two companies to market overseas
computer products and services, and medical supplies. The NEB has
been particularly active in the electronics field, which was one of the
five sectors picked out by the Government for special attention early
in 1977.

This activity appears largely to be the result of the detailed work
being undertaken by NEDO and the SWPs. There was thus some limited
evidence by mid-1977 that the Chequers strategy had begun to produce
tangible results. The extent to which this was the first stage of the
implementation of sectoral plans or the development of a wide-ranging
industrial strategy was still uncertain.

The Problems of Implementation

While it is easy to see the logic of moving towards integrated sectoral
plans with different aspects of industrial policy being fully co-ordinated,
recent experience has shown that there are difficult problems for
governments when it comes to the implementation stage. It has been
quite possible for Whitehall to stand back and draw up a plan for a
particular sector. One of the arguments behind the nationalisation of
steel in 1967 was that it would be possible to integrate what had previously been fourteen separate company investment programmes. Yet
successive governments have been deterred from implementing a grand
development strategy for the British Steel Corporation because of the
extensive costs, and because of the problem of closing outdated works
in areas of high unemployment. The problem of disagreement between
industrial management and the government has also arisen with one of
Europe's biggest machine tool companies. The company, Alfred Herbert,
wanted to close a factory but was overruled in March 1976 by the government as it was the only plant in Britain making heavy grinding
machinery for the steel industry and its loss would have led to increased
imports. The input of the public interest thus altered the plan at the

implementation stage.

The same sort of problem confronts government when an industrial crisis flares up suddenly. For example, in December 1975 the Government was ready to provide aid on a massive scale to Chrysler, rather than create unemployment in sensitive political areas like the West Midlands, and—because of the Scottish National Party—in West Central Scotland. The fact that the government was no more prepared in 1975 than it was for a similar crisis at Chrysler's in 1967 shows how difficult it is for Whitehall to be prepared for such a crisis.

Governments have found it extremely difficult to take a long-term view when implementing a development strategy for a sector, or responding to a crisis situation. The pressures of the short term undermine the attempt to plan even within a sector. This often arises out of the conflict between promoting industrial efficiency and preventing further regional unemployment. The central problem for government is that the process of implementing a policy can and does change the policy that was originally put forward.

This throws into higher relief the problem of machinery that Whitehall uses to implement its industrial policies, where they relate to the future investment planning of the sector. Project appraisal can be done by an independent agency like the NEB, or within the sponsoring government departments, as with the arrangements under the 1972 Industry Act which gave greater accountability to Parliament. Experience between 1972 and 1976 suggests that when ministers are responsible for the decisions, uncommercial political factors, like the protection of jobs, are very influential. The decision to order the Drax power station showed how long-term plans for a sector can be sacrificed in the face of short-term political pressures. In this case C.A. Parsons Ltd, MPs and local authorities in the North East and some unions had more influence over the Cabinet than the combined advice of the Treasury, the DoI, the Central Policy Review Staff, the Central Electricity Generating Board, the NEB, NEDO and other companies in the power engineering industry.

It seems that there is thus a fundamental conflict of objectives underlying the industrial policy of successive governments since the dash for planning and the development of much more detailed industrial policy-making in the early 1960s. On the one hand they have based their policies on the commercial independence of the firm. On the other, however, they have found that systems of project appraisal that have been developed do not by themselves lead to the successful conclusion of the scheme in which the government is financially involved.[31] Governments have found that their involvement is continuous and that they cannot avoid the need to be ready to intervene in the internal affairs of an industrial company, thereby breaking down its commercial independence. Governments thus face an appalling dilemma. They rely on the commercial and managerial independence of the firm to help achieve their broad ends. Yet bitter experience has shown that independent, private sector firms cannot be relied upon to complete projects partly sponsored by the government.

Notes

1. I have been grateful for the chance to talk to people inside and outside government about issues raised here.
2. I have avoided getting involved in the complex issue of what is an industrial plan. *An Approach to Industrial Strategy* (London, HMSO, Cmnd 6315, November 1975) makes an interesting contribution to this ongoing debate.
3. For a fuller explanation see S.C. Young with A.V. Lowe, *Intervention in the Mixed Economy* (London, Croom Helm, 1974), pp. 31-7.
4. *Ibid.* chs. 11-13.
5. See the Annual Reports made under the Act: HC 429 of 1972/73; HC 339 of 1974; HC 620 of 1974/75; and HC 619 of 1975/76.
6. For a typical example, see 1974/75 Report, p. 8.
7. 1975/76 Report, pp. 11-14, and *Trade and Industry*, 17 September 1976, p. 706.
8. 1972/73 Report, pp. 10-11; 1974/75 Report, pp. 11-13; 1975/76 Report, pp. 14-17.
9. 1973/74 Report, p. 16.
10. Reprinted in 1975/76 Report, pp. 35-40.
11. Cmnd 6393 (London, HMSO, 1976), Table 2.4.
12. *Machinery and Production Engineering,* 21 March 1973, pp. 400-1; 30 May 1973, p. 11E; and 4 July 1973, p. 32.
13. Cmnd 6315, op.cit. para. 24.
14. *Ibid.* para. 14. See also paras. 12-13.
15. Peter Shore, Secretary of State for Trade, changed the arrangements in 1975. This section is based on the *Report of the Task Force,* BOTB, 1972; the *BOTB Initial Report,* 1972; and the Board's Annual Reports, 1973/75.
16. *Initial Report,* para. 22.
17. See the Reports of the Yorkshire and Humberside Industrial Department Board in the 1972 Industry Act Reports; *Growth Industries in the Region,* Yorkshire and Humberside Economic Planning Council, 1972; *Trade and Industry,* 24 October 1974, pp. 157-74; and *The Times,* 1 March 1973.
18. 1974 HIDB Report, paras. 38, 79 and 88.
19. HC 81 of 1974, Development Commission Reports 1965-73.
20. Cmnd 5710 (London, HMSO, 1974).
21. National Enterprise Board Report and Accounts 1976, pp. 2 and 10.
22. *Ibid.* pp. 5, 44-8.
23. NEB Report, op.cit. pp. 7-19 and 33.
24. *The Contents of a Planning Agreement: A Discussion Document,* DoI, 1975, para. 5.
25. Cmnd 6315, op.cit. para. 22.
26. See for example Cmnd 6315, paras. 2 and 7 (v).

27. 1975/76 Report of 1972 Industry Act, pp. 11-12.
28. 1975 BOTB Report, p. 11.
29. See BSC annual reports. For a brief summary to 1974, see *Crisis in Steel*, Young Fabian Pamphlet 38, 1974.
30. The evidence for this paragraph is in the *NEB Report*, op.cit. pp. 3, 5, 6 and 18.
31. This argument is more fully developed in Stephen Young with A.V. Lowe, op.cit. ch. 7.

5 PERFORMING AND PLANNING: COMPLEMENTARY ROLES IN UK INDUSTRIAL PLANNING EXPERIENCE

Phyllis Bowden

This chapter has been written by one who worked for 34 years in the Civil Service: in the Board of Trade (1941-64), the Department of Economic Affairs (1964-9), the Ministry of Technology (1969-70) and the Department of Industry and successor departments (1970-5). The first phase of my career was concerned with the exercise of wartime controls, designed to limit supplies to the civilian population, the consequential policies of price control and utility schemes, and their subsequent dismantling. There followed four years (1953-7) working on the problem of an industry—the film industry—which the government was, exceptionally and substantially, concerned to protect and support. From 1958 until 1972 I dealt with a variety of general policies (e.g. export promotion), and my last three years (1972-5) I spent (as Regional Director, Department of Industry North West) in the most difficult task of all: seeking to implement regional policies upon which I had so authoritatively pontificated some ten years earlier.

So, to read the account by political scientists of a period in which one was engaged in the daily struggle is rather like looking at an aerial photograph of one's home town: the basic structure is clearly discernible, but the familiarity of the landscape on the ground is chillingly absent. In the chapters written by Stephen Young and Jacques Leruez, I find accurate records of events, thought-provoking analysis and sensitive insight. But like M. Jourdain, who did not realise he was speaking prose, I did not fully realise at the time that I was living through such a history. The experience of my career was, among other things, salutary. I emerged with an acquired and much-needed humility; sympathy for Ministers, colleagues, trades unionists, economists and planners; and a profound conviction that, whatever our troubles and their cause, it is not wickedness, idleness or idiocy. Instead, I believe that the circumstances of our country—resulting from a combination of our history, geography, and political philosophy—are exceptionally difficult and complex. I also believe that the application of the concept of industrialisation and land use planning (in combination) in the British context poses unique problems for all who are concerned with decision-taking, in central and local

101

government, in individual companies, in employers' and employees' organisations.

It is noticeable that the impetus towards industrial planning is not a spontaneous native product. Those who think that the process has something to offer the British economy tend to draw their inspiration from the sophisticated economic management practices of the United States, the state planning systems of Eastern Europe, the government/ industry partnerships of France, Germany and Japan, or the fully integrated tripartite Swedish system. A transplant operation is always difficult: the exact duplication of the natural habitat cannot always be guaranteed, even with the most strenuous efforts. It is my general proposition that those who work hard to extract, for the benefit of British society, the advantages to be gained from the application of the techniques of planning, have to battle with some strong currents which make their task singularly difficult.

Such a wide generalisation is difficult in any case to test, and can certainly not be even sketchily probed within the limits of a single essay. But perhaps I can make some modest contribution to a most important subject by pulling out of my recollection of 34 years' experience some of the incidents which, cumulatively, have left me with this impression. Throughout, the common thread of that experience has been, as it is for all public servants, the need to ensure the smoothest possible operation of the policies and aspirations of successive governments.

A very big problem for any individual or organisation is assessment of the length of time an operation is likely to take, if it is to be successful. The larger the number of people involved, the more complicated the chain of communication, the longer it is likely to be before all are certain of the direction in which they are moving. Any family going on holiday or even a day's outing can confirm this. So I make no apology for starting as long ago as 1941.

I was told then that the Board of Trade, needing (for the purpose of controlling supplies in wartime) to compile a register of manufacturers of cotton cloth, sent 20 forms to Manchester, and was both surprised and overwhelmed by requests for forms from 7,000. Since I myself was at the time completely ignorant of any current economic or industrial facts (having newly graduated and being fairly expert in the history of Florence, 1507-13), I was fascinated by what this incident revealed about the relations between government and industry at the time.

Certainly the Board of Trade had a long history of administering legislation which affected the operations of individual companies. But the role was one of setting a general framework within which the majority of decisions taken by those companies could be arrived at without oversight. So detailed information was neither collected nor needed, and the provision of it was resisted. I believe there are, to this day, more than lingering traces in many minds of the concept of such a relationship between government and industry: even the operations of nationalised industries are basically 'at arm's length', which poses considerable problems for government and nationalised boards.

It is important to remember, in this context, that the Statistics of Trade Act 1947 stands, unamended, on the Statute book; and that this Act provides severe penalties for government statisticians who might use, or allow to be used, information collected under the Act about the affairs of individual companies for purposes other than general analysis of the economy. When it comes to detailed industrial planning the provisions of this Act can be a major complication, certainly so far as the government contribution is concerned.

The pressure for a rapid turn-round to meet wartime needs meant hard and wearying work for industrial management and government administration, both robbed of many of their ablest young men. The grind was, however, relieved by two factors, of which the most important was a common objective—winning the war. The Board of Trade and Ministry of Food had the more depressing task—that of limiting supplies to the civilian market and then trying to provide for fair distribution (by consumer rationing) and the equitable control of inflation (by price control and the subsequent utility schemes). The Ministry of Supply had the more positive and invigorating role, that of ensuring that the instruments of war were made and delivered on time. All could count on the willing, or at worst, uncomplaining co-operation of the public at large.

The second advantage (and one which has been repeated in a number of forms since, but most dramatically in the composition of the Department of Economic Affairs) was the bringing together, within government administration, of people with much more varied experience: businessmen, university dons, accountants, engineers, public relations experts, wet-behind-the-ears young recruits like me. I fear we gave the hard core of seasoned government administrators—unrivalled in their discipline and orderly habits—a very difficult time. Heated arguments frequently occurred, but the weaving together of different ways of thought and methods of conducting business were intensely valuable.

Despite these advantages—a common objective and teams of varied expertise—I thought I discerned, even then, a basic cause of continuing friction between what are conceptually described as 'government' and 'industry'. Such phrases are a form of shorthand. Neither are monolithic structures but are composed of people seeking to arrive at decisions in different but inter-related environments. Central government and the individuals in it are inevitably concerned with abstractions: they do not actually make goods or sell them. So the difference between the civil servant and the manufacturer (in particular, although much the same applies—more dangerously—to the provider of services) is the different viewpoint of one who is performing and one who is, in a sense, watching. The civil servant, however sympathetic he may be in temperament and experience to the workings of industry, is, nevertheless, observing the behaviour of a company or an industry. Certainly, the inclusion in government of people who are familiar with the different pace of business operations helps to reduce friction with industry, even if that friction is transferred to the body of the government department. However, the extent to which this happens is much less, I suspect, than it is in those countries towards which planners look as examples of what can be done.

There are two dangers in the watching role, combined as it is with the (undefined) government role of ringmaster. The first is that the nature of the job is different and the second is that there may be too many watchers and not enough doers. As to the nature of the job, it is certainly very demanding to have to produce, generally in a hurry, and inevitably with insufficient information, that Churchillian sheet of notepaper, neatly filleting a complex issue for consideration by the Cabinet; but it is equally demanding, in a very different way, to be on top of the thousands of details (and hourly changes in them) which is the very essence of business. An informed and sympathetic observer can often see ways in which things could be done differently and probably better; but if he has not had the experience and were in the arena himself, would he be as good?

Analogies of strategic and tactical commanders, or even holding companies, do not seem to me relevant to the working of a complex economy, providing as it does for its domestic market an enormous range of capital and consumer goods; dependent on overseas suppliers for half its food and nearly all its raw materials; and needing, therefore, to export, as it does, some £2,000 million worth of goods whose range is so varied that even the infinite detail of the Customs Classification lists cannot completely define it. (Somebody, for example, is making a living, or part of one, from shampoos, made of dried nettles and imported from Bulgaria!) Unless government administration is wastefully to replace the whole of manufacturing and commercial expertise, it can never keep up with the movements of the myriad activities involved.

Three periods of my career brought this home to me with considerable force: these were time spent on wartime utility schemes; government support of the film industry; and a wide range of services provided for the promotion of exports.

The utility schemes were evolved as a consequence of price control. A ceiling price for socks was not effective and fair unless tied to a definition of the quality of socks subject to price control. The definitions in the Utility Orders were of immense and complicated detail, but they served the civil home market well. Goods were available of reasonable quality at reasonable prices, and manufacturers found the schedules useful and comfortable. Indeed, they were too comfortable and the need to return to the competitive environment of world markets after the Second World War enforced their abolition. For, in the end, they acted in restraint of innovation. I well remember a hot summer's day in 1952 when an irate managing director flung open my office door, threw an armchair across the floor, and asked, in bellowing terms of wrath, what was wrong with it. The cause of this *contretemps* was that his company was a leader in methods of mass producing upholstered furniture; the utility specifications were geared to hand-made products. I cannot but think that, however well-organised, flexible and refined the utility orders might have become, they would not, ultimately, have been a constricting straitjacket.

The British film industry did not, and does not, account for a very large sector of the economy but it is an industry in which the government has been closely and substantially involved since the twenties. Not the least of the government's problems was the need to steer clear entirely of the *content* of films, so as to avoid giving any impression of censorship. (I once hit the headlines by saying, 'We in the Board of Trade do not care if it is rubbish, so long as it is British rubbish.') Successively, measures were introduced to ensure adequate showing of British material in British cinemas; the channelling of a specific slice of the box office take directly to the producer; and the provision of government money for the initial financing of film production. The intellectual and emotional demands made on government officials involved were considerable. The finances of film production are, in themselves, complicated, even for a wholly native product. Participation by American and European interests (which tended to be at variance with each other as well as with their British partners) frequently involved the judgement of Solomon. I was the recipient of confidences from everybody, from Los Angeles to Rome, and had to be infinitely careful never to reveal them. Needless to say, it was impossible to please everybody all the time, and I had to learn to bear with equanimity the public disapproval of one or other disappointed client, expressed with that eloquence and fire which is a natural characteristic of the industry.

Here was a case in which I was not merely a watcher, and I was certainly not a strategic commander. Whilst other industries may be less dramatic in expression, the possibility of the extension of this close government involvement to the whole range of British industry and commerce does postulate the need for rather large numbers of fairly intelligent and patient people to fulfil the role expected of the government partner. They may not exist in the right numbers at the right time; or, if they do, they may be required by other partners, i.e. management, trades unions, or consumer representatives.

Another area of long-standing and rather closer association between government and industry is that of the provision of services to support exports. I did my stint in this field in the early sixties. Among many activities (which kept me working at least twelve hours a day) and together with a Foreign Office colleague, I examined the market services provided by Embassies. We started with a 'market survey' (which we did ourselves) of a small sample of large and small exporters, supplying capital, component, and consumer goods, distributed throughout the country from (nearly) Land's End to (nearly) John o'Groats. My method was to select a recent market survey and confront the Managing Director with it, on the somewhat arrogant assumption that it had probably been received down the line and merely filed. I well remember presenting a biscuit maker with a well-written piece headed 'Opportunity for Sales of Biscuits in the Trucial Kingdom of Kuwait'. Very detailed it was, and, I thought, pretty expert, especially for an officer who, I guessed, had to cover in time, say, ladies' stockings, electric generators, suitcase locks, matchbox toys or, indeed, any other commodity. True, the Managing Director had not seen it; and he read it immediately. Yes, it was very good indeed, very thorough, very painstaking. But although it referred to biscuits (both sweet and plain), the market in Kuwait was for sweet biscuits. His firm specialised in plain. I felt very humble, for I had temporarily overlooked the fact that the successful exporting company will keep their export manager in orbit for up to nine months in any one year. Government services can help that work; they can never rival industry's detailed knowledge.

An arm's length tradition of relations between government and industry sharpened by secrecy on both sides; the friction between watcher and doer; the complexities of a mature economy and of world-wide international trade: enthusiastic proponents of national, regional, or even local planning will undoubtedly expostulate that surely such problems must be common to other Western industrial democracies, who have yet managed to operate effective planning arrangements and construct fruitful partnerships between government and industry. My submission must be that the mix is different by tradition and history. The German federal system of government breaks down the geographical scale of decision-taking. French and Japanese industry have developed within a more centralised political ethos. In these and in other Western countries, there is much greater and more fluid movement of decision-takers from one sphere to another. In America there is much more open availability of information from both government and industry. In all these countries, there is much freer movement: the movement of individuals into and out of politics, the civil service, industry, banking, and trades unions. I submit that the habitat for ideas of economic planning and management is much more congenial than it is in the UK.

Above all, I believe that a major component is the characteristic I thought I detected during a year (1957/58) I spent as a Harkness Fellow in the United States: a much more successful amalgam of intuitive and analytical thought processes, particularly in the sphere of industrial and economic decision-taking. I was persuaded then that in the United Kingdom, by contrast, there is a very uneasy relationship between the analyst and the creative thinker, the planner and the improviser, the theorist and the pragmatist. And this view was reinforced by my subsequent experience with the organisation of regional economic planning in France and with the practices of the member countries of the European Free Trade Association.

One familiar battleground which may illustrate the point is the unending argument about the provision of management training. I remember that even an otherwise friendly report about the Business Schools reflected ruefully that students were 'not taught to take decisions rapidly on the basis of inadequate information, in a less than perfect world.' The general complaint is that the output of the Business Schools too frequently goes into the planning groups of larger companies, into merchant banks, teaching or the civil service but rarely into production, or line, management. Moreover (and I have often talked to companies about this), the outcome of the activities of companies' planning groups—handsomely presented, statistically logical, well-written and researched—does not always make the impact on Board decisions that one would expect from its excellence.

My experience has led me to regret what the French call *cloison-nement*—compartmentalism—which seems particularly to have affected the application of theoretical economic thinking to the practicalities of daily economic activity. If my recollection serves me accurately, it was only in 1945 that the Board of Trade acquired, for the first time, an economic adviser. (The Treasury had done so somewhat earlier.) His role was undefined and difficult and after a while it was handed over to a generalist administrator. Nearly twenty years were to elapse before the Board of Trade (and successor departments) recruited a variety of economic specialists and sought to amalgamate their activities with those of yet further specialists, the statisticians. The 1977 Civil Service Year Book shows that the Department has six divisions entitled 'Economics and Statistics'; but there is a separate 'Industrial Planning and Commercial Policy' Division. There is a perhaps even more dramatic division between theory and practice when it comes to regional affairs, with the Department of the Environment being responsible for regional economic planning and the Department of Industry for regional industrial development.

Some of this compartmentalism is undoubtedly due to the structure of government. In the light of my own efforts in the Department of Economic Affairs to secure the co-ordination of the components of regional development, through the mechanisms of the Economic Planning Boards and Councils, I read with fascination that, as long ago as 1930, the young Mosley's plan was condemned by the Snowden Committee because it 'cut at the root of the individual responsibilities of Ministers.'[1] The same conditions certainly bedevilled the work of the Department of Economic Affairs and is a major factor in current administration. Moreover, the association of planning with authoritarian governments touches a deep and sensitive fear: Lord Roll, at the very birth of the DEA, warned the whole staff of the complaint 'Scratch a planner, and you find at heart a dictator.' Some of the cloistering must be due also to traditions of education, with their cleavage between apprenticeship and professional or university education. But I wonder if it does not reach even further back to the fact that as leaders of the world in the Industrial Revolution we performed brilliantly with men who had little or no formal education and succeeded through individual genius, empiricism and common observation.

It may be the case that we can still manage too well through the mechanisms of common sense and experience. A recent homely example came my way when a distinguished civil engineer told us that he awoke sweating in the night to the realisation that, through weariness, he had miscalculated the components of a factory roof. He rushed to his office and confirmed his worst fears. He rushed to the site: the roof was correct. His highly experienced, non-graduate, non-professional foreman had felt that the specification was wrong, and, without fuss, had put it right. Being (through my American experience, but I suspect my temperament too) a systems and organisation man (even domestic shopping is listed by meat, groceries, greengroceries, and 'other'), I have often been asked, particularly by superiors, why I have burnt the midnight oil in such elaborate exercises of analysis as I have frequently performed. The answers have been little different from those provided by the shrewd, informed and intelligent guess. I could only agree, but point to my higher degree of certainty. What a pity that I had not then heard of that judgement of Nelson: 'No-one was ever better served by the inspiration of the moment: or trusted less to it!'

A closely related problem is the very rapid increase in the amount of information which can be made available by the use of computers and the demands which can be made for large numbers of highly-qualified people to handle it. This afflicts both companies and government institutions, particularly when we are not creating enough wealth to be able to support the effort. It is all too easy to thirst after an American system of statistical analysis without remembering the cost, perhaps without remembering also that any institution in the USA which requires a refinement of standard government statistics has first to pay the cost of a feasibility and cost study.

Much more could, I believe, be achieved if we could follow more closely the French and the German practice of integrating the findings of university and private fact finders with the results of government workers in the same field. Once again, our traditions of independence seem to be a stumbling block. I have personally lived through several exhausting experiences in the commissioning of economic research projects: from the framing of the original terms of reference to the completion of the final report much time and effort was spent in securing agreement to a common objective. There are some outstanding successes, notably the work of the National Economic Development Organisation, but down the line one cannot escape the depressing conclusion that much time and effort is wasted by cloistering.

The basic scepticism about the value of analysis of the past and present is nothing compared with the suspicion to be met about forecasting, or any form of planning for the future. This is partly due, as I have said, to a deep suspicion that planning results in dictatorship; and partly to the earthy, common sense view that plans can be comfortable, so that individuals may work blindly to them, instead of being constantly on the *qui vive* about unforeseen happenings. The British may overwork their capacity for improvisation, but there is certainly a need to keep the instrument bright and shining.

There is a great deal of confusion about language relating to the difficult art of looking to the future. 'Plans' seem automatically to be qualified with the word 'rigid'; and I have seen a great deal of time anxiously spent discussing the difference between 'forecasts', 'mere extrapolations' and 'predictions'. Yet no British explorer would have set out without at least a sketch map, close questioning of the locals, and some idea of the direction in which he was going. The 1965 National Plan suffered a great deal from this semantic confusion, so that the hard and useful work which was put into it was not exploited.

Moreover, it cannot be denied that the first people to accept that forecasts are more likely to be wrong than right are those who produce them, and I have myself heard this from Russian planners at the highest level. Businessmen have had their enthusiasm blunted also. It was generally said that 'when the statistical position of wool was at its strongest, you knew that the market is about to break.' The Chairman of a large complex producing one of the world's valued raw materials once said ruefully that, having employed the best economists to be found, at considerable expense, when it seemed reasonably certain that demand was on a healthy rising curve, the market broke within six months.

One of the country's greatest problems is the proper deployment of intelligent and expensively trained manpower. Charles Babbage, the great nineteenth-century mathematician who first envisaged a machine capable of mathematical computation, remarked that men who can effectively base their decisions on a proper appreciation of a complicated situation are very rare. The Duke of Wellington possessed this ability to an outstanding degree.[2] Analysis, forecasting, and the inter-relationship of one factor with another are brain-cracking and exhausting, especially given the complexities of the British economy, which can be stated, in brief, as dense population, major dependence on overseas trade, the inheritance as leaders of the Industrial Revolution, and bitter memories of unemployment. How many Dukes of Wellington have we got, and where are they best deployed, from the viewpoint of society as a whole: in management, in trade union leadership, in planning departments of local authorities, in the Civil Service, in politics, in the professions? Many ideas, valuable in themselves, may fail at their first application and be thereafter damned for a long time to come. The main reason for failure is most probably the demand made on the intelligence, energy,

time and experience of those called upon to carry the ideas through.
I will take one example from the many with which I have wrestled.
Many people have supported the idea that, with so much purchasing
power in the hands of central and local government departments and
agencies (not to mention the nationalised industries), goods and
suppliers should be chosen so as to encourage such general concepts as
efficiency, innovation, export potential—all in addition to securing maximum quality at minimum price. I have seen purchasing officers who,
although very able at their job, are not necessarily top-flight analysts
or policy-makers, struggling with such objectives in the course of their
difficult day-to-day job. It faces them with well-nigh unendurable conflicts. Very often they are buying in millions, and this dictates suppliers
of a certain size. Innovators, on the other hand, may be quite small concerns, with ideas but no development capital or capacity or expertise.
True, there is the National Research and Development Corporation but
from drawing board to first prototype there may well be a long lead
time, and the order for, say, babies' bottle tops needs to be fulfilled in
a maximum of four weeks. I felt very sorry for colleagues grappling
with such problems. If, specialising in exports as I did, I could not
follow the infinite subdivision of markets, what hope was there for the
busy purchasing officer to keep up with it, whilst at the same time
encouraging innovation, efficiency, quality and so forth.

A similar kind of practical hurdle confronts the industrialist and the
civil servant seeking to work out the concept of planning agreements
with the government. The industrialist has to slot in practical issues
arising from the dispersal of his sites geographically, the pattern of his
local and national union consultation arrangements, and the rhythm of
his investment decision-taking. At the same time, the civil servant has
to make arrangements for proper consultation with other departments,
under the pressure of a rigorous time-table. Practice and experience
may well lighten the load but the initial hump is formidable.

In wartime we managed, and at short notice, a fair degree of national
coherence in the manufacture and supply of goods. But it was under
pressure of the unarguable single objective of the need to survive. A
modern example of a similar performance is that of one Eastern European country which has, for 25 years, achieved a fantastic annual growth-
rate in industrial output, at the expense of a minimal increase in consumption. But this has been, in essence, a cold-war response: the need
not to be over-dependent economically on a gigantic neighbour.

In peacetime, certainly in a democracy and—even, as I have learnt
from Russian colleagues—in more authoritarian regimes, there is no

such clear objective. Who, for example, decides the relative importance of efficiency and productivity, or full employment; pollution control or internationally competitive prices; regional industrial development or physical planning requirements; import saving or the goodwill of the country's foreign trading partners; growing food or developing mineral resources; digging coal or conserving an oasis of a calm and beautiful countryside; the need to reduce public expenditure, as a condition of an IMF loan, as against legitimate aspirations for, say, a better health service and proper pay for people doing unpleasant and dangerous jobs? In principle, it is, of course, the Cabinet, but beneath it, thousands of people in town halls, board rooms, trades union offices and government departments must work out the detailed steps. It calls for the maximum of intelligence, foresight, patience, negotiating skill, experience, learning and stamina. When the whole complex is transferred to the dimension of future possible or likely developments, it is small wonder that energy and imagination flag.

Moreover, it is not a national, intellectual characteristic to think *en principe* or to discuss objectives in theory. This has been my experience throughout my career. Most frequently, I have had to deduce the underlying objective from the facts or the legislation involved. This particularly affected me when, in the late 1960s, I was set the task of considering the outline of a government paper on industrial policy. When I started to think about this, it seemed to me that there was no generally accepted concept, but that, instead, there had grown up a highly complex system of regulation of industrial and commercial activities. It must have started in the early eighteenth century (after the South Sea Bubble) with laws designed to protect the investor, and continued, throughout the nineteenth century (and very slowly at first), to protect the safety and health of workers. Towards the end of the nineteenth century, given the increasing sophistication of products, came legislation designed to protect the consumer. Laws to protect the environment (principally air and water) came much later. Protection of the land itself (embodied in physical planning control) emerged only in the 1940s. Last, but not least, there have been requirements on private industry—some statutory, some 'moral'—to protect the economy. The first phase of this very broad and diffuse area was government encouragement, by services, exhortation and incentives, to export more. Contribution to the 'health of the economy' is now expected in the training of operatives and management, greater efficiency, greater productivity, counter-cyclical investment. At the same time, greater attention to safety and health at work, better service to consumers (including lower prices), greater stability of employment, more investment in pollution-avoiding equipment have become statutory obligations. As a *quid pro quo*, so to speak, the government now offers a variety of monetary incentives for a variety of purposes. I felt that to refine and develop thinking about all this I could do with a Royal Commission. Indeed, it seemed almost surprising that, at a time when government or private reviews and enquiries have been launched into nearly every aspect of life, there has never been a Royal Commission on Industrial Policy and relatively little has been written in the academic world on the general theme. For example, what is the basic difference between the relations of the government with private enterprise, subject as it now is to a considerable corpus of legal control or moral requirement, and the nationalised industries? I mention the basic objects of industrial policy, because they seem to me to be a prerequisite to any attempts at national industrial planning, which, in my submission, could and should be no more than a general outline of direction and a rough order of priorities.

For in my end is my beginning. Those who are responsible for decisions large and small in our country work in a fast-flowing river, with strong cross-currents. Society places a heavy burden upon them and is too often inclined to blame individuals or groups of them for failures which are caused by the complexity or immensity of the task rather than by incompetence, ignorance, laziness or stupidity. There are many ideas which have been successfully carried into effect in other countries which might serve us well. But they cannot simply be lifted as they stand and made to work in our environment without proper adaptation. If progress is to be made, a sustained and co-operative effort is required by all concerned with major decision-taking, drawing on all the rich resources of our research and academic institutions. In this field, as in others, we have too often suffered from stops and starts.

Notes

1. David Marquand, *Ramsay MacDonald* (London, Jonathan Cape, 1977), p. 536.
2. B.V. Bowden, *Faster than Thought* (London, Pitman, 1953), p. 331.

6 ASPECTS OF SOCIAL PLANNING IN FRANCE
Bruno Jobert

The notion of social planning varies a great deal according to the type
of society to which it is applied. Sometimes it is used in connection with
local forecasting and planning but in France it is the central planning
authorities—are there any others in France?—which have taken it up.
So we shall be concerned with the emergence of these new social preoccupations in a body principally devoted to economic planning. We
shall successively consider: the plan as a subsidiary forum for political
actors and the erosion of the plan's hegemonic role; the context in which
the intellectual formulations of social planning are produced, dominated
by macro-economic factors, with the effects this has on the definition
of what is social; finally considering some hypotheses on the linkages
between planning and social policies.

**The Gradual Extension of the Social Element in National French Plan-
ning**

In the immediate post-Second World War period and almost throughout
the Fourth Republic, French planning had been first and foremost, if
not exclusively, economic planning. At the liberation, a programme of
nationalisation and the takeover of the state by new political forces
gave the state a new power. This new political power was faced by
archaic and divided employers, sometimes compromised by their support for the Vichy regime. Nevertheless, it was with these enfeebled
employers that the government negotiated the economic reconstruction
programme. This involved, in particular, sharing out the Marshall Plan
funds as nationalisation embraced only certain, albeit strategic, economic sectors. So the First Plan was based upon a 'concerted economy',
expressing a compromise between political and economic power.[1] This
was the origin of one of the peculiarities of French planning. Lacking
a well-organised business partner and faced by lively competition among
the trade unions, the French state could not rely upon the permanent
and often informal consensus-building structures between social forces
that existed in some other European countries. The state had itself to
create an official consensus-building institution. Thus the first three
plans were essentially economic in character and were mainly the basis
for a dialogue between business and the state, with the trade unions

largely looking on with indifference.

It was only with the Fourth Plan (1962-5) that social elements made a striking entry into the plan. Previously dubbed a 'modernisation and investment plan', it was renamed an 'economic and social development plan'. In this period of triumphant Gaullism, the plan was regarded as the selected instrument thanks to which political power would assert its supremacy over the blind economic mechanisms. Having become an 'ardent obligation', the plan intended to promote growth and place it in the service of 'a less limited conception of man' by giving priority particularly to public consumption. Furthermore, the trade unions—including the CGT—gave a new dimension to consensus-building by playing a more active part in its commissions. The Opposition itself reinforced the legitimacy of this idea of the plan as a charter of development, taking up the idea of democratic planning which had been launched by the Catholic CFTC (now CFDT) trade union. But eighteen months later the 'stabilisation plan', adopted by the Finance Minister to combat inflation and a balance of payments deficit, ignored the Fourth Plan and undermined its ambitious pretensions to subordinate the logic of the market to social objectives.

In subsequent plans, the only question considered was how to correct the imperfections and stresses caused by the working of the market. In the plan's rhetoric, the correct working of the market, thanks to the cold winds of foreign competition, would henceforth be the best way of attaining the more basic social objectives. In the next three plans, the instruments capable of taking account of social phenomena as they related to economic phenomena were developed. At the same time the state-business dichotomy, which dominated the early plans, became more homogeneous. The same social forces occupied the commanding heights of the economy and the state and attempted to spread through various channels, such as the plan, the same world view. This state of affairs accounts partly for the trade unions' sulkiness since then on the score of the plan, notably their withdrawal (apart from *Force Ouvrière*) in the second phase of the preparation of the Sixth and Seventh Plans. After the failure of the Fifth Plan's attempt to launch an incomes policy, this aspect of social policy was not directly dealt with until the Seventh Plan's discussion of social inequality; although the treatment of self-financing, levels of employment and minimum wage norms in subsequent plans sketched the outlines of an incomes policy.

Even if the strategic choices embodied in successive plans rooted the French economy increasingly in the competitive market economy, social concerns occupied an ever more important place in planning. It was as if the increasing internationalisation of capitalist production rendered attempts to influence firms ever more illusory and made mastery over the development of social matters increasingly necessary. It was first and foremost the problem of unemployment which was the focus of these new concerns and which received the closest attention. After the Fifth Plan's mistake of seeking to guarantee the international competitiveness of French prices by maintaining a sort of pool of unemployment, which was a contributory factor to the crisis of May 1968, the plan once again became the constant advocate of a policy of full employment through economic growth. This brought it into conflict during the Sixth Plan with the Ministry of Finance, which was worried about the fiscal and monetary consequences of a high growth-rate. The Seventh Plan stressed the need to overcome the growing French dislike for industrial jobs—which rapid growth would increase—as a way of achieving full employment.

Mastery over the accelerating growth of public expenditure in the social field was also one of the major preoccupations of the Fifth, Sixth and Seventh Plans. As we shall show in greater detail, the increasing distinctions drawn between types of social service was aimed at obtaining a more precise idea of their cost and of their contribution to growth and to the objectives of social policies.

The activities of French planners has been described by Shonfield as that of a 'pressure group for growth' and it is the case that many observers have given them the credit for the crystallisation and spreading of development norms and attitudes among French businessmen and civil servants.[2] Over and above the mere promotion of quantitative growth, however, French planning became increasingly concerned about the many social conflicts, bottlenecks and social changes which have resulted from, yet sometimes stopped or slowed down, economic growth. The effects and limitations of this concern must now be dealt with. We shall first of all show how the range of social matters covered by planning is restricted both by political factors which minimise its significance and by the predominance of a macro-economic perspective in planning. This double constraint is expressed in a special way of representing the social sector and social matters. Lastly, we shall examine the paradoxical situation of the French plan, which, despite being itself organised in a very centralised way, has sought to promote a large measure of administrative decentralisation.

The Plan as a Subsidiary Political Forum

Rejecting the idea of planning as an 'infallible prediction of the future' as well as 'an illusory way of developing the economy by constraint', President Giscard d'Estaing defined in his preface to the Seventh Plan its true role in these words:

> It consists first of all in fixing France's direction of advance up to the end of 1980. To fix this direction precisely is especially important because otherwise, in a turbulent environment, the passively undergone might, because of day-to-day necessities, predominate over the deliberately willed. Only persevering action in the service of a consistent project would make it possible to secure the resources necessary to maintain national independence and attain our social objectives.

The head of state located the plan's true role at the level of the resources to be mobilised, the definition of a strategy, progress towards objectives that have been fixed for it. This definition is not new, even if a certain conception of the French plan presents it as the place where the most opposed social objectives can be formulated. We can only recognise with Georges Delange that French planning has refused to face up to the major problems of the modern economy.[3] As a planner has put it, the forecasts and economic alternatives envisaged during the preparation of the Seventh Plan were all more or less in conformity with the political choices of the coalition in power. It was not permissible or legitimate for the planners to use any other framework.

The relative indifference of Fourth Republic governments towards planning has given way to increased political control under the Fifth Republic,[4] especially since the presidency of Giscard d'Estaing. He has created alongside the Planning Commissariat an exclusively governmental Central Planning Council, whose role includes fixing the guidelines and exercising political control over the planning process. More generally, the Seventh Plan seems to have been characterised by an intensification of the relations between ministers, their private staffs and the planners, as if the latter's purpose were less to secure agreement between the various social partners than to translate into consistent economic terms the political preferences of the coalition in power.

This view is confirmed by the very much more restricted consultation of interested parties in the Seventh Plan, which was characterised by a considerable reduction from twenty-eight to nineteen in the number of commissions called upon to discuss the plan in the second phase of its preparation. This figure does not mean much since it is generally agreed that the development of consultation in previous plans had led to a top-heavy structure involving about 3,000 people. More significant was the short time that elapsed between the two consultative phases and especially the discontinuity between the consultative procedure and the programming procedure used to draw up the priority action programmes (discussed below).

Furthermore, the very content of these priority programmes seems to suggest that some problems have been excluded from planning in the light of these political considerations. Leaving aside social planning, the fact that the priority given to military expenditure is not mentioned in the plan is significant. So is the lack of a programme for immigrant workers or the total neglect in the plan of the crisis in higher education. It would appear that in a number of especially sensitive areas, the government did not want its freedom of action restricted by forecasts or public norms written into a plan.

More generally, the Seventh Plan seems to mark a turning-point in the development of French planning. Until then, concertation in various forms appeared to play an important part in the whole planning process. Planning helped to produce norms that were indispensable to the intellectual domination of those in power.[5] While planning was certainly not the only place where the ideology of the dominant class was marked out and communicated, it was without doubt a most important political forum where this ideology could acquire the practical form of norms capable of providing a common vision and guidelines for action by the various classes that share power. To be carried out successfully, this hegemonic function requires a certain distance and independence from the government of planning institutions. The decline of consensus-building and the increased political control over planning indicates the opposite: a decline in the intellectual hegemony of the plan, which should be investigated.

Social Planning as Intellectual Production and Social Representation

Limited by political constraints, social planning is largely structured by the economic preoccupations that predominate in French planning. This is evident in the collection of data, in the specialist studies of social planning, as well as in the general conception of the 'social' transmitted by planning.

This dominance of economic concerns manifests itself first of all at the statistical level. The National Institute of Statistics and Economic Studies (INSEE) has the task of centralising and co-ordinating the whole public statistical system. This Institute comes under the aegis of the Ministry of Finance and it plays an important part in the technical side of the plan's preparation. This is not surprising as the French statistical system was built up and developed to suit the needs and requests of those responsible for economic policy.[6] Despite important improvements since the mid-1960s, the development of social planning continues to be handicapped by the relative underdevelopment of social statistics, as the report by OECD experts on the social sciences in France has shown. It asserts that social indicators remain inadequate despite the improvements made thanks to Jacques Delors.[7] Furthermore, the ministries other than Finance lack adequate sources of information. This is true of matters such as labour disputes, hours of work, absenteeism, the analysis of works committee election results and the extent to which social legislation is respected by firms.

The development of social statistics has itself been very uneven.[8] In connection with the Fifth Plan, some important work was done in the field of employment. In the various social ministries, progress is much slower despite the efforts of various statisticians. They tend particularly to concentrate upon resource indicators, such as the number of hospital beds per inhabitant, as if an increase in these resources could be equated with the attainment of objectives. Furthermore, the statistical apparatus of the social ministries tends to deal only with abstract citizen-consumers. ignoring social inequalities in the use of services and thereby contributing to their perpetuation. Lastly, it is difficult to ascertain precisely the inequalities in the geographical distribution of public service infrastructure. However, the situation here is rapidly improving as the planners secure the drawing-up of maps indicating where it would be desirable to locate hospitals and schools.

The difficulties are much greater where private firms are concerned. More than a decade has elapsed since the creation of a Research Centre on Incomes and Costs (CERC), following the breakdown of the 1963 Incomes Policy Conference, yet the Seventh Plan's Development Commission in 1976 acknowledged the size of the gaps in statistical knowledge about the cumulative processes by which inequalities are reinforced.

So the strong and weak points of the statistical system do not coincide with a well-serviced productive sector and a neglected social sector. Some of the most important parts of the productive system—the allocative structures and labour disputes—can also be passed over in the statistical systems on which planning is based, seriously prejudicing the very possibility of a close integration of economic and social planning. However, since 1968 an attempt has been made to broaden and diversify the possible users of the statistical system, especially through a change in

INSEE publications (notably the appearance in 1973 of *Données Sociales*), the creation of Regional Economic Observatories to facilitate access to statistics and lastly the establishment of a National Statistics Council open to consumer associations, trade unions and trade associations. It will be interesting to see how the work of this Council develops in the matter of statistics necessary to social planning.

The uneven development of the statistical system is only the first of the brakes on the development of social planning. Models, whose importance in the search for a consistent economic strategy is generally acknowledged, have not seemed to be able—at least until the Seventh Plan—to take into account the social dimensions of economic development. This is because models only deal with agents linked by functional relationships and not groups or social classes. Only averages are picked up, which sometimes leads to the neglect of fundamental disparities.[9] Economic models are also hesitant in defining the status of public infrastructure in economic development. If models can account for the cost of public services, it is much more difficult for them to measure the social effects of these services upon growth. Lastly, we must mention, in connection with this matter of models, the fundamental problem of the structural inequality of the various classes and social organisations when faced by economic terminology and its connotations.[10] Without being able to show how the Seventh Plan overcame these difficulties, the planners' strategy was clearly expounded in a report entitled 'For a better integrated social planning'.

> The common purpose uniting all our proposals, concerning instruments, themes and procedures, is to ensure a better integration of social planning into the whole process of the Seventh Plan's preparation, at every instant and in all the places where it is prepared.[11]

The first choice was to abandon the attempt to include all the concerns of the social planners within existing economic models. Not that this was impossible in many matters. But this integration would have required a great deal of work and would have stressed the economic cost of social policies rather than their social advantages. The use of social indicators in macro-economic forecasting certainly continued. But the keystone of the initial edifice was elsewhere. The planners had intended to build a synthetic means of embracing social reality corresponding to the role of an economic model in the definition of economic policies. In short, it was intended to prepare a social report which would attempt a selective and as synthetic an approach as possible of the state of society and of social problems. It would be based in particular upon a certain number of social indicators regarded as essential but it would try to escape the analytic logic of the functional approach and try to operate from the overall social level with themes that cut across functions as much as possible.

This attempt at an overall diagnosis would enable the planners

to draw attention to the possible effects of certain planning choices, such as the rate of growth; public expenditure and the level of taxation; the choice between transfer payments and public services and between public services; the national, regional and local level of decision-making.[12]

The social report constituted a key part of what was envisaged to achieve a better integration of social planning, as it would have both counterbalanced the economic syntheses and fitted the partial priorities determined by functional rationalisation into a whole. It was to have been followed by an annual check on application along the lines of the report on the plan's implementation. This important scheme, which had the support of the planners, was not accepted, even though many other suggestions made in the same report were applied. While we do not know the precise cause of this refusal, it appears that the planners' right to prepare a social report was questioned. In the name of what and of whom could the planners lay claim to sit in judgement upon society, even if they submitted this judgement to the interested parties? If this was the case, it would amount to additional evidence in support of our hypothesis on the decline of the plan's intellectual function.

The Planning Commissariat also plays a very important part in the stimulation of economic and social research. A whole series of research centres have been created or encouraged by the planners: CREDOC, the Centre for Research and Documentation on Consumption; CERC, the Research Centre on Incomes and Costs; the Study Centre on Employment; CEREQ, the Study and Research Centre on Qualifications; without forgetting the whole system of economic research very closely linked with the Plan, carried out particularly by INSEE teams. The Planning Commissariat, notably through CORDES, Organisation Committee for Applied Research on Economic and Social Development, plays an important part in the allocation of public money to support research. On the whole, the Plan has not confined itself to financing short-term research. Many young researchers have, thanks to its support, been able to escape university constraints. In the social sphere, the Plan has played an important part in encouraging research on both social indicators and the theoretical conditions of social modelling, as well as studies of the social ministries and agencies. Thus CORDES financed the main studies on hospitals. Centralisation is the counterpart of this dynamism. In the field of social research, most projects are financed by one of the two or three main supporters of public research.

The linkage between this rather eclectic research policy and the Plan's medium-term work is not very clear. It is certainly not by a deductive process, such as theoretical research yielding general concepts which specialist studies will operationalise and present for consensus-building discussion. In the social field, research has mainly had the function of exposing new tensions, new aspirations, secretive institutional processes or experimenting with new ideas. Its role has been to take soundings or highlight particular problems rather than to reinforce the consistency of socio-economic strategies directly. It was probably in the long-term planning commissions that the closest link between research and social planning activities was established, for example in the field of long-term family policy in the Seventh Plan. But the link between these long-term planning groups and the quinquennial planning process seems as problematical as the link between research and planning.

What are the characteristic traits of social planning as they emerge from the planning process? The plan seems to have played a part in the conception of the 'social' as a unified field of action and reflection, in the transition from the 'social' conceived as assistance to the 'social' conceived as an aspect of the quality of life, going beyond the concept of infrastructure as the foundation of public action. We shall show the inevitable ambiguity of the 'social' ideology by indicating the persistent gap between some of these norms and the state's activities.

Until the Fifth Plan, France only had particular social policies for health, education and so forth. Then a social affairs department was created within the Plan, charged with participating in and co-ordinating the work of the separate employment, public investment and social services commissions.[13] However, this new department was for a long time perceived as a 'collector of needs or at least of social demands, the spokesman of these demands to those responsible for reaching the final synthesis, particularly the financial synthesis.'[14]

Nevertheless, a number of concepts gradually unified these disparate policy sectors. First of all, there was the notion of public infrastructure consecrated by the Fourth Plan.

From the advice received there emerges the idea of greater resort
to public infrastructural services. It might be thought that the consumer society, which is foreshadowed by some aspects of American
life . . . leads eventually to futile pleasures, which themselves give
rise to malaise. Doubtless, it would be better to use the anticipated
increasing affluence to promote a less limited conception of man . . .
The opportunity should be seized of accomplishing a major, durable
achievement so that men can live better.[15]

Thus most of the social policies are united in a single category. Thereby,
they should go beyond the myriad specific needs they are supposed to
satisfy and be embraced within a vast scheme: provide a better life for
the whole man, far from the futile satisfactions of a consumer society.
Through the concept of public infrastructure, the 'social' loses its outdated connotation of assistance and becomes a prestigious foundation
of the quality of life. Thus, one no longer talks of social and cultural
assistance but social and cultural activation. But this more integrated
conception of social policy comes up against the extreme fragmentation of French social administration, each part of which is very jealous
of its autonomy and its monopoly over its own sphere of action. So the
planners have made a major contribution to the development of administrative ideas and practices, challenging the boundaries within social
administration. At the conceptual level, the idea of public infrastructure is quickly replaced by public function. Within this framework, all
the public activities related to the same objective can be studied; not
just infrastructure but resources in personnel or regulatory activities.
    The Sixth Plan attempted

to make explicit and to reformulate the objectives pursued in each
field: systematically studying the most efficient alternative ways of
achieving the ends; systematically analysing the consequences of
applying the means in a particular field, as well as in other fields.[16]

Through this ambitious effort, the Sixth Plan's social planners sought to
challenge the identification often made between a particular administrative service and a particular need, by analysing the effects of all forms of
public intervention in a field, without bothering about administrative
boundaries. In the same spirit, these planners tried to promote the
theme of integration or at least the general utility of infrastructures.
Similarly, the planning commissions were so organised that in many
cases there was no identity between the commission's sphere of com-

petence and that of a particular part of the administration. In this connection, the establishment in the Seventh Plan of a Commission for Social Life was significant as it embraced a number of neighbourhood services involving numerous ministries, including Justice, Youth and Sport, Health and Social Action.

These attempts at internal integration within the social sector implied that the fundamental dichotomy between capital and current expenditure should also be surmounted. After the 'bricks and concrete' Third and Fourth Plans, it became increasingly clear that planning had to include not only capital investment but current expenditure if many miscalculations were to be avoided: new hospitals without the personnel to staff them completely or an uncontrolled growth of operating expenditures arising out of investments, for example. In the wake of the Sixth Plan, the Seventh Plan organised the selective programming of priority activities as a whole, providing the investment and recurrent resources, sometimes even the necessary regulations. At the same time the programming of all social investment was abandoned. So twenty-five priority action programmes (PAP) were established, involving 15 per cent of state civil expenditure. We shall return to them later.

This elaboration of a set of concepts common to all kinds of social intervention was combined with a gradually closer relationship between the economic and social spheres of action. It is true that from one plan to the next there is the same fundamental choice: economic growth is the prime objective whose attainment conditions the pursuit of the social goals, which are claimed to be the ultimate objectives of the plan. Yet a marked change is evident in the Seventh Plan, with its stress upon social hindrances to economic growth. The need is to

modify growth to retrieve expansion . . . In the present state of society, it would be vain to try to increase happiness by reducing overall consumption. It must be combined with the goal of quality. Growth can only be great provided it can become markedly more pleasant.[17]

It did not seem likely that the relative full employment objective of the Seventh Plan could be attained unless the dislike of French labour for industrial work could be overcome, as this was where most new jobs would be located. Such a change required a policy aimed at the reduction of inequalities and the improvement of the conditions of manual labour as proclaimed among the plan's objectives.

In the event, despite some modifications of detail, planning continues to treat need as a datum whose permanence it recognises, without really questioning the origins of social demands or the processes by which needs and social structures are linked.[18] When these links were mentioned in some commissions, they do not appear to be reflected in the text of the plan.

Thus the Seventh Plan Health Commission, taking up arguments already expounded in the preceding plan, emphasised the need 'to improve the conditions of social life so as to reduce the need to give the French health care', stressing in this connection some of the unhealthy features of work and urban life. It therefore proposes that the criterion of health as a public good should be more systematically taken into account by development agents. However, on this point, it could only be very brief. 'Action at this level involves the most varied fields which were outside the terms of reference of the commission.' So the activity of the Health Commission was from the start restricted to prevention of illness and care of the ill. It was outside its terms of reference to question the social genesis of health needs and the possible changes in social organisation that might make it possible to contain the growth of health needs. Because it refuses to deal with the contradictions of capitalism, French planning can only have a very limited influence upon the sources of social needs. At most, it can organise the flight forwards (based upon the circular process of contradictions–tensions–needs–production–contradictions), dubbed growth, through which capitalist society tends to respond by a further increase in production to the tensions engendered by production.

Social planning in France has therefore been better able to identify certain new needs when they have been connected with the working of the economy. It has been one of the places where the new, broader conception of social policy, going beyond the traditional compartmentalism of social sector bureaucracies, has been worked out.[19] But it has not given pride of place to the fundamental processes that decide the genesis of social needs.

The Plan and Social Policies

The idea of an intellectual function of the plan, closely related to consensus-building, clearly renders redundant any attempt to separate the plan rigidly into phases of preparation and implementation. It is during the preparatory phase that the hegemonic function of defining and spreading the values underlying the plan is carried out. Nevertheless, the accentuation of the French plan's programming role makes it necessary to pay more attention to the link between the plan and social policies. We shall start by considering the regularity with which certain social goals have been fixed without any action to achieve them in previous plans, before examining the new procedures adopted in the Seventh Plan's link between plan and budget.

The conception of a harmonised social and economic development asserted by French planning has not been fully reflected in the economic and social policies in which it is supposed to be embodied. One is compelled to recognise that, with monotonous regularity, French plans have suffered from substantial short-falls (notably in the Fifth and Sixth Plans) or at least from very severe sectoral distortions (the Fourth Plan) in the implementation of social investment programmes. The reasons for this divergence have sometimes been sought in 'the lack of any real co-ordination between the Ministry of Finance and the Planning Commissariat, particularly the absence of any links between the budget and the plan.'[20] It is certainly true that social investment projects have often been the first victims of the crises that have occurred during each plan. But we must also bear in mind the 'growing antagonism between market forces and collective needs'.[21] This antagonism reveals itself through increased pressure to restrict public expenditure—in the name of competitiveness—and the devotion of these limited resources primarily to those public goods that come closest to being the immediate environment of market activity.

The failures of planning in the sphere of incomes policy are even clearer and more significant. Everything works out as if reference to growth concealed an implicit assent to inflation which appears to be 'a general anaesthetic for all inequalities, all attempts to obtain compensation by some social groups . . .'[22] The Seventh Plan, for its part, seeks to define a strategy that takes account of the acceleration of inflationary tendencies in a context of unemployment and promises measures aimed at reducing inequalities. But the programmes remain timid and the fate of a bill to tax capital gains in 1976 is not calculated to make one optimistic about the future. The power of market forces seems once again to threaten one of the social purposes of planning. So, apart from the employment sector and more marginal sectors, where planning seems to have contributed more clearly to the formation of social policies, plan-devised harmonies between the economic and the social constitute an unreal duet. But is it really possible to shift the social sector from its residual status without challenging the basic structures of capitalism?

Anyway, in the absence of a social report structuring long-term social objectives, the fragmentation of plan programming into twenty-five more or less homogeneous programmes marks a turning-point in plan preparation and, it would appear, a retreat from the very general object-

ives of previous plans. These plans are characterised by the replacement
of a general investment programme by a complex priority programming
involving recurrent as well as investment expenditure. The overall total
of programmed expenditure does not appear to have fallen but its character has been substantially changed.[23] On the basis of the priorities
defined in a preliminary report, the ministries were called upon to define
their PAPs in the summer of 1975. These proposals were sorted out,
reclassified and reformulated into the twenty-five programmes that make
up book two of the Seventh Plan. This exercise was carried on without
any serious discussion except among officials of the ministries concerned,
the budget division of the Finance Ministry, the planners and the *cabinets
ministériels*. In this long process of adjudication between competing
claims, the salient feature is the almost absolute priority given to telephone investment, which received nearly half of the funds for all twenty-
five priority programmes.

Over and above the rationalised linkage between planning and investment programming, social planning exerts an influence that is indubitable
but difficult to assess as a stable reference point for public—and probably
governmental—action. The head of the Plan's social affairs division put
the matter this way:

> the [Seventh] plan itself devotes half a page to the general policy on
> health in book one, while book two sets out the financial commit-
> ment and the activities in which the Ministry of Health participates
> ... But in all this involves at most two or three pages, whereas the
> report of the Health Commission amounts to 240 pages. Even if it
> does not have the same binding force, the latter illuminates the policy
> direction chosen by the government. In particular, there is a great
> likelihood that most of its recommendations will be carried out in
> the years to come.[24]

Planning and the Regulation of the Political Market for Social Resources

The reinforcement of the links between plan and budget will only resolve
part of the difficulties of plan application because local authorities are
in charge of almost two-thirds of public investment. It will not be possible even to outline the territorial arrangements for programming
public investment in France. However, we wish briefly to demonstrate
the very centralised character of French planning and, paradoxically, its
original contribution to the establishment of more deconcentrated or
decentralised institutions.

The centralisation of planning is on the same scale as French central-

isation. It is based upon the extreme centralisation of the social information system in France. The share of towns and other local authorities
in financing research is minute. Statistics, generally aggregated at the
département level, are extremely difficult to use locally. However, it is
also true that local authorities or the most influential local councillors
profit from this obscurity because it conceals the privileged treatment
they receive in the competition between local authorities for the allocation of social resources.

But in France's recent period of rapid urbanisation, this political
market for social resources necessarily worked against the recently
urbanised areas. The lack of public services in these new areas was
connected with what was described in the early sixties as the high-rise
housing estate problem. It was consequently logical of the Planning
Commissariat, which sought to promote rapid and harmonious development, to initiate the main instructions defining the content of the co-
ordinated investment programmes of the major urban areas in June
1959, October 1961 and February 1969.[25] Similarly, the plan played
an important part in the establishment of regional institutions. The
Sixth Plan attempted a very complex exercise in the harmonisation of
the various levels of planning. Urban modernisation and investment
plans had to be made compatible with regional economic development
plans, which themselves were to provide the basis for a regionalisation
of the national plan. The Seventh Plan's strategy was simpler in that it
abandoned the attempt to plan all public investment. Its premise is not
the integration but the autonomy of the various levels of planning:

> Regional bodies will prepare their development plans by autumn
> 1976. Local authorities which so desire may also prepare such pro-
> grammes. Drawn up by regional and local authorities on their own
> responsibility, these programmes will be neither a part nor an exten-
> sion of the national plan. They are not submitted for state approv-
> al.[26]

In practice, these provisions led to a serious decline in the interest of
local authorities in the programming process. In a large town that played
an active part in Sixth Plan programming, the preparation of the Seventh
Plan was confined to drawing up an inventory of investments, without
any clear fixing of priorities or evaluation of their consequences upon
recurrent expenditure. In one *département* the Prefect prepared a development plan which also included all investments without any evaluation of
the recurrent costs or the financial capacity of the local authorities to

meet them. The Seventh Plan's selective logic did not reach the local level. The local authorities ran the serious risk of becoming the passive receptacle for the partial priorities fixed at the regional or national level. Any independent social planning by the local authorities is bound to reveal the size of the gap between the needs felt and the means available to satisfy them. In a period when the national finances are under severe strain, it is doubtless not desirable to organise a systematic mobilisation of social demand.

At the regional level, the preparation of the Sixth Plan, with the a more intense activity, closer to the spirit of the Seventh Plan, with the preparation of regional priority programmes. It should be noted that the central government did not intend to make a substantial contribution towards regionally-initiated programmes, since only ten per cent of all PAP funds were devoted to them.

Conclusion

French social planning is, therefore, a good example of the extreme centralisation of French public administration. This centralisation is expressed in a very intense concentration of expertise. It is paradoxical to recognise that French social planning originated from economic planning agencies and not the local authorities who are responsible for an ever larger part of social investment. This centralisation is also evident in the state's relations with its 'social partners'. The French state is not confronted by united business or worker organisations, equipped with adequate expertise. In a way, 'concertation' seems to be an attempt to place at the disposal of the interests affected an expertise largely monopolised by the central government.

The emergence of social planning from within the bosom of economic planning has also made it possible to pose publicly and more clearly the problem of the integration of social policy into an overall economic strategy. It remains to be seen whether publicising social goals in the context of developing a market economy represents the line of future progress or a new planner's illusion.

French planning seems to be in a very fluid state. The more limited character of social consensus-building, the semi-independent development of inter-administrative programming and increased political control over the process, all seem to suggest that the plan's hegemonic or socialising function is declining in favour of a more limited function of co-ordination within the machinery of government. It is too soon to say whether this is a temporary aberration or a permanent feature in the development of French planning.

Notes

1. Georges Delange, 'Evolution de la planification française face aux contradictions sociales' in *Planification et Société* (Grenoble, PUG, 1974), p. 379.
2. L. Nizard, *Changement social et appareil d'Etat* (Grenoble, CERAT, 1975).
3. G. Delange, op.cit. p. 391.
4. Jack Hayward, 'The changing political context of French economic planning: a British view' in *Planification et Société*, op. cit. p. 542.
5. L. Nizard, 'De la planification: socialisation et simulation', *Sociologie du travail*, 1972, no. 4.
6. A. Desrosière and P. Nardin, 'Planification, information économique et groupes sociaux' in *Planification et Société*, op. cit. p. 504.
7. Jacques Delors (ed.), *Les indicateurs sociaux* (Paris, Futuribles, 1971).
8. See 'Matériaux pour un historique du système statistique depuis la deuxième guerre mondiale' (Paris, INSEE, June 1976), vol. I, *Statistiques Sociales*.
9. R. Courbis, J.P. Pagé, 'Méthodes de planification et tensions sociales' in *Planification et Société*, p. 351. For a more general critique of the economistic reduction of social phenomena, see B. Jobert, J. Revesz, *Représentation sociale et planification* (Grenoble, CERAT-IEP, 1972).
10. Claude Seibel, 'Modèles et stratégie des acteurs dans la planification', *Revue française de science politique*, XXIII, no. 2, April 1973.
11. Groupe planification sociale, *Pour une planification sociale mieux intégrée* (Paris, Commissariat général du plan, 1973), p. 3.
12. Ibid. p. 19.
13. J. Fournier, 'Quelques réflexions sur la planification sociale et contradictions sociales à partir de l'expérience du VIe Plan' in *Planification et Société*, op. cit. p. 412.
14. Y. Ullmo, 'Pratique de la planification', *Revue française de science politique*, XXIII, no. 2, April 1973, p. 234.
15. *IVème Plan*, p. 6. See CERFI, 'Les équipements du pouvoir', *Recherches*, December 1973, ch. V.
16. Atreize, *La planification française en pratique* (Paris, Editions Economie et Humanisme, 1971), p. 194.
17. Seventh Plan, Book I, introduction, p. XII.
18. For a more complete discussion of this topic, see B. Jobert, B. Revesz, 'La planification et la production sociale du besoin', *Sociologie et sociétés*, April 1974.
19. See B. Jobert, 'Bureaucraties sociales et planification locale', *Aménagement du territoire et développement régional*, 1977.
20. M. Devaud, 'Le devenir de la planification française'. Report presented on behalf of the Economic and Social Council, *Journal Officiel, Conseil économique et social*, no. 4, 1974, p. 1262.
21. Atreize, *La planification française en pratique*, op. cit. p. 190.
22. M. Rocard, 'Debat sur l'avenir de la planification francaise' in *Planification et Société*, op. cit. p. 661.
23. Service du Financement, *Premières estimations de l'enveloppe quinquennale globale des programmes d'actions prioritaires*, Commissariat général du plan, 20 October 1975.
24. Jean de Marcillac, *La conception et le contenu du VIIe Plan*, duplicated, p. 10.
25. P. Cornière, 'Les PME', *Aménagement du territoire et développement régional*, V (Paris, la Documentation Française, 1973).
26. *VIIe Plan*, p. 79.

7 PUBLIC PARTICIPATION AND SOCIAL PLANNING IN BRITAIN AND CZECHOSLOVAKIA

Barry Hills

Public participation in planning decisions can scarcely be dismissed as a transitory political fad. Whether the cause is a greater civic sophistication, irritation at bad planning decisions, or increased potential militancy amongst the members of the 'mass society', it is clear that modern societies are under pressure to provide genuine public involvement in the preparation and formulation of plans affecting the lives of citizens. In Britain strong pressure groups have demanded and obtained the right to be consulted. However, the recent experience of public inquiries illustrates that all is not well. Government-inspired programmes of public participation have not prevented well-founded accusations of 'foul play' and a widespread sense of grievance concerning social planning matters. Czechoslovakia, with its ideological commitment to political and social ends, has relied on a system of local government that emphasises mobilisation and close contact with the citizens who exercise formal political control over the planners. However, public attention has turned increasingly to the role of the planner, to the mistakes resulting from the power that has accrued to planning offices, and to the possibility of asserting, by clearer priorities endorsed by public debate, the primacy of social ends over economic means.

It is by now commonplace to demand that planners explain what they mean by 'planning'. However, the question has not always been gratuitous; the recent development of planning in Britain, responding to depression in the thirties, wartime needs and recurring post-war economic crises, has understandably emphasised varying aspects of our economic needs. The constant factors have been the emphasis on the economic, and the limited conception of the role of planning or, to put it another way, the reluctance or (in a politically pluralist society) the inability to postulate a 'social end' to be achieved by a 'planned society'. Hence planning in Britain has two basic aims: the improvement of deteriorating, stressed, or 'crisis' areas, and the opening up of new regions of development. This is not to suggest that the socialist and free enterprise states cannot share a definition of planning as 'the making of an orderly sequence of action that will lead to the achievement of a stated goal or goals.'[1] It is a matter of limited or total ideological goals.

There can be little doubt that in Britain the whole tone of planning is generally aimed at economic needs rather than social needs and social considerations tend 'to be filed away as one of the many "other things" that are conveniently "being equal".'[2] Increasingly, and especially since 1968, social planners are being consulted during the early stages of plans but there is no shortage of planning horror stories involving economic juggernauts with little or no social consideration. Public outrage at various cost-benefit analyses have confirmed stereotypes of the heartless and amoral planner comparing costs of deaths and traffic lights to see if road safety expenditure can be economically justified. In general, transport policy has provided the worst illustrations of contempt for social concern:

> ... how shoddy is the treatment pedestrians get from transport planners. They are made to scuttle under dark subways through a stench of urine, to climb bridges or walkways, anything rather than interfere with the essential flow of motor traffic ... borough engineers like to enclose pedestrians behind guard rails ... it speeds up traffic and makes people walk twice as far. But the engineers love them.[3]

The environmental/conservationist line-up has now become of course the classic contest between the forces of good and evil with the planners usually, but not always, in the role of the evil; although no one has yet been able to castigate British planners with the sheer depth and intensity of hatred that Daniel Moynihan, when President Nixon's chief planner and urban problems adviser, attracted for his policy of 'public unity and common purpose' buildings in America.[4] In fairness it should be said that political parties have not encouraged environmental concern, and the Labour Party in particular has a very bad record.[5] Even in the field of economics, social planners often have something valuable to say. In Stoke-on-Trent the contraction of the pottery industry has resulted in an over-supply of female labour (traditionally holding the lower paid and boring jobs). Plans for regeneration of the region have not taken note of this need for female employment and consequently stand a lesser chance of success as well as promotion of consensus among the population.

The planners' task has not been made easier by the confusion over the structure and functions of local government. A vast range of functions have been removed from the control of local authorities or transferred to higher levels[6] and local government itself has become less 'local' after the 1972 Local Government Act. Indeed the situation has become so critical that the Layfield Committee, reporting in May 1976, suggested that either local government must accommodate itself to centralisation and discard illusions of independence or central government should hand over new powers, including financial powers, to local government. The latter proposal met immediate resistance from the financial establishment including the Governor of the Bank of England.[7]

Not all the faults lie in the system. If there is no increase in the number of councillors genuinely connected with and interested in the locality they represent, 'it will not be long before local government withers away.'[8] This withering affects the relationship between councillor and officials (including planners) and each can negate the efforts of the other, not necessarily consciously or wilfully. Many would consider the councillor/elector relationship irrevocably withered. Research undertaken by Olga Narkiewicz and myself in Stoke-on-Trent during 1975-6 indicated that only 24 per cent of the city's population claimed to be able to name any of the councillors. Unfortunately 54 per cent of those who thought they knew were wrong, leaving only 11 per cent able to name at least one councillor (as opposed to 26 per cent naming their MP correctly). Only 13 per cent of the citizens had something favourable to say about the council or its policies, but not all the comments ('they got us in the Common Market') were relevant. This last factor is hardly surprising; it is increasingly difficult to know which functions belong to which authority. (Even the political legitimacy of local government is confusing for the citizen: county elections are every four years; metropolitan district elections every year for one-third of the council except in a county council election year; and district elections every four years or as for metropolitan districts, in single member wards or three member wards or a combination.)

> The local council, the county council, the regional boards and hospital committees, the arrangements for consumer consultation in the nationalised industries are not part of a faceless bureaucracy. This is, however, how they must often seem . . . a complex maze of officialdom. Because of this, the person who wants help turns first to the most familiar part of the system—the town hall—only to find that the power lies at a different level of government or with an entirely different kind of public authority.[9]

Admittedly, the lack of comprehensive planning in England and Wales noted by the Redcliffe-Maud Commission has been mitigated by the requirement that structure plans (prepared by county councils and covering employment, housing, transport, conservation, shopping and recreation) and local plans (usually prepared by district councils) be produced and submitted to the appropriate Secretary of State. However, this limits integrated planning to problems within the scope of individual local authorities. One academic study has noted that this allows individual and private interests to dominate structure plans, particularly in the fields of housing, industry and commerce, transport and environment.[10]

Obviously regional planning must accompany the development of structure plans. At the moment there appears to be no will at the higher levels of government to decide what the regions are. The standard regions are commonly assumed to be the eight economic planning regions plus Scotland and Wales but no less than twenty-four public agencies (including government departments) have invented their own regions, choosing to ignore partially or entirely the 'standard regions'. As it is, the eight planning regions have a poor history of co-operation and co-ordination with local authorities, and their (unelected) boards and councils have not been popular voices articulating coherent regional strategies as opposed to pragmatic responses to specific problems.

Of course the question of regionalism is now considered controversial. Firstly, it is often confused with nationalism, although there are regions where many inhabitants claim to be a separate nation, not just a regional variant. In Britain the claims of Shetland Islanders and the Cornish, for example, are met with the same abusive defensiveness, incomprehension and forced amusement as those of the Scots and Welsh some years back.[11] Not infrequently the confusion is deliberate and can be considered a political trick, as when some form of English regional government (as opposed to English national government) is demanded as a sort of compensation for allowing the Scottish and Welsh nations a limited degree of self-government. Secondly, an overall regional policy has not been formulated and it is not clear whether rural regions are would-be industrialised regions, or whether old industrialised areas (like North Lancashire) are capable of former glories. There is no shortage of harsh but valid criticism in this respect: 'The redevelopment of "obsolete areas" (in planning terminology), and the rehabilitation of the less worn areas of urban Britain were undertaken with an arrogant disregard for human and social consequences.'[12]

With the advent of the social planner 'human and social consequences' are now given their due. This befits a system guided by administrators who, since the 1950 Report of the Committee on Qualifications of Planners, have had so long to cultivate a 'creative and imaginative' mind, the 'power of synthesis and broad human understanding', appreciation of 'good design', 'courtesy, human understanding, the sense of service', and, of course, a university education![13] But the controversy has not abated. Two basic criticisms have been voiced. The social planners, theoretically concerned with the relation of human needs and planned environment, have devoted themselves to the 'deprived', thus becoming a twentieth-century version of the nineteenth-century 'Good People' helping the 'poor, honest and dim'. (This is a planner's equivalent of the 'democratic' managing director: 'I don't give orders, but I do demand prompt, unquestioning, obedient response to my suggestions.') In America such individuals have been known, not entirely affectionately, as 'Housers'; at their worst they represent an inefficient throwback to what the Romans understood by planning.[14]

A second criticism is that 'good works' or a sophisticated grasp of social theory is irrelevant. 'Housers', for example, did not realise that the enemy was not bad conditions but the inadequate economic system. This theory has been pushed further and the idea that planning is an instrument of oppression has gained devotees in several planning schools throughout Britain. Certainly the bias towards 'establishment consensus' —the cosy clique administering 'development' at the expense of a commitment to planning which at its very least would involve more than a cautious updating of the *status quo* for the benefit of the wealthy and powerful—has been noticed by several writers.[15] One American critic has generously allowed that planners may be too naive or stupid to realise this tendency:

> . . . it is in that very ability of a social organisation to promote a repressive ideology while masking its effects in the mannerisms and rhetoric of freedom, 'democracy'and 'opportunity' that we find one of the unique forms of repression in both this country and the Soviet Union. The planners' own . . . methods have contributed to this repression. Through this posturing, the real bias behind their plans, whether the bias is intended or not, has been obscured from the people they have affected.[16]

The picture of the planner as oppressor is not entirely convincing especially as public participation is now required before plans are approved by the Department of the Environment (DoE). In July 1969 the report of the Skeffington Committee on Public Participation in Planning was published and its conclusions widely welcomed although the concept of participation was limited. Public involvement was seen as a useful method of reducing hostility:

where information comes too late and without preliminary public discussion there is the likelihood of frustration and hostility. *It may be that the plan produced is the one best suited to the needs of the community* but the reasons for the decision do not emerge . . .[17]

This idea that the participation concept should be used to ease planners' work by lulling the public into a false sense of involvement is perilously close to Moynihan's concept of the planner as a 'doctor' who should positively *try* to keep his 'patients' ignorant. Similarly, the DoE's chief planner has emphasised the fickleness of public opinion and claims to remember the public demanding more office blocks and motorways.[18] Skeffington's report scarcely tries to conceal a condescending tone:

. . . delays could become worse through the injection of public involvement into the intricate process of preparing a plan . . . Each authority should, therefore, prepare a time-table making clear the stages at which they hope to secure *positive* reactions from the public.[19]

But who decides which reactions are 'positive'? Therein lay the seeds of the authoritarian approach which later manifested itself in the banning of the public from public enquiries and the hiring of stewards to remove from enquiries members of the public whose opinions were presumably not considered 'positive'.

This disastrous misunderstanding still regularly leads to ungrateful citizens rejecting the bewildered planners' 'persuasion exercises' as too limited and too late. The suspicion has arisen that a regular set of mechanisms are used to deceive the public, namely: the exclusion from discussion of genuine (and usually noisy and radical) community groups; restricted meetings (uninformative posters or leaflets delivered the same night as meetings); uninformative or over-technical exhibitions; arbitrary and peculiar 'constituencies' for meetings (cutting across natural communities); biased and incompetent surveys (biased questions, no relevant questions, biased response categories, 'other' responses not coded, etc.); and sudden and mysterious appearances of conservative, establishment-orientated Residents' Committees.[20] Enquiries are seen as offering only the most limited debate: 'inviting a condemned man to appeal against his death sentence on condition that he confines himself to comments about whether the eggs in his final breakfast should be poached or boiled.'[21] Even allowing for the natural limits to participation that a society based on representative democracy requires, any corrective should be cherished that prevents planners from seeing themselves as 'new gods, as the inspired creators for whom politicians are merely necessary to provide the means'.[22] At its most limited, participation merely requires adequate communications and in a post-Skeffington age there is evidence that this still causes trouble and annoys people. In a 1976 Consumers' Association study of planning, the most common reason for dissatisfaction (nearly two-thirds of the sample) was the difficulty in obtaining information. Other major complaints were that it was difficult to contact the right people, objections were not taken seriously, enquiries were not answered properly and letters were not acknowledged.[23]

This is, unfortunately, a different world from Skeffington's. A neat programme is suggested that for structure plans, for example, would go as follows:

The Council	The Public
Announcement of programme	
	Hear about it
Planners collect data	
Include special requirements	Collect data
Analyse it	
	Discuss and comment
Publish survey report and define objectives	
Sketch out alternative plan	Public discussion
Publish and state preferences	
Consider comments	
Prepare statement of proposals	
Publish	
Explain it	Come to a view and submit representations
Consider representations	
Revise, publish and submit to Minister	

Formal objection and public enquiry

However, well-established and important pressure groups such as the Council for the Protection of Rural England are frequently ignored and the Skeffington programme implies too simplistic a concept of a 'consultable' local community. Consequently, if 'the community' possesses no instant means of offering an official spokesman with one authoritative viewpoint, it is likely that any consultation will be minimal. Thus the exclusion of dissidents (even at, or especially at, public enquiries) leaves the planners out-of-touch with the real fears and informed wishes of the community. Attempts to penetrate the complex structure of a local community need not always lead to *impasse*. Although those wishing to be consulted need not of course agree amongst themselves, it is quite possible that active opponents of a small part of a plan may be content with an alteration that leaves intact a larger plan generally though lethargically supported by a wider community.

One of the greatest dangers before the 1970s turbulent public enquiries was the increasingly well-documented belief that by the time any planning issue came to a public enquiry, it was all over.

> If megalomaniac civil servants take it into their heads to knock your house down there is precisely nothing you can do about it. The best you can hope for is that the Secretary of State . . . will set up an enquiry into some irrelevant detail of his department's plans. The results of this enquiry can be blandly ignored and will carry little weight as against the advice of his road-besotted civil servants.[24]

All pressure had to be outward-directed and the planners themselves or elected representatives could not or would not do anything. Consequently loud screams might just possibly help but involvement in the planning process was a waste of time. The Skeffington report recognised this lack of interest arïd suggested one answer: that participation in planning is presented as an important aspect of participation in government. This is without doubt democratic in theory, but is it a sufficient inducement? Bernard Shaw's King Magnus had his doubts:

> . . . not one of them will touch this drudgery of government, this public work that never ends because we cannot finish one job without creating ten fresh ones. We get no thanks for it because ninety-nine-hundredths of it is unknown to the people, and the remaining hundredth is resented by them as an invasion of their liberty or an increase in their taxation.[25]

So what happens when 'the people', at least in theory, rise up, establish a people's or socialist democracy and govern the country themselves? In the socialist state a different philosophy of planning prevails: planning is the basis of the state and the means to a social goal desired by all. This is not to state that from a regional point of view the objectives need be different. The major objective of the Yugoslav first five-year plan was in general shared by Czechoslovakia and other East European countries: 'to ensure a faster rate of development of economically backward republics and to remove all consequences of uneven development.' In Czechoslovakia this emphasis on regional development and the reduction of regional disparity (the two do not automatically coincide) was present in the immediate post-war period of socialism and was shared by the Czechoslovak Communist Party (KSČ).[26] However, socialism is not just high-powered planning and a 'critical second attribute' is the ideological devotion to a desired end, in this case the socialist society.[27] Socialist planners seldom fail to emphasise the political aspect of national and regional planning and indeed claim that, basically, planning is a shambles without a socialist background.

> ... The principle of rationality is limited in a capitalist economy to enterprises. In the macro-economic field—that of the entire economy —conditions are lacking for its consistent application ... only with the advent of socialism does the principle of rational operation and economic calculation find conditions for its full implementation.[28]

A British socialist agrees:

> How can the most expert town planner make a reliable plan without some knowledge of the future population of a town, and how can he estimate the future population when the industrial prospects of the town depend on the vagaries of private enterprise?[29]

The importance of ideological definition can be seen here. If rationality is defined as the total devotion of resources to the greatest market demand regardless of national or ideological considerations then Goldmann and Kouba's capitalist economy can be 'rational'; but of course this is not rationality in the sense of a just or fair society.

> Socialism implies the existence of superior aims and objectives which govern the whole country's development consistently. The implementation of the integrated system of local, regional and country-wide plans serves the achievement of these aims and objectives.[30]

Housing policy is an instructive example. Despite the severe shortage of accommodation (not surprising in the aftermath of the war) rents remained frozen after 1945. This policy, especially by the mid-fifties, meant that rents were extremely low and respect for market forces would normally have indicated a long-overdue need for sharp and substantial rent rises. Rents in state-owned housing accounted for only a tiny fraction of the cost of maintenance and repair; turnover of accommodation was extremely limited and private building was almost non-existent. However, erudite economic analysis is inappropriate. Social and ideological considerations outweighed the 'rationality' that, in a strictly economic sense, would have dictated certain solutions in a market economy. In the case of Czechoslovakia, low rents in conjunction with the low wages of the time became a cardinal tenet of government policy. When, by 1959, extra measures were sought, the government encouraged 'co-operative construction', a system of housing that was promoted by generous subsidies and loans. Provision of housing by enterprises was similarly assisted by tax allowances and subsidies.

When in 1964 a major rent revision took place it was primarily aimed at introducing uniformity of rents in accommodation of similar quality. Discounts for those with children could reduce the rent by as much as 50 per cent and subsidies and credits were offered to those building their own homes. Since 1973 married couples can take advantage of a loan of 30,000 kčs (Czechoslovak crowns) at one per cent interest to obtain a flat, with large amounts of the loan written off when a child is born to the couple.

Economic growth mania in the 1950s (not confined to the socialist countries) took its toll, of course. The 'loss' on housing made it a target for priority relegation whenever the economy was sluggish, and low investment in construction led to shortages and delays. However, it is not clear that the ideological commitment to housing, as a social service not affected by market forces, has caused a situation noticeably worse than that to be expected from the 'rationality' of the market. Perhaps one valid criticism could be that housing was not planned *enough*, that its priority as a national objective deserving of steady investment was not sufficiently emphasised as an ideological commitment to be included as a central principle of any plan purporting to serve a social purpose.

It is of course well-known that social considerations or the desired end of planning can become forgotten. Czechoslovak citizens know well enough that a plan can become transformed from a means to an end, and one Czechoslovak economist has suggested that this is a major attribute of Stalinism.[31] This is now being rectified and development priorities have changed from the total commitment to economic growth characteristic of the 1950s and early 1960s to a recognition of the pressing importance of social objectives.

Naturally this calls for a different approach to planning. Planners already have controls (the socialist background they claim is essential) and access to the 'ears of the mighty', but room for flexibility is needed. In 1968-9 abundant evidence came to light showing that an appalling lack of flexibility lowered the quality of life for citizens throughout the republic. Architecture and the environment suffered in particular[32] and one dogmatic, ill-considered decision could affect whole towns. One example will be quoted here. In 1954 a Party functionary visiting Banská Bystrica

> was approached by a delegation of district and municipal officials who asked him to approve a certain change in the plans for the big new cement plant to be built outside the town. In a detailed memorandum experts had proved that the plans had not taken into account the direction of the wind: if the plant was to stand on the spot proposed, Banská Bystrica, the jewel of all the Slovak towns . . . would be showered with ash and heavy cement dust. The delegation put forward an alternative plan . . . it should stand on the other side of the town, to leeward, in a valley where conditions for obtaining the raw materials were ideal. The local draftsmen promised to do all the necessary work in their own time, without payment, so that there would be no increase in costs.

The suggestion was summarily rejected.

> The cement plant was built. In the years since then it has covered the town with a blanket of heavy white dust. After you have been there for a few hours, if you rub your hand over your face, it may leave a bloody scratch as you rub the sharp particles of the ash into your skin.[33]

As no geological research had been done, the inadequate limestone deposit was soon exhausted and now is quarried on the site recommended by the experts and laboriously transported across the town.

Mistakes were neither all wilful nor noticeably worse than those made in Britain. Standard 'block-style' housing was thought to be cheap and, quite rightly from a short-term point of view, dirty industrial plant was considered cheaper than non-polluting plant. With the greater range of controls available to planners in Czechoslovakia and the greater sensitivity to the social and ecological consequences of development, there has been much improvement in the last ten years, especially as neglect of pollution has been recognised as an expensive mistake.[34] Perhaps most important, citizens have become increasingly concerned and are prepared to voice their concern and lobby their local government officials and representatives.[35] The *občanský výbor* (citizens' committees or 'neighbourhood committees')—the lowest level of local government—has a right to be consulted on matters affecting the community and it seems that citizens do indeed identify most closely with this institution.[36] Research by Olga Narkiewicz and myself has indicated that few citizens could name town councillors but nearly all knew some, if not most, of the neighbourhood representatives on the *občanský výbor*. It is open to debate whether formal public participation in the planning process is better or more effective than a representative political system in close contact at its lowest levels with the public.

Like its British counterpart, Czechoslovak local government has experienced major reform, reducing the number of authorities and leaving a trail of wounded feelings and embittered towns. In 1960 the nineteen regions were reduced to ten and the 308 districts became 108. The system is uncomplicated and most people know where to go but, apart from the immediate level of their *občanský výbor*, they are, not surprisingly, disinclined to bother. The National Front/united party method of election and the pressure on citizens to vote discourage a psephological approach but it can be mentioned in passing that local elections have in every case recorded a lower percentage of votes than federal elections.

Inasmuch as the regions are precisely defined, there is no equivalent of the British confusion. The regions are supposed to plan their development in full knowledge of the national requirements as formulated in the national plan. An idyllic picture has been presented by some planners:

> An implicit requirement of planning continuity is the existence of a relevant institutional system responsible both for planning and for the implementation of plans; country-wide plans are prepared by specialised bodies within the central planning authorities. Regional plans are prepared by planning offices associated with regional administrative and economic authorities or sometimes by the central planning level . . . Local plans including urban as well as rural areas are prepared by organisations subordinated to the relevant local authorities.[37]

Control is very much at the top although the Prague-centred hierarchy
that has annoyed the Slovaks so much has been avoided; the Czech Planning Commission and the Slovak Planning Commission are responsible
to their respective national governments (although both governments
are subordinate to the Federal government with its Ministry of Planning). This still leaves the Moravians and Ruthenians without special
consideration. It is noticeable that the research institute set up to
examine the question of special 'urban regions' in Czechoslovakia (a
scheme to provide special development plans for overpopulated industrial centres—12 are proposed for Bohemia/Moravia and 7 for Slovakia[38])
has been tactfully situated in Brno, capital of Moravia. Apart from local
planning, the councils at the regional level see planning primarily as an
information service for a better informed centre although close liaison is
maintained and, whatever happens to the public, the politician-planner
relationship is close.[39] This obviously has its dangers. What is manifestly
'good' to the politician and planner is often a resented policy to the
community involved. Two Czech sociologists have pointed out that
those in apparently dire situations (for example, living in old, sub-
standard homes) are often content, or at the most desirous only of
improvement not redevelopment, because of 'community atmosphere'[40]
—a situation not unknown to British planners.

The danger for Czechoslovak planners is their exalted status. The full
resources of the state are at their command, industrial development is
state-controlled and market forces can be resisted by 'a society that possesses all the pre-conditions for truly scientific management';[41] the new
society is round the corner if priorities are ordered correctly. So who is
to blame if disparities remain and the just society does not materialise?
Chinese planners have an excuse—the structural revolution, political
and economic, is not enough; it is only the right *framework* for the
cultural revolution that leads to a new relationship between citizens,
namely the socialist society. The hapless Czechoslovak planners have no
let-out; they face the wrath of those who have toiled according to plan
and do not see spectacular results. The irony is that their power may
mean *less* control:

> Experience has shown that when the planners seek to embrace too
> many activities, they fail to keep them in their grasp. Spontaneous
> activities go on at lower levels . . . because the plans are too inaccur-
> ate . . . The prescriptive nature of the plans, backed up by the
> sanction of law, reinforces the planner's mental prejudice against
> programmes providing for alternative cources of action to meet

a variety of contingencies

or as Brecht's Mother Courage declared: 'The finest plans have always been spoiled by the littleness of them that should carry them out.'[42] British planners are scarcely better off. They face the wrath but do not have the powers either. The solution need not be to push vast powers onto probably unwilling planners, but, if planning is here to stay as part of our scheme for national advancement, a less coy approach to Britain as a planned society is called for. Planning acting as 'rationalisation of the system rather than a process of socio-political change from within . . . keeping the system on course without enquiring too closely into the ends it is serving'[43] or planners planning as they wish within an acephalous order does not safeguard democracy. Nor does it improve the quality of life, as when theatres refused licences by planning boards are encouraged by the same members sitting as county council arts committees, and tourist boards promote parts of the countryside where the Countryside Commission is attempting to restrain visitors. It would be wrong, however, to suppose that the occasional blustering and inappropriate 'unplanned' response represents the unjust society at its worst. It *could* be worse:

Starving aboriginal children in the town of Wyndham, West Australia, have formed commando raiding parties to search for food in rubbish bins. This has touched the hearts of the local council. 'We are considering ways', they say, 'of dealing with the problem. We intend, for instance, to build a high fence round the area'.[44]

Notes

1. P. Hall, *Urban and Regional Planning* (Harmondsworth, 1974), p. 6.
2. M. Broady, *Planning for People: Essays on the Social Context of Planning* (London, 1968), p. 65.
3. J. Buglar, 'Knockout tournament', *Guardian*, 8 March 1976, p. 14. The cost-benefit analysis is an actual case: see L. Allison, *Environmental Planning: A Political and Philosophical Analysis* (London, 1975), ch. 7, esp. pp. 82-3.
4. See in particular R. Goodman, *After the Planners* (Harmondsworth, 1972), pp. 142-8 and 203-6. Goodman points out the amazing similarities between Moynihan's planning policies and Hitler's in *Mein Kampf*.
5. 'Labour in power gives every appearance of taking political decisions on the basis that environmentalists are opposed to the interests of the working man', J. Buglar, 'The Left and the Environment', *New Statesman*, 16 April 1976, pp. 500-2.
6. For an account of this see P. G. Richards, *The Reformed Local Government System* (London, 1973), ch. 1, and J. Norton, *The Best Laid Schemes?* (London, 1970), ch. 1. However, it should be noticed that confusion and deadlock existed before the reorganisation. An admit-

tedly antagonistic source claimed as early as 1950 that 'there are no local authorities in existence capable of carrying out regional plans', R. Darwin, 'Town Planning under Democratic Socialism', *Communist Review*, January 1950, pp. 26-32.

7. For a summary of the Layfield proposals see *Guardian*, 20 May 1976, p. 12 and for the reaction: 'Money men will oppose Layfield', *Guardian*, 19 June 1976, p. 5.

8. G. Mallaby, *Local Government Councillors–Their Motives and Manners* (London, 1976), p. 2.

9. D.M. Hill, *Participating in Local Affairs* (Harmondsworth, 1970), pp. 42-3.

10. North East Area Study Group, *Social Consequences and Implications of the Teeside Structure Plan: Summary Report* (Working Paper no. 37), July 1976. See also J. Ardill, 'University fails council plan', *Guardian*, 8 March 1976, p. 7.

11. Rev. D. Jenkins, for example, has managed to convince himself that the enthusiasm of some Welsh for their own Welsh community is reminiscent of fascism. 'The Ecumenical Dimension of Devolution', *Crucible*, October/December 1975, pp. 156-60. Antagonistic reactions have not always been a standard response to nationalist demands. In 1918 the Labour Party at its annual conference called for separate Scottish, Welsh and English legislatures and in 1895 the House of Commons passed a resolution favouring separate national legislatures.

12. J.A.D. Palmer in Introduction to R. Goodman, op.cit. p. 26.

13. Ministry of Town and Country Planning, *Report of the Committee on Qualifications of Planners*, Cmnd. 8059 (London, HMSO, 1950), pp. 70-1.

14. ' . . . the maximum population and size were determined before construction began. The planners then allocated adequate space for houses, shops, squares, and temples. They decided how much water would be needed and the number and size of streets, pavements and sewers. By planning this way they tried to satisfy the needs of every individual–rich and poor alike', D. Macaulay, *City: A Story of Roman Planning and Construction* (London, 1975), p. 5.

15. A Broadbent, 'Planners' Plight', *New Society*, 20 November 1975, pp. 426-7. See also M. Watson, 'A Comparative evaluation of planning practice in the liberal democratic state' in J. Hayward and M. Watson (eds.), *Planning, Politics and Public Policy* (London, 1975), pp. 445-83. For grassroots opinion: 'Local Power and Who Controls it', *Community Action*, no. 15, 1974, pp. 23-8 and 'The Democratic Charade Exposed', *Community Action*, no. 16, 1974, pp. 27-31. One response of planners concerned with this situation has been to form an Association of Socialist Planners.

16. R. Goodman, op.cit. p. 52.

17. *People and Planning: Report of the Committee on Public Participation in Planning* (London, HMSO, 1969), p. 3. Italics added.

18. *Guardian*, 8 July 1976, p. 4.

19. *People and Planning*, op. cit. p. 5. Italics added.

20. For a full discussion of such methods see Chapeltown Community Centre's *Planning to deceive: A critique of Leeds Council's 'participation planning exercise'* (Leeds, 1975).

21. R. Boston, *Guardian*, 2 October 1976, p. 11. See also R. Batley, 'An Explanation of Non-Participation in Planning', *Policy and Politics*, vol. 1, no. 2, pp. 95-114.

22. B. Jobert, 'Urban Planning and Political Institutions' in J. Hayward and M. Watson (eds.), op.cit. p. 378.

23. 'Planning' in *Which?*, June 1976, pp. 133-8.

24. R. Boston, op.cit.

25. G. B. Shaw, *The Apple Cart* (Harmondsworth, 1956), p. 75.

26. F.B. Singleton, 'Problems of Regional Economic Development: The Case of

Yugoslavia', *Jahrbuch Der Wirtschaft Osteuropas*, vol. 2 (Munich, 1971), pp. 375-95. See also the paper prepared by Hungarian planners: Economic Commission for Europe, *Seminar on National and Regional Planning as Frameworks for Local Planning, Document HBP/SEM. 7/R. 7*, 27 September 1974. For the pre-1948 period in Czechoslovakia: Central Planning Commission, *The First Czechoslovak Plan: Explanatory Memorandum and Text* (Prague), pp. 6 and 75-8; and for the KSČ attitude: Czechoslovak Ministry of Information, *Long-Term Planning in Czechoslovakia* (Prague, 1947), p. 14. (Speech by KSČ President K. Gottwald.)
27. This is discussed in full in R.L. Heilbroner, *Between Capitalism and Socialism* (New York, 1970), esp. pp. 79-114. See also M. Lavigne, *The Socialist Economies of the Soviet Union and Europe* (London, 1974), pp. ix and xi-xvii.
28. J. Goldmann and K. Kouba, *Economic Growth in Czechoslovakia* (Prague, 1969), p. 116. For a Polish viewpoint see Economic Commission for Europe, op.cit., *Document HBP/SEM. 7/R.2*, 2 August 1974.
29. R. Darwin, op.cit. p. 29.
30. Economic Commission for Europe, op.cit., *Document HBP/SEM. 7/4*, 15 September 1975, p. 73; R.L. Heilbroner, op.cit. p. 91.
31. R. Selucky, *Czechoslovakia: The Plan that Failed* (London, 1970), esp. pp. 79-87. The problem was not unrecognised by top Party leaders: see the speech by J. Lenárt (then Czechoslovak Prime Minister) to the KSČ Central Committee, *Rudé Pravo*, 2 February 1965, p. 3.
32. See the entire issue of *Architektura ČSSR*, no. 3, 1969, and for a discussion of the problem in general A. Lindbeck, 'The Efficiency of Competition and Planning' in M. Kaser and R. Portes (eds.), *Planning and Market Relations* (London, 1971), pp. 83-107.
33. L. Mňačko, *The Seventh Night* (London, 1969), pp. 139-40.
34. Costing Czechoslovakia about 4,000 million kčs per year, *Životné Prostredie*, no. 4, 1973, p. 203. Also *30 Let Československého Hospodářství a Všeobecného Rozvoje ČSSR* (Prague, 1975), p. 68.
35. *Životné Prostredie*, no. 4, 1973, p. 199.
36. M. Malý and A. Friedl, *Národní Výbory a Občan* (Prague, 1973).
37. Economic Commission for Europe, op.cit., *Document HBP/SEM. 7/R.2*, 2 August 1974. See also J. Haliena, 'K. Otázkam oblastného plánovaia', *Nová Mysl*, no. 2, 1976, pp. 120-4.
38. *Architektura ČSR*, no. 2, 1974, p. 98. Decentralisation in Czechoslovakia before the federalisation of 1969 did not always mean greater autonomy or advantage for Slovakia; J.M. Montias, 'Economic Reform in Perspective', *Survey*, no. 59, 1966, pp. 48-60, esp. pp. 52 and 59.
39. J. Matoušek and V. Uhlíř, 'Úloha národních výborů v řízení a plánování rozvoje národního hospodářství', *Plánované Hospodářství*, no. 10, 1974, pp. 1-8. Also O. Žúrek, 'Oblastní plánovaní a národní výbory', *Plánované Hospodářství*, no. 8, 1969, pp. 33-40.
40. J. Musil and M. Pozderová, *Společenské Požadavky a Důsledky Vyplývající z Asanaci Obytných Čtvrti* (Prague, 1965).
41. O. Sik, *Czechoslovakia: The Bureaucratic Economy* (New York, 1972), p. 51.
42. J.M. Montias, 'A Plan for all Seasons', *Survey*, no. 51, 1964, p. 74. B. Brecht, *Mother Courage and her Children* (London, 1962), p. 48.
43. M. Watson, op.cit. p. 459.
44. Reported in *Punch*, 3 February 1971, p. 175.

8 SPATIAL PLANNING IN POLAND AND LOCAL GOVERNMENT REORGANISATION, 1961-75

Danuta Jachniak-Ganguly

The Administrative Structure before and after the Reforms of 1972-5

The economic and political developments in Poland in the last two decades have made it imperative that local government be changed in order to meet the needs for spatial planning. How such change is to be carried out, whether by decentralisation, or by a change in the degree of centralisation, has been the topic of political discussion for a long period. In the event, the recent changes have produced a dramatic restructuring of government bodies at all, except for the central level, but such changes appear to owe little either to centralising or decentralising factors. In order to understand them, one must take a brief look at the historical events which shaped Polish local government.

Despite frequent changes of frontiers, partitions by foreign powers and occupations during the last two wars, certain features of Poland have remained constant for centuries. These were the geographical regions, each with distinctive borders, characteristics and traditions. The geographical regions dated back to the late middle ages, before the state was centralised, and they retained vestiges of former regional governments. To institutionalise such traditions, and also to allow a voice in local affairs to the Lithuanian and Ruthenian parts of the Polish Commonwealth after it was created, a wide network of local institutions existed up to the partitions. These were based on local diets: assemblies of gentlemen which met at regular intervals to elect a deputy to the central Seym, as well as to discuss local affairs. The cities, granted a wide measure of autonomy, had similar self-governing bodies. The central state had never been very strong, the gentry having seen to it that a minimum of taxes were collected, that there was no standing army, and that there was no central apparatus to enforce either tax collection or military service. The elective monarchy had a particularly difficult task, and unless a monarch could command wide respect by his military abilities or a large fortune, he found it almost impossible to recruit troops in time of war or invasion.

This state of affairs, as is well known, led to the partition of Poland by Russia, Prussia and Austria in the late eighteenth century. But there was another aspect to it: more than in any other European state, with the exception perhaps of the United Kingdom, where local government has very strong traditions, the Poles were accustomed to the fact that regional government was the most important authority in decision-making and they regarded central government as an imposition. A citizen with full rights (i.e. a gentleman or a burgher) had the inalienable right to decide matters of importance without the interference of central government, particularly in local affairs.

The admirers of a strong centralised state, on the French model, deplored this tendency, but the attempts at reform in the second half of the eighteenth century showed that it was so deeply rooted as to be almost impossible to eradicate. The strong local traditions, described by the centralists as 'parochial', were clearly of more importance than a modern centralised state could ever be, and the divisions between regions did not grown any less. This was reinforced by the partitions, when Poland was divided among three different states for a period of nearly one-and-a-half centuries. It probably saved the country from total extinction because, accustomed to provincialism, the Poles continued to live within their units, dealing with the foreign governments with only slightly more distrust than that which they had exhibited towards their own. The partitioning powers did not attempt to break down the regional barriers, mostly leaving them intact and imposing their own administration above them.[1] The cities were still left with a measure of autonomy in all partitions, and the only really radical change at local level occurred after the emancipation of the peasants. Because of this, the magisterial powers of the landlords were abolished or modified and new institutions had to be created.

This brief outline may serve to explain the fact that in 1918 the Polish Republic emerged with a remarkably similar administrative division to that of pre-partition days but with an extremely mixed system of administration at the lowest levels. This mixed system had four different sources: the Prussian administration in the German partition; the Austrian administration in former Galicia; the administration of the semi-autonomous Kingdom of Poland within the Russian Empire; and the administration of the Russian partition proper (outside the Kingdom of Poland, but within the borders of the old Polish Commonwealth). The Republic was divided into sixteen regions (*voivodships*), all based on the old territorial divisions. Each region was headed by a *voivoda*, a chief executive, appointed by the President of the Republic. Each region was divided into districts (*powiat*), headed by a *starosta*, appointed by the Minister of the Interior. The division into districts was very uneven as there was unwillingness to break up the traditional regions and some regions had only nine while others had 36 districts. As a result, not much change was introduced at these upper levels. But at lower levels, the situation was much more difficult. During the partitions local government systems had been created which the Republic felt unable to abolish overnight, though in the twenty-one years of its existence some changes were made and a degree of unification achieved. There were two types of lowest unit: a rural borough (*gmina*), equivalent to one village, and a collective rural borough (also called *gmina*), equivalent to several villages. Collective rural boroughs were divided into smaller units, called *gromada*. In every former partition area there was a different system of rural borough administration; in some instances by an appointed official only, in others by a mixture of appointed officials and elected representatives. In some instances the same person served as an appointee and an elected representative of the people. The system was in abeyance in the period of 1939-45 and the People's Republic in 1945 was faced by a considerable dilemma. The new administrative system had to be established under new territorial conditions. The four eastern *voivodships* had become part of the USSR. In their place five *voivodships* were created in the western territories.

By 1946 the state was divided into 14 *voivodships,* 268 districts and 3,236 collective rural boroughs (*gmina*) which were subdivided into 38,347 communes (*gromada*) with the addition of towns which had the status of districts. Some changes occurred soon afterwards and, in 1954, before the first significant administrative reform, there were 17 voivodships, 276 districts, 2,956 collective rural boroughs and 40,098 communes.[2] In 1954 an administrative reform was carried out, abolishing collective rural boroughs and communes. In their place, a collective commune (called *gromada*) was set up, comprising several villages. These new communes were to have from 1,000 to 3,000 inhabitants instead of the 5,000-18,000 inhabitants in the former collective boroughs. Each commune would constitute an entity, where good communications and centrally-placed commune offices would facilitate the running of the unit. This reform was not successful and several ministerial decrees of 1954, 1955 and 1956 attempted to improve the existing communes, create new ones, abolish the unsuccessful ones and create new districts and townships. A drastic reduction in the number of communes was carried out on 1 January 1956[3] and more changes were introduced when the new law on People's Councils was promulgated in January 1958.[4]

To underpin the system of local administration, the People's Republic quickly established a system of People's Councils. The first decree was issued by the Polish Committee of Liberation on 21 September 1944. According to this, the deputies to councils were to be appointed by political parties, trade unions, co-operative organisations and other bodies. They were to function alongside the offices of the *voivoda* and the *starosta*, who were the heads of regions and districts respectively, and were appointed by the central government, as formerly. The councils were given the task of supervising the activity of the administrators.[5] However, the first elections to the councils did not take place till 1954, after the adoption of the Constitution of 22 July 1952. Article 37 of the Constitution stated that 'the People's Councils direct, within their competence, the economic, social and cultural activities, linking the needs of the locality with the principles of the state.'[6] All administrative tasks were now entrusted to the councils, the offices of *voivoda* and *starosta* having been abolished in 1950. However, the councils were very closely controlled by financial limitations, because their budgets were established at the central level. In October 1956 a decree of the Council of Ministers broadened their rights considerably. They were still only allowed a global sum from the central budget but they could now use it as they wished, according to local needs. They were also empowered to raise their own income from taxing industrial enterprises, co-operatives and private enterprises in their area.[7] A law passed in 1958 further widened the councils' financial powers by allowing them to vote their own annual budgets but subjected this to the approval of the Ministry of Finance. In addition, the councils at lowest levels were subject to the old regulations about ratification by a higher body.[8]

The law on the People's Councils, promulgated in January 1958, defined their functions in an attempt to regulate and improve their activity. This was agreed to be poor at the highest government levels and was given prominence by Ignar's pronouncement in 1956 that 'We have called the commune councils a great achievement for the working people. Simultaneously, we have arrived at the conclusion . . . that the councils do not carry out their tasks. They have many functions, but few possibilities.'[9] Cyrankiewicz stated in the Seym that the commune councils 'have become the executors of the higher offices, mostly in the field of taxation and contracts. They do not show any initiative in the economic, educational and cultural fields.'[10] The 1958 law established that the councils were the main agents of the government in their area; that they could control all enterprises in the area; that they could supervise both the institutions which were subject to them and those which were not; and that they could raise their own sources of income.

However, the law did not abolish the right of the Supreme Chamber of State Control to supervise the councils, nor the right of the Ministry of Finance, the State Procurator, or 'other control organs' to control their work. It also broke new ground by allowing the Council of State to dissolve the councils when a breach of political or legal regulations occurred.[11] In 1961 additional powers of formulating and executing annual and long-term economic plans were added to the councils' powers.

The structure of the councils prior to 1975 was as follows. There were three tiers of administration—voivodship, district and commune. At each level all administrative tasks were carried out by the councils. Five cities were independent of their respective voivodship and many towns had the status of a district. The councils were made up of elective deputies, committees (whose members were co-opted) and the praesidium as the chief executive body of the council, as well as various executive departments which were dually subordinated to the council and to their own ministry. The machinery tended to be top-heavy, slow and inefficient; nevertheless, it was reasonably democratic. However, because of the structure of the councils, too many functions were left to the appointed officials and the collective responsibility of the praesidium made decision-making difficult.

Partly because of these shortcomings and partly because of the change of leadership in 1970, a radical change was introduced in 1972, when a new law transferred the functions of the praesidium to the chief executive of the council. This was a professional administrator who was appointed for an unspecified period. With the help of a small independent staff, he was to carry out a dual function: as the council's management executive and as the local administrative officer. This change was introduced at commune level first, and later (in November 1973) extended to the voivodship and district levels. In the 17 voivodships the title of the *voivoda* (abolished in 1950) was given to this administrator. In the five cities of voivodship status, his title was that of the president of the city. In the districts, he was usually called the chief executive.

The reasons advanced in favour of this reform were that, firstly, the praesidium had too often come under the control of administrative specialists, such as department heads; secondly, the praesidium did not really perform a praesidial function, i.e., instead of directing council work, it was concerned with its executive management functions; and, thirdly, the praesidium, as an intermediary between councillors and specialists, obscured the lines of responsibility. The role of the deputies *vis-à-vis* the administrators would be strengthened if it were clear who took the responsibility for administrative work. The People's Council would now be seen in the wider context of the entire economic system, at the same time as greater authority was given to directors of state enterprises. And, finally, one-man management would be efficient and stronger than collective management.

The newly-appointed administrators were given all the powers previously belonging to the praesidium and some additional ones. The general pattern of giving councils a greater say in the co-ordination of the work of all enterprises in their locality was demonstrated in the increased powers given to the *voivodas* and city presidents, especially over institutions not subordinated to the council. They could now, with respect to centrally-controlled industry, suspend enterprise directors if they considered they were not carrying out their duties, and they had to approve of any plans for creating or liquidating such enterprises. In locally-controlled enterprises they were to appoint all department heads, directors, deputy directors and chief accountants. They were also now the chief representatives of the central government in their area and were to carry out tasks entrusted to them by the Council of Ministers. In individual administrative cases their decisions were to be final and in times of danger to life, health or property, caused by 'spontaneous disasters' or economic disorders, *voivodas,* presidents and executives of districts and communes were empowered to issue a wide range of directives. It was thought that as a result of these changes, administration would be the personal responsibility of one man and would make him more responsive to the influence of the elected deputies.[12]

The basis for such changes had been laid down by the Sixth Congress of the Polish United Workers' Party (PUWP) in December 1971, when a number of resolutions were passed affecting the system of People's Councils. These were: that central control over the balancing of local budgets should be relaxed; that higher tiers of government should concentrate on basic economic and social objectives; that the main functions of the central organs should be the planning of economic and social development, the provision of resources to ensure that they are carried out and the supervision over the process of implementation; and finally that the local administration should be modernised.[13]

In order to solve these problems a joint Party-Government Committee for the Modernisation of the State, Economy and the Management Systems was established after the Sixth Congress of the PUWP. The ideas for such reforms were a sequel to long years of political and technical discussions which sought to interpret the socialist concept of administration and relate it to the conditions of everyday life in Poland. Five basic strands of thought behind the reform can be identified:

(1) In socialist economies the efficiency of the system is to a large extent determined by that of the smallest production and administrative unit. Thus the strengthening of the lowest level of administration and the delegation to it of more economic and administrative resources is of importance.

(2) Socialist democracy can be strengthened by providing the best possible service to the population. In practice this meant allowing the towns and rural communities more power and thus a greater say in the running of their own lives.

(3) There was a need to make management and administration more efficient and responsive. This belief gained support during an experiment in 1970, when decisions at the regional and commune levels only were taken, and it was thought that a two-tier system of administration was likely to be more effective in the decision-making context. The reorganisation of the system into a two-tier one was seen as a mechanism for obtaining greater public participation and for streamlining the decision-making process.

(4) The demand for an increased rate of economic development. Previous experience seemed to suggest that the highest growth-rates were achieved in urban agglomerations and it was noticeable that the administrative set-up was a spur to development and to urbanisation processes. This prompted the project to form 32 new voivodships.

(5) Local government was to be an integral part of the economic development of the country. Thus its aims and objectives had to be in harmony and it was felt that the existing administrative structure was inadequate in the light of the emerging spatial patterns over the last 30 years.

Such arguments and other similar ones, were instrumental in the final local government reorganisation which was introduced in three stages: in 1972, 1973 and 1975. On 29 November 1972 a law was passed which abolished the old communes, replacing them by larger ones. 2,365 larger communes were established (now called *gmina*) which were on average twice the size of the former commune with an average population of 7,000 and an average area of 130 sq.kms. This was a striking reversal to the pre-1954 administrative division, but was justified by Gierek's vision of the communes as an 'economic micro-region' which would act as an organ of local self-management, with considerable financial authority. It also meant the second tier of local government, the district, would no longer be a basic administrative unit.[14]

The new commune would now be big enough to be an effective economic entity and would be able to cope with the problems of modern farm production and to provide the necessary facilities for the well-being of the community (schools, health centres, marketing co-operatives, farm machinery, repair centres, co-operative banks and so on). To facilitate this, the communes were given more powers and wider sources of revenue. They could now raise turnover tax on local industry; examine and co-ordinate the investment projects of local industry; dispose of budget surpluses as they saw fit; influence the drawing-up of local economic and social development plans; set up special funds from local revenue to undertake projects of an economic or cultural nature; and embark on joint ventures with neighbouring communes, or form a joint council with a neighbouring town. In addition central subsidies were to be awarded for longer periods. The overall effect aimed at was the curtailing of the powers of the old voivodship and a corresponding increase in the powers of the primary tier, i.e. more democracy and less centralism.

In the following year administration in districts and voivodships was simplified by the separation of the administrative organs from the elective bodies and executive officers were appointed at all levels. The voivodships abolished their departments (sometimes as many as thirty or forty) and the chief executive with a small staff, responsible directly to the Prime Minister, took over the task of administration. To counteract his personal power, the principle was introduced that the first secretary of the PUWP would be elected the chairman of the People's Council and the leaders of other parties would become deputy chairmen. (This had in fact been the case at higher levels before, but was not legally enforced.) The new arrangement was intended to enhance the consultative power of the councils in their new task of concentrating on policy problems concerned with economic and social development.

To complement this change, an electoral reform was carried out in September 1973 with a view to broadening the representative nature of the councils. Council elections were no longer to be held concurrently with those of the Seym; electoral commissions at commune level were set up for the first time; and the size of the councils was increased considerably in order to encourage self-management.[15]

The final stage of the reform was introduced on 28 May 1975 when the district tier of local government was abolished and a new Ministry of Administration, Regional Economy and Environmental Protection was set up. From 1 June 1975 the basic units of administration became the communes, towns and, in bigger cities, neighbourhoods. Voivodship borders were redrawn to act as unified city regions, so that they had more homogeneous socio-economic profiles. Some were to specialise in selected sections of industry, others in agriculture, yet others in tourism. Their immediate task was to act as planning authorities for their areas. The bulk of their previous powers had been transferred to the commune level. The 17 voivodships had been increased to 49. Most former districts were incorporated into voivodships as complete units in order to minimise confusion and preserve continuity of operations. Of the 314 districts, 76 needed slight adjustments and only 29 were broken up. The population of the voivodships still varies from 280,000 to almost 3,400,000 while the number of local authorities in each ranges from 28 to 96 with the exception of Katowice, where there are 136.

Another new institution was the metropolitan area. These have been formed in big cities: Warsaw, Łódź and Kraków, where old divisions into boroughs, towns, settlements and districts have been retained. Each of these, like the boroughs, has its own council which is a primary level unit, the supervisory body being the council of the metropolitan area. In addition, Wrocław has retained the status of a city together with a division into boroughs, but it now shares a council with the separate Wrocław Voivodship. Poznań, the smallest of the cities, has been made a town at primary level, no longer with wards, but with its own urban council, subject to the Poznań Voivodship council.[16]

These three different solutions were treated as pilot schemes to provide information as to the best arrangement for other large cities, when they began to acquire national significance. The new voivodship authorities have become the sole link between the central and local authorities. Local and voivodship administration is responsible to the Prime Minister, while ongoing supervision is carried out by the Ministry of Administration, Regional Economy and Environmental Protection.

As can be seen from the above account, many of the 1972-5 changes were merely a reversion to former practices: these include the restoration of larger communes and the reintroduction of the office of the *voivoda*. Others were new to the socialist state but were in direct line with the administrative system in the Polish Republic; these include the separation of the executive and legislative bodies and the introduction of personal responsibility for decision-making. Yet others were completely new. For example, the abolition of what appeared to be the middle tier of local government involved the *de facto* break-up of the top tier of local government. The requirement that each local council be chaired *ex officio* by the First Secretary of the PUWP introduced a degree of political control that had not been thought necessary previously.

The sweeping nature of the reforms makes one naturally wonder why, in a state which is short of resources and is suffering the effects of inflation and shortages resulting from the oil crisis, such measures should be introduced, particularly since there had been frequent local government reforms in the previous thirty years (two major ones and four minor ones). Apart from the obvious reasons that the reform may increase the efficiency of the administration and possibly local democracy, the answer appears to be the necessity to improve the system of planning and harmonise it with that of local administration. Under the old system, planning was the weak link in the chain of command, with one exception—that of economic planning, which took precedence over all other activities.

If the foundation of a socialist state is to be an efficient planned economy combined with a participatory government, then the changes carried out in Poland appear to be aimed at such a solution. This hypothesis is supported by the fact that extensive changes in the system of planning, with an upgrading of non-economic planning, have been carried out concurrently with the administrative reforms. One must now consider these in the context of the reform of the structure of local government.

The System of Spatial Planning

Spatial planning in Poland has always been regarded as an aspect of the comprehensive system of planning. In the early post-war period it was almost completely independent of the still underdeveloped economic planning; then, for some time, it was dominated by the latter. The slow process of integrating the two organisationally separate sub-systems of planning began after the promulgation of the 1961 Spatial Planning Act. While spatial planning had its inception in the period before the Second World War (such as the Building Laws of 1928 and the Regional Planning Law of 1939), economic planning is more recent, having begun after the war because of the need to create an industrial base suitable for a socialist economy. The basis for such planning was the social ownership of capital and the predominant role of the state in directing economic activities. There were several economic plans between 1947 and 1956, all of them directed at the restoration of the economy first, and the expansion of industrial development in the second place. In 1957 long-term perspective planning was introduced (after the governmental changes of 1956) and, while this helped to create the right conditions for

regional planning, it was not till the introduction of the Spatial Planning
Act of 1961 that the legal framework of spatial planning was created.[17]
The Act took into account past experience and the methodological
results of spatial planning and brought together, at regional level, spatial
and economic plans in the context of long-term national plans. The
most important provisions of the Act were as follows:

1. a methodological and organisational division of spatial planning
into national, regional and local (or town) planning;
2. the incorporation of regional planning into the perspective socio-
economic plan;
3. the extension of regional planning over the whole of the country
by means of general plans.

The economic goals of the 1961-5 plan stressed the development of
the base of raw materials—especially fuel, energy and chemicals—and
the process of balancing production and consumption. However, the
spatial plan at the national level had not been elaborated and the regional plans had the character of a set of recommendations. A great effort
has been made since to link the local spatial plans with plans and economic policies at regional level. Since 1963, too, there has been an
emphasis on the modernisation of agriculture.

The 1966-70 plan aimed at working out detailed employment policies for the regions, with a view to balancing regional employment and
creating more jobs. In 1967 a special office was created within the Planning Commission with the responsibility of preparing the national economic plan. It was also to draw up, in co-operation with regional planning offices, ministries and scientific bodies, a draft plan for spatial development of the country which was to be an integral part of the perspective plan for the development of the national economy up to 1985 and
strategic developments up to 2000. So far, however, only studies and
drafts have been completed.

The 1961 Spatial Planning Act defined the aims of spatial planning
as follows: it was to ensure proper development of the various regions;
it was to establish spatial relations between the production and service
facilities in the regions; and to create the spatial conditions necessary
for economic development, social consumption and protection of the
natural resources and environment. Land-use plans, considered as specific
planning tools to implement these aims, were based on economic plans
and various studies. The Act made a distinction between spatial planning
at the national and regional levels, which was to be exercised within long-

term planning at the appropriate level, and spatial planning at the local level, which was to be organisationally separate from economic planning. In practice, however, national and regional planning had a comprehensive (spatial and economic) character, and alongside it there existed sectoral and territorial economic planning.

Since spatial planning is a process of interaction between various levels of planning and various institutions, it has in general been the task of several bodies to carry it out. In the 1961-72 period two different ministries were engaged in the planning processes: the Planning Commission at the Council of Ministers (PCCM), responsible for spatial-economic, sectoral-economic and territorial-economic planning, and the Ministry of Building Construction, responsible for local spatial planning. The PCCM drafted the economic plans on the basis of proposals made by the ministers and People's Councils, and from 1967 began to prepare national spatial plans. The regional planning offices at the Voivodship Economic Planning Commissions, subject to the PCCM, worked out long-term regional plans for voivodships. The departments of PCCM and the relevant ministries elaborated at the central level the development plans of the sectors and branches of the national economy.[18] The draft plans were prepared first at the union and enterprise levels. Sectoral-economic planning was the most important type of planning in Poland but it had a limited use in spatial planning as it only gave provisional locations of proposed investments and proposals were made for five-year periods only.

The 1961 Spatial Planning Act established that at each level spatial planning should be undertaken within the framework of the economic plan at the national, regional and local levels. All spatial plans were to be inter-related and to complement one another. At regional level the plan is to be treated as a guideline for all the detailed plans which are limited to elements included in the general plan. Each plan has a slightly different character. National plans, although prepared in close connection with the long-term plan of socio-economic development, are concerned mainly with determining the functions of particular towns and regions of the country; with creating the basis for the territorial distribution of particular types of activity; and with the shaping of the systems of technical infrastructure. Regional plans are, primarily, socio-economic plans for the development of the regions. Local plans concentrate on the decisions concerning utilisation and the physical and technical development of a given area. Although they are based on the analysis of intentions maintained in the economic plans, they are, formally at least, autonomous in relation to those economic plans.

By the late 1960s there were discussions at the highest level about the role of planning as a tool for co-ordinating the investment activities of the various decision-makers. More particularly, there was the problem of extending the spatial planning functions within the system of planning as a whole. Until the period 1972-5 only a few regional plans had a comprehensive (spatial and socio-economic) character. There was no national spatial plan, despite the fact that several specific studies had been carried out. At the regional level, two separate sub-systems existed: one for spatial planning at the local level and another for economic planning at territorial level. Because these plans covered different periods of time, they were not linked at all. The need for co-ordination arose from the fact that economic activity was carried out by a very large number of relatively independent economic units at different levels. Though these units were state-owned and their activity already co-ordinated within the sectoral planning sub-system, this made little difference, as the aims of these sub-systems were purely economic and often contradicted the national, or even the regional, social plans.

The territorial plans were concerned only with economic activities subordinated to the regional level, whereas regional plans were more general and covered all activities in the region, economic as well as non-economic. Therefore, neither the territorial nor the regional plans were capable of horizontal co-ordination of economic activities, which is necessary to create conditions in which various activities can be rationalised, so as to achieve the best results from a given amount of resources. The problem became even more acute following the increased autonomy granted to the economic units in the 1960s and the increasing decentralisation of planning and management. The existing regional planning structure revealed problems in the co-ordination of plans of neighbouring voivodships and the financing of joint projects. These problems of regional planning led to the reformulation of the aims of spatial planning and to structural changes in the planning system.

Since the late 1960s the specific objectives of spatial planning have been seen as part of the aims of general planning, i.e.:

socially, to secure the best conditions for the people's life and work and to eliminate differences in living conditions in the various regions;

economically, to optimise the productive capacity of an area by the most fruitful exploitation of its resources and the enhancement of its value;

environmentally, to protect the natural environment and to increase its resources.

Two other tasks have been added to those specified by the 1961 Spatial Planning Act: to distribute spatially the processes of production and consumption; and to provide guidelines for co-ordinating the actions, in space and time, of the various decision-makers taking part in the development process. In this way spatial planning became the basis of all spatial policies.

To attain these new objectives and to bring about a more effective use of resources, a White Paper in 1972 called for plans to be prepared on a 'macro-regional' basis, in order to have the means of tackling problems in areas with similar development characteristics. Thus, depending on the aims of a particular project, 'macro' plans would concentrate on the problem, rather than trying to sum up the individual regional plans. Initially three macro-regions were designated: northern, southern and south-eastern. These plans and the existence of a few agglomeration plans which did not belong to any of the three tiers of planning destroyed the symmetry of planning.

While one of the main aims of the administrative reforms of the seventies has been to create better conditions for planning, the reforms themselves caused some new problems of planning. These were as follows: the necessity of co-ordinating the regional system of planning at a level higher than the new voivodships; the adaptation of the local and regional plans to the new functions of local government; the establishment of planning offices in local authority offices; and the takeover of planning duties previously carried out at district level. To cope with these problems and in order to strengthen central strategic planning, local medium-term planning and the spatial approach, it has been found necessary to redefine the existing planning structure at all levels.

Under the new definition, plans at the national level are to be prepared as before with the following aims:[19] the long-term socio-economic development of the country; the long-term spatial development of the country (this now being recognised as of equal importance to the previous aim); medium-term socio-economic development, until then inclusive of the spatial plan; the development of sectors and branches of the national economy (these plans have again acquired a long-term and spatial character).

In addition, new forms of planning have been initiated, in order to prepare: forecasts of strategic problems (i.e. social consumption patterns, technological advances and so on), and long-term programmes to meet basic social needs (housing, food production, recreation and culture); macro-regional plans, which have been extended both in their range and function (in this way, they have become a part of national planning); the so-called 'national regional' plans, which differ from the 'regional' plans proper, as envisaged by the regions.

Planning at macro-regional level was also established.[20] For planning purposes only eight macro-regions were created, each consisting of four to eight new voivodships. This was done because it was argued that with the change from 17 to 49 voivodships, there was a need to create larger, more viable planning units, to provide guidelines for the new regions and to co-ordinate the implementation of the national strategy. It was also stated that the smaller voivodships would find it difficult to operate the entire social infrastructure and services, e.g. schools, hospitals, transport services and so on. To be more effective, some of these services had to serve more than one voivodship. In addition, it was argued that it would be too time-consuming to prepare perspective plans for the many new voivodships, and that under the macro-regional system problems common to the whole country, such as tourism, sea trade, agrarian structure and others, could be systematically examined.

Macro-regional planning is to be implemented in two ways: by the advisory Commission for the Development of Macro-regions and by the Joint Planning Group. The Commission is to provide a platform for discussions and is to formulate proposals relevant to the development of the whole macro-region. Its members are the secretaries of the voivodship committees of PUWP, the deputy-*voivoda*, the head of the planning commission, representatives of scientific bodies and two representatives of the public, who are actively engaged in economic or social problems. The head of each commission is also the deputy chairman of the Planning Commission at the Council of Ministers.

The commissions meet at least twice a year, each time in a different town in the voivodship of the macro-region, in order to provide a parity of treatment for all voivodships. Their aims are to present a periodic summary of socio-economic development of the macro-regions and the achievements of each voivodship, to identify inter-regional problems which need a joint solution, and to formulate policies for the central and regional authorities on this basis.

The Joint Planning Group consists of regional teams of the PCCM. They work in the region, are financed and supervised by the PCCM and their functions are confined to long-term and spatial planning. It is not anticipated that they will prepare one-year and five-year plans, although they will make medium-term studies. Their main aim is to provide studies and possible solutions of such problems as the distribution of population, the labour force, protection of natural environment, urbanisation, tourism, infrastructure and so on. They act as advisory bodies to the PCCM and cannot initiate projects.

These changes necessitated appropriate changes at the regional and local level.[21] The voivodships have transferred many of their tasks to the PCCM and are now only concerned with the preparation of perspective development plans, within the context of macro-regional plans, as well as urban and commune plans and detailed plans of a spatial nature for specific areas. A new body has been created, the Voivodship Board for the Development of Towns and Settlements, of which the Spatial Planning Office is a part. It is also intended to set up planning offices at the commune level but, as there is a shortage of qualified planners, these offices will only be set up initially in communes of over 20,000 people.

The new planning system is so designed that all the plans are interrelated and are prepared in several versions so that they are consistent in detail and fit in with each other. The long-term nature of planning is obvious from the fact that in September 1976 the medium-term plans for the 1976-80 period have been completed and the process of preparing plans for the 1980-2000 and 1980-5 periods will start after preliminary studies in two or three years' time.

The Changing Nature of Local Administration and Planning Functions

In order to understand the planning system in Poland, the political nature of planning decisions must be recognised. A clear indication of this was seen in resolutions of the Sixth Congress of the PUWP in 1971, when for the first time definitive objectives were stated in terms of improved housing standards for the population. The achievement of these and other socio-economic objectives was stipulated by the party as a pre-condition for further rapid economic development of the country. As a result of this PUWP initiative, more emphasis began to be placed on the manufacture of consumer goods and on the increase of agricultural production. Planning priorities were shifted to an increased supply of housing, health service, education, cultural facilities and to better protection of the environment.

This new emphasis on improving the quality of life and raising the standard of living was used to justify the changes in the organisation of planning and administration (which entailed a considerable loss of power by certain rungs of administration and a reduction in the number of administrative posts) and to raise the status of spatial planning within the state planning machinery. Spatial planning now became the basic framework for the spatial economic development of the country. The national plan would now be administered by a special planning unit in the Planning Commission at the Council of Ministers. A wide range of specialists from relevant ministries, planning experts from technical and scientific bodies and representatives of people's councils were brought together to complete the drafting of the plan by 1974. The PCCM also asked for advice from the Committee for Spatial Economic Development of the Country and the Committee for Forecasting Poland in the year 2000, within the Polish Academy of Sciences (PAN). A collection of some of the comments[22] indicates a general concern within the group about the lack of guidelines for such a study. The commentators were unclear as to the purpose of such analysis and, without some objectives for the research, many felt that the development of a conceptual framework for the study would be impossible. There was also a strong feeling that the existing system of administration with its weak boundary definitions, was unable to deal adequately with special needs.

The most important of these was the efficient management and implementation of large-scale investments. So many administrative units were involved in such decisions as the location, infrastructure needs and the whole local economic support system, that co-ordinated spatial planning proved to be extremely difficult to implement. An example of this was the unsatisfactory development of the sulphur region of Puławy, on the border of the Lublin-Kielce voivodships. Another serious problem was the planning and administration of urban agglomeration areas, which lacked self-government and were to be included in the voivodship plans, because the voivodships lacked resources and powers of implementation in the urban areas.

Apart from theoretical and conceptual difficulties, the practical difficulties were immediately obvious. The new administrative structure would be unable to perform its tasks because macro-regional planning was unworkable unless there was a political unit at the macro-regional level to implement policies developed for the area.[23] As an example, the plan for the coastal regions which covered several pre-reorganisation voivodships was almost impossible to implement, as no single administrative unit existed for the plan area and the voivodships involved acted competitively. Fears were also voiced about the split between economic and spatial planning in the new voivodships. It was now argued that both the new, smaller voivodships, and the reconstituted, larger communes, were too small to fulfil their planning functions effectively.

These criticisms, as well as an objective appreciation of the working of the reforms, can now be discussed in the light of practice. It seems that the aims of the reforms were twofold: on the one hand, the government and party authorities were concerned about the apparent 'amateurishness' of the people's councils in their dual legislative/executive role, their slow and inefficient implementation of planning and administration. On the other hand, they were also concerned with the power structure of the country and with the apparent independence of the larger voivodships in their decision-making. It is now clear that when the new structure was put into operation, the elimination of the above features was the main aim. However, by implementing these changes, the leadership appears to have departed from the democratic ideal of the people's councils legislating, executing their own legislation and checking up on it, and it has laid itself wide open to the accusation that the administrative division of the country into small units was a classical strategy for the strengthening of the central government.[24]

The other aims of the reforms were: integration of economic and spatial planning at every level; reduction in the number of local government employees; a similar reduction in the number of buildings used by local government offices; greater efficiency through a simplified decision-making process; equalisation of industrial and agricultural voivodships in economic and demographic terms; increase in the number of new houses; a better development of infrastructure (piped water, public transport, shops, schools, crèches, roads); and an improvement in environmental protection.

On the first count, the position has already been indicated above. Instead of increasing the links between spatial and economic planning, the reforms seem to have made them even more difficult. At the 1976 conference of urban planners it was claimed that the voivodship plans, which ought to be treated as spatial-economic plans, were proving to be difficult to implement, because of methodological difficulties; the main difficulty being that the harmonisation of such plans was beyond the competence of the *voivoda.*[25] At the same conference a call was made to enforce the view that spatial and economic planning should be treated as an indivisible whole. Lack of co-ordination between the two types of planning as well as lack of contact between the two administrative tiers come up constantly in the opinions of those in field work.[26]

A reduction in the numbers of administrative employees has, indeed, been achieved by the reforms. All the employees from the district offices have been directed to the following areas of employment: 20 per cent to voivodship offices, 39 per cent to commune offices and 34 per cent to other enterprises and institutions. Three per cent retired because of age (4 per cent are unaccounted for). However, the problem of acquiring properly-trained cadres for the new offices and, most particularly, highly-trained planning personnel, has not been overcome. As a result the new administrative and planning offices suffer from lack of personnel. At the same planning conference it was said that the cadres are weak and because of a faulty structure 70-80 per cent of their time is spent on administrative functions.[27] Furthermore, institutions of higher education do not take into account the training of appropriate specialists and it takes a minimum of five years, though more often eight years, to train an urban planner after he has completed his higher education. There was a marked lack of teachers of planning in the institutions of higher education, so the problem was self-perpetuating.[28] Similar opinions came from field workers. It was said that the problem of providing specialists for the commune offices was very difficult, particular shortages being in the field of specialised planning. Though short-term solutions, such as the secondment of such specialists from voivodship offices, were being attempted, the basic problem still remained to be tackled. One solution would be to provide good housing for such specialists, and the Prime Minister decided that the voivodships would be obliged to build 40,000 homes in the communes for specialists in the period of 1976-80, in order to alleviate the shortage. Another solution adopted was the partial transfer of some duties to other (town or commune) offices, which had sufficient personnel.[29]

The third aim of the reforms was to provide more space in buildings vacated by district offices. This appears to have been done to a certain extent but was more than compensated for by the need to provide offices at the commune and new voivodship level. An example of this is the problem of the new voivodship of Biała Podlaska, an underdeveloped region, which had the task of building some seven thousand homes in the voivodship, in addition to providing office space for the voivodship offices (a new single-purpose building was already planned) and for the new communes (at least ten communes needed offices).[30] Hence the creation of so many new administrative units has increased, and not decreased, the need for office space and living accommodation. Planning here generated its own spatial problems!

The equalisation of agricultural and industrialised voivodships in economic terms (whether through the encouragement of agricultural development or through the gradual introduction of industrialisation) was one of the main aims of the reforms. However, it seems clear that the new division did not favour such developments but, on the contrary, appears to have emphasised the differences. The smaller voivodships which are highly industrialised tend to isolate themselves from the underdeveloped ones, with which they have a common border. The underdeveloped voivodships lack the means and the experience of spontaneously creating economic development. Urbanisation proceeds along former lines: the

already overcrowded towns and cities continue to attract more inhabitants; the underpopulated areas become even more underpopulated.[31]

It is possible that the management of the region by the *voivoda* has
produced more efficiency—or at least speed—than the former collective
management. However, there are many complaints about inefficiency,
old-fashioned methods, lack of unified direction and lack of co-ordination.[32] There are signs that the provision of new homes is planned,
though it remains to be seen how many plans are actually put into
operation. The provision of new infrastructure will no doubt take much
longer. Similarly, the protection of environment is still in its early stages.
Some advances have been made by enterprising and energetic action,
but, to give one instance, the purification of the river Warta in the
voivodship of Czestochowa, where biological life was restored by the
joint action of planners and industrial enterprises[33] was an isolated
action, rather than the rule in the country as a whole.

In practice, industrial enterprises are still in a position to bring pressure on local authority and spatial planners, once they have obtained permission from their own ministry to set up a new enterprise. While local
authorities now have the powers to insist on strict adherence to the
spatial plan, they are also interested in attracting industry to the area.
Holding up a decision to build a new factory may mean loss of cash and
delays which the local authority is not prepared to incur. Hence, spatial
planning still lags behind economic planning and is not co-ordinated
with it, despite the resolutions of the Sixth Congress of the PUWP.

While it is too early to make a general assessment of the reforms, the
following opinions can be advanced: politically speaking, the reforms
reduced the element of participatory democracy in local government by
dividing the people's councils from professional administrators, though
they may have improved the decision-making processes by doing so. The
number of offices and employees has been reduced at the district level,
but this was done at the expense of increasing the number of voivodship
offices and the size of commune offices. The reforms did little to improve
the staffing of all offices with highly-qualified personnel. They did not
produce an equalisation between less-developed and better-developed
regions. And, lastly, the reforms introduced an element of institutional-
ised party control into local government, through the linking of the
office of the chairman of the people's council with that of the first
party secretary, a feature which has not been known in Polish administrative usage before. So, far from producing an improvement, local
government reforms have, paradoxically, had retrograde effects upon
Polish spatial planning, an effect that has also been attributed to the

1972 local government reform in England and Wales.

Notes

1. This is made explicit in a book on the government system during the Partitions: A. Ajnenkiel, B. Leśnodorski, W. Rostocki, *Historia Ustroju Polski (1764-1939)*, see particularly Part II.
2. L. Kosiński,'Ludność', *Wielka Encyklopedia Powszechna P.W.N.*, volume: *Polska* (Warsaw, 1967), p. 69. For figures on administrative changes, see A. Burda and R. Klimowiecki, *Prawo Państwowe* (Warsaw, 1959), pp. 393-4.
3. Burda, op.cit. pp. 395 and 399.
4. Ibid. p. 398; also see *Dziennik Ustaw*, no. 5, 1958.
5. Burda, op.cit. p. 92.
6. Ibid. p. 134.
7. Ibid. p. 410.
8. Ibid. pp. 411-12.
9. *Rada Narodowa*, no. 22, 1956, p. 2.
10. *Sprawozdanie Stenograficzne z IX Sesji Sejmu*, col. 40.
11. Burda, op.cit. pp. 436-9.
12. *Dziennik Ustaw*, no. 47, 1973. Decree on the role of the People's Councils.
13. 'O Właściwą, Realizację, Zadań Zawartych w Wytycznych na VI Zjazd Partii' in *Nowe Drogi*, no. 12, 1971, pp. 93-9.
14. *Dziennik Ustaw*, no. 49, 1972. Decree of 29 November 1972 on the establishment of *Gminas* and changes in the People's Councils.
15. *Dziennik Ustaw*, no. 47, 1973. Decree of 22 November 1973 on the role of People's Councils.
16. *Dziennik Ustaw*, no. 16, 1975. Decree of 28 May 1975 on the Two-Tier System of Administration.
17. *Dziennik Ustaw*, no. 7, 1961. Spatial Planning Act of 31 January 1961.
18. About two-thirds of the Polish economy is subordinated to the central level, whereas the other one-third is governed from the regional level. The smallest units are the enterprises which have a managing director and are financially responsible for their own activities. National economy enterprises are mainly state-owned and are subordinated to the national unions and other types of economic organisations, e.g. union of coal mining, union of sea fisheries and so on. Several of these unions cover an entire sector or branch of the national economy and are subject to a relevant ministry. Regional economy enterprises (mainly co-operatives, often privately-owned) are organised into voivodship unions or corporations. The role of ministries here is limited to co-ordination and indicative management.
19. K. Secomski, 'Najbliższe Zadania Planowania Przestrzennego w Polsce', *Biuletyn PAN KPZK*, no. 85 (Warsaw, 1974), pp. 17-25.
20. Directives of the Chairman of the Council of Ministers of 30 June 1975 on the creation of eight macro-regions. Three macro-regions (northern, southern and south-eastern) had been established in 1972 as an experiment.
21. Act no. 111 of the Council of Ministers, 28 June 1975 on Process and Methods of Regional Plans.
22. *Biuletyn PAN*, no. 85, op.cit.
23. Zarzycki, ibid. pp. 139-42.
24. Rybicki, ibid. quoting Napoleon's division of France as an example of a similar process, p. 109.
25. Kachniarz, *TUP Komunikat* 35, 2, 1976, p. 26.
26. Richert, ibid. p. 29. Also see C. Kotela, 'Rozbudowa miast i osiedli wiejskich w nowym podziale administracyjnym kraju', *Rada Narodowa*, no. 17, August 1975, pp. 6-7.

27. Zarzycki, *TUP Komunikat* 35, 2, 1976, p. 29.

28. Skibniewski, ibid. p. 35.

29. T. Bejm, 'Terenowe organy władzy i administracji państwowej po trzecim etapie reformy', *Rada Narodowa*, no. 25, December 1975, p. 9.

30. J. Piela, 'Problemy rozwoju województwa bialskopodlaskiego', *Rada Narodowa*, no. 17, August 1975, p. 10.

31. A. Mijakowski, 'Poziom urbanizacji województw', *Rada Narodowa*, no. 17, August 1975, p. 15.

32. Buszkiewicz, *TUP Komunikat* 35, 2, 1976, pp. 73-7.

33. D. Pietrzyk, 'Przykład koordynacji', *Rada Narodowa*, no. 24, November 1975, p. 42.

CONCLUSION: EUROPE AT A CROSSROADS— THE FUTURE OF PLANNING

Olga Narkiewicz

The Issues in Planning

Though Europe is a small continent in global scale, it has pioneered in industrial development and modern urbanisation. As a result it has become 'a vast testing ground, where a variety of policies and measures aimed to improve the human habitat have been tried out.'[1] Urban planning in Europe is not new and can be traced back to ancient Athens, where the city was designed so that all amenities—the public square, the markets, the schools and the living areas—were within easy walking-distance, as much as to the medieval cities, walled to produce maximum security from outside and maximum space inside the walls. The political demands of a slave-owning oligarchy produced a different city than those of a feudal society but they were very clearly defined and expressed all the same. This long history of civilisation has played a large role in European development.

Europe is unique in many other respects as well. The variety of its nationalities and political systems, and the sophistication of its population are self-evident. What may be less well realised is the way in which the Europeans have always been ahead of the events, and well ahead of their governments, in their assessment of realities. Many examples, both political and social, could be quoted. Perhaps one of the best is the mass emigration from Europe to other continents at the end of the nineteenth and beginning of the twentieth centuries, when it became obvious that the continent was unable to feed the growing population and the governments were preparing for a major war. Another is the way in which the Europeans have, despite a variety of measures designed to increase the birth rate in almost every state, reduced their birth rate to the lowest in the world.[2] Such response to the plight of an overcrowded continent shows that the population adopts forward-planning techniques, which most governments have yet to follow. Similarly, European attitudes to economic development have been ahead of the rest of the world. Having been the first to start the industrial revolution, the Europeans were also the first to call for a curb to industrial growth. Growth is no longer considered to be the most important factor in Europe. The standard of living measured in *per capita* figures of GDP and other factors has given way to the notion of the 'quality of life'. In the most developed states the process has reached the stage where the population assesses its well-being in terms of 'leisure time' and 'job satisfaction' instead of earnings.[3]

Nevertheless, such planning as is being carried out in Europe depends either on individual effort or on some specific national or regional initiative. There are planning bodies both in the states with a socialist-type economy and in those with market-type or mixed economies.the socialist states have comprehensive planning bodies, which are, in theory at least, expected to provide for each eventuality in planning. The other states have organisations devoted to sectoral planning: physical, economic or social. There are also two international planning bodies: the EEC and the CMEA. Each of these is limited to one area of Europe alone and is concerned with economic planning in the first instance, though some social planning is dealt with. There is one body which is concerned with the whole of the continent: the Economic Commission for Europe, which is an integral part of the United Nations Organisation, but it has purely advisory functions and has no executive power and no financial means even to institute research activities on a larger scale. It may be concluded that the population of Europe is well ahead of European governments in establishing planning patterns for its own needs. On the other hand, that same population is distrustful of the traditional type of planning as applied by the governments and appears to be ready for the setting-up of a truly international planning body, which would fulfil present-day needs.

The distrust is quite justified. From a historical point of view planning in Europe has not been associated with spectacularly successful ventures and has not always been notable for its degree of concern for people's best interests. Indeed, it is doubtful if any planning authorities have so far established what the people's best interests are (as opposed to what they *think* the people's best interests are). A brief glimpse at past examples will be sufficient: when the broad boulevards were planned in Paris, in place of the warren of narrow streets, the aim was simply to make revolutions impossible. Similarly, when the walls of Vienna were torn down and a wide ring-road installed, the aim was to prevent a repetition of the 1848 revolution. The incidental effect was that this political venture into town planning helped produce two of the most beautiful cities in Europe; but the aims were clearly regressive: to stop the spread of democratic ideas any further. Similarly, social and economic policies in the late nineteenth and early twentieth centuries were designed to stop the growth of socialism. This applied equally to the agricultural policies of the German Empire and to the Stolypin Reforms in the Russian Empire. In each case, the policies were designed to support what was considered to be the most conservative sector of the population at the expense of the sector most likely to become socialist. The blunders of the First World War and of the subsequent revolutions and abolition of both Empires have shown the futility of planning for regression.

The aftermath of the War reinforced, rather than changed, some attitudes. The rise of the European dictators may not have been planned (though some may think it was the inevitable result of nineteenth-century policies), but the dictators' policies—the repression of the working classes, the stress on developing the war machine, the persecution of intellectuals—all stemmed from a negative type of planning. Even where the planning purported to be positive, as in the USSR, it had negative values built into it. As Jack Hayward so rightly points out:

> In the Soviet Union, the institution of a comprehensive, collectivist and centralised system of planning was part of a deliberate desire for intransigent polarisation to give the political leaders maximum support for the tasks of mass mobilisation for industrial modernisation.[4]

In socialist economies, planning techniques were used to mobilise the masses and to industrialise. In the market economies, various techniques were used to stifle legitimate public opinion, to create or support unemployment in the name of a 'balanced' budget and to produce a stagnating economy which the inept governments of the day could manage more easily. The classical examples of such negative planning were the smaller Central and Eastern European countries but other states could be cited as well.

The aftermath of the Second World War brought about a complete change in European attitudes to planning. The socialist bloc expanded and the Soviet-type system of planning was imposed, willynilly, on the newly-established People's Democracies. This made it necessary for the other European states to adjust their attitudes in any case. But there were other reasons for the changes. The sheer volume of the war damage had made physical planning a necessity in most countries affected by military action. It was also realised that the social policies of pre-war governments had worked to the detriment of democracy. Social planning was updated, in order to provide welfare, education and health services for all, or most of, the population. In order to make good damage to industries, many had to be nationalised, which involved the state in planning techniques, with or without an ideological content. Economic and industrial planning became respectable. Socialism in a moderate form became an accepted part of the ideology of most political parties in market economies, including the parties which professed to be conservative. The result was that within some fifteen years of the war ending, there was a considerable degree of economic and social convergence between the various political systems.

A period of indecision followed. European systems hung in balance for a decade, while the politicians were wondering how far such convergence would proceed. Then old habits reasserted themselves. Instead of working for a united and democratic Europe, various power interests began to press their own solutions. On the one hand, the socialist bloc was prepared to use military strength to stamp out lack of discipline (as in 1968); on the other hand, the *laissez faire* lobbies, equally devoid of a sense of historical perspective—and hence always tending to work against their own best interests—began to reassert their right to get rich at any cost. The result did not take long to materialise: the policy of expensive food, soon followed by widespread unemployment due to a recession, produced a revival of extreme politics in Europe. The dream of a few post-war idealists became distorted out of all recognition: in the seventies Europe is as disunited as it was in the nineteenth century. Social benefits on a large scale, whether in the form of unemployment benefits in market economies, or of overmanning in socialist economies, stop the people from starvation or from revolution-making. But such measures are very far from solving the basic problems—problems which are still virtually the same as in the nineteenth century.

These problems are as follows: Europe is a small continent, it is overpopulated, it has a worked-out soil and a large, but abused, industrial potential. Europe's natural riches are puny by comparison with those of Asia, Africa and the Americas. Its one asset is its people; over the last ten centuries they have proved their assertiveness, cleverness, adaptability and adventurousness. Despite this, millions of Europeans have been killed in the twentieth century alone, waging futile wars against fellow Europeans. And, periods of prosperity apart, millions have been expected to live their lives out on social security benefits, instead of being encouraged to engage in productive work. Europe's other asset, environmental beauty, has been all but eroded in the twentieth century. A traveller in Italy, Switzerland or Norway will be shocked by the pall of industrial smoke which air currents are unable to move from the mountain valleys. The rivers have suffered in an equal way. If Lorelei

still visits the Rhine, it must surely be to weep tears of bitterness over
the destruction of the most beautiful river in Europe. The Danube, the
Seine and the Thames have all suffered similar damage.

European buildings have not fared any better. At its best, European
architecture has no equal. There are no continents where architecture
has been practised on such a scale over the last twenty-five centuries.
There are no continents where such a variety of styles, changing to
demonstrate technological advances, has survived over such long periods.
Yet many of these monuments to man's religious faith, engineering skill
and sheer audacity, have been eroded by industrial pollution and traffic
fumes, or have been demolished to make way for industrial or commercial development. Should anyone protest at this deliberate destruction
of the European heritage, he is immediately branded as being regressive and either anti-proletarian or anti-capitalist (depending on whose
immediate interest he is threatening). There are various voluntary
bodies which have sprung up to prevent such destruction. Unfortunately,
they are elitist and weak, and in most cases lack any powers. They cannot act in a positive manner and make their voices heard by unseemly
demonstrations. As in the case of population control, it is left to individuals to put up a resistance to the vandalism of destruction, even
though here, clearly, is a strong case for official action. The action of
some individuals, such as John Styme, is merely an exception which
proves the rule.

It is not the intention of this essay to sound dire warnings. They are
evident to every forward-thinking European. It will be sufficient to say
that if the process is not stopped, in the twenty-first century our contemporary destruction will be rated above that created by the barbarian
invasions or by the Second World War.

The issues in planning, as they appear to this author, are as follows:
how to preserve the natural environment in Europe; how to balance
industrial population with agricultural population; how to produce
enough food for the people without damaging the environment; and
last, but not least, how to introduce political systems which are democratic and participative, yet orderly. It may be that the functions of
the state cannot become so technical as to make politics appear as a
kind of applied statistics, as Hayward argues,[5] but the Saint-Simonian
dream is the same dream as those cherished by Plato and by Rousseau,
forgotten in the twentieth century, as Europe became poor and dis-
pirited. It may also be that it is already too late; that only preservation
is possible, without any development. Even if this were so, if Europe
were to become a vast museum of past human progress, with its people

acting as resident custodians, the other continents may still think it worthwhile to keep it so. But it seems far more likely that with well-developed planning techniques, many present-day problems can be solved by the Europeans themselves. All the essays in this book suggest that this is the case.

The Divisive Politics of Europe

There are two strands in the European heritage which appear to work against each other. One is the common heritage: the Roman Empire, the Roman Church, Latin as the language of the educated elite. The other is the divisive heritage; some thirty different states, many more different nationalities and languages, different religious faiths and political systems. To the ideology of the French Revolution, which worked for European unification, one can juxtapose the ideology of nineteenth and twentieth century nationalism, which worked for divisiveness. With the strengthening of the national state, attitudes in the twentieth century hardened. The establishment and solidification into two mutually opposed political blocs in the second half of the twentieth century completed the process of division.

The contemporary European is at present assailed by two contradictory viewpoints. On the one hand, he is told that the two blocs have no meeting-point. On the other, he has proof before his very eyes that Europe is one whole. The Norwegians, plagued by acid rain, find it hard to distinguish whether the pollutant is of Eastern or Western European origin; all they know is that the pollution is threatening to extinguish their river fish. The Danube flows through market economy countries and socialist countries, without altering its ancient flow. The oil-polluted and over-fished seas border on many countries, with various political systems. And any radiation which the nuclear power stations could allow to escape at any moment will poison Eastern Europe just as surely as Western Europe.

Environmental dangers apart, many other factors bring the Europeans together. Despite travelling restrictions still extant in the socialist bloc, the ease of modern travel has brought more people together than ever before. The uniform youth culture has affected the East almost as much the West, and the young are particularly appalled by the division into political blocs. The infrastructure of roads and railways has yet to be developed fully on a continental scale but it is already well on the way towards linking all parts of the continent. Educational, social and welfare policies have produced a generation which, while still at different stages of economic development, at least knows which way it is heading:

towards greater uniformity. Industrial culture has produced more equalisation than all the above factors taken together. Similar problems and
the similar life-styles it created have been accompanied by similar desires:
at first, to join the highly-paid urban population; later to escape urbanisation by transplanting oneself and one's family into the simulated
country surroundings of the outer suburbs. In view of all those common
factors, one would imagine that the political systems (which have already
reacted by degree of convergence) would begin to lose their significant
differences. If they refuse to do so, they could be helped by the pressure
of public opinion.

This is not an unrealistic assessment of the position. The continent
was populated for a long time before any of the current systems were in
operation. The Europeans pioneered in evolving various political systems
and in abolishing them, as they became useless and oppressive. The common bond of all the Europeans has persisted over centuries and governments which refused to heed the people's warnings have seldom survived
for long. It may be timely to remind all European governments of the
immortal words of Tsar Alexander II of Russia, that it is better to introduce reform from above than to wait for it to rise on a revolutionary
tide from below.

Naturally, the reform one has in mind has nothing to do with old-
fashioned political revolutions. One needs a reform of attitudes and of
habits. An absolutely essential part of this reform would be a change of
governmental attitudes to planning. It is not only that, in Hayward's
words, 'it is even more difficult to separate politics from planning than
it is to separate politics from administration'; or that 'The planner, both
in Communist and non-Communist societies, is a technocrat, whose
expertise is adapted to suit political purposes.'[6] It is a much more fundamental problem: what is the political purpose with regard to planning;
and, how is this political purpose carried out?

So far as it can be established, planning is confined to either national
or sectoral interests. Even in the case of socialist-type economies, with
a centralised planning machinery and with a theoretical political purpose,
such planning is sectoral. Perhaps the best contemporary example of the
nature of planning in both blocs is the failure of both the CMEA and the
EEC organisations to effect economic fusion, despite a strong ideological
commitment to fusion. To an observer it appears clear that while, even
within each state, governments have been unable to establish a reconciliation of regional interests, it is fruitless to attempt such reconciliation
between states and between blocs.

There are various reasons for this, not all of which can be blamed on short-sighted governments. It may be that there is a strong feeling among the Europeans that the variety of languages, states, nations and systems, which exist at present, is preferable to a uniform planned society. In a century where there are ever-growing tendencies towards uniformity, this would be an understandable sentiment. One would need to produce a framework for planned development, which would assure each nationality and each state of optimum development within the existing systems. Such a framework would not be detrimental to the basic interests of each state, would not change the basic nature of states, and would yet be harmonised to produce the best overall result. The alternative to such planning may well be growing chaos.

Such ideas are not outside the field of 'realpolitik'. While they are not totally acceptable at the moment, one must remember that, up to the middle of the twentieth century, few Europeans would have accepted the small measure of planning which the EEC and the CMEA have established. The need for such planning is being increasingly recognised. There are serious technical difficulties. If planners are 'technocrats' the objections are that there is a lack of democratic apparatus to underwrite planning. But such objections are relatively minor, compared with what is at stake. It has been proven over centuries that, when mankind's survival is at stake, the peoples as well as the governments exhibit extraordinary maturity in preserving their own heritage and that of the future generations. This was the case in the cessation of gas warfare, after its full effects had been demonstrated in the First World War. It has been shown in the caution about the proliferation of nuclear reactors for peaceful use, after nuclear potential had been tested in war. It is an accepted fact that when confronted with the greater prospective evil of total extinction, the majority of the people will choose the lesser actual evil of some form of control over damaging activities.

A recent assessment of the chances of control of nuclear fission stated: the ordinary citizen

> must . . . bring his reason and commonsense to bear on his country's whole approach to the problem. The first act of sanity is to insist, with all possible urgency and influence, on the need for caution . . . Men are not making simple estimates of gain or convenience. They are confronting their own survival and that of their children and grandchildren and the whole race of men. Caution in general is the beginning of wisdom.[7]

What applies to the use of nuclear reactors is equally applicable to the damage done to the environment by all the factors which at present work on it: the excessive desire for a quick profit, leading to dirty over-industrialisation, overpopulation, soil erosion, water and air pollution through the extraction and use of oil, and manifold other problems. While all mankind is at risk, the solution is as yet impossible on a global scale, simply because of the enormity of the task. As Hayward says, the 'Sysiphean' solution appears more realistic than the 'Promethean' solution. Hence, one must look at the task on a smaller scale. A partial answer lies in tackling it on a country-by-country basis. But sometimes this is insufficient. The sensible fishery-protection policy pursued by the UK will have little effect if all the other European countries over-fish in the same waters. Other examples could be quoted to support an argument for planning on a continental scale. Such planning, in a small continent, which is yet a 'vast testing ground', could prove to be of value not only for Europe, but could make Europe a laboratory for future global maintenance.

This book has been concerned with demonstrating some of the problems and some of the possible solutions. Lessons learnt from the practice of planning in many European countries could be applied, either across the board if necessary, or in specific cases in various political and economic systems. There will, of course, be opposition to such approaches. Change is always resented, when it threatens to upset the established norms of action. When the US Navy introduced a new tech-nique which was thought to threaten the position of officers and men operating ancient skills, there was strong opposition to the innovation because:

> The threat to stability of established institutions carries with it a threat to the stability of established theory and ideology because institutions like the labour movement, the church, social welfare agencies, all carry with them bodies of theory, ways of looking at the world and when the institutions are threatened the bodies of theory are threatened as well. Most important, when the anchors of institutions begin to be loosened, the supports which it (*sic*) provides for the personal identity, for the self, begin to be loosened too.[8]

Evidence for such behaviour is well-attested. This is why, when a change is too sudden, too big and not immediately beneficial, reactions are violent and negative. When the Soviet planners first introduced a central plan in the twenties, they were swiftly purged, because of 'fail-ures'. When the First Five-Year Plan failed, Stalin, on whose insistence the plan was 'maximised', found his position severely threatened by other contenders for power. Khruschev's measures to change the Soviet planning apparatus were rewarded by his being removed from power, without giving him a chance to rectify the supposed mistakes. When the British public was persuaded of the benefits of joining the EEC, it reacted by voting in favour. As soon as the association began to appear to be less beneficial, public opinion turned against the EEC. The former reaction was no more logical than the latter, but such feelings tend to turn nations away from experimentation and any possible improvement in the way of life. Therefore, any programme to plan on a continental scale must exhibit a great degree of caution and must avoid sudden upheavals. It will now be necessary to examine what can be accomplished within these parameters.

Can Planning Succeed?

Hayward has looked at this question from the point of view of political science and has come to a pessimistic conclusion, namely that comprehensive and democratic planning is virtually impossible:

> In the absence of an overriding public purpose, governments can be expected to rely upon expeditious solutions that do not disturb existing power relationships and therefore adapt to rather than overcome the situational constraints.[9]

An historian is in a different situation. Unlike the political scientist, he can proffer guidance on the basis of many years, or even centuries, of past experience. The politicians usually take little heed of either the political scientists or the historians; recent experience has shown that when political scientists become politicians, they do not depart from this rule. It is the force of events, the 'situational constraints', which compel governments to adopt new measures. Such constraints arise when there is historical necessity for them. In other words, the pressure of events and public opinion effect what the advice of scholars cannot do.

This is particularly true of planning techniques. Centralised planning on a national scale has so far only been practised in the USSR for some sixty years and in the countries of the Eastern European bloc for some thirty years. This experience of planning has been distorted by its dogmatic application in underdeveloped countries, with a small reservoir of skilled cadres. Hence, because such planning has not been spectacularly successful, the belief grew that centralised planning is intrinsically impossible to operate. This belief can be disproved by quoting examples where the Soviet centralised planning techniques have been extremely successful; i.e. in the field of building up the armed services and sophisticated weapons, as well as in the field of space research. Another such example is the Soviet and Eastern European success rate in achieving gold medals in Olympic Games—long-term social planning alone can achieve this. Rather less success has accompanied Soviet political planning, which resulted in the integration of Eastern Europe into the socialist system. But this provides a good example of what happens when planning techniques are geared to what is an *ad hoc* solution. On the whole, where Soviet planning is allowed the full use of the state's resources— the best-trained cadres, goods and services backed by sustained support— the results are very rewarding. This makes one wonder why such means are not used in less spectacular fields, as, for instance, in the field of the economy.

Whereas Soviet planning for growth in the armed services has been carried on without a break since 1945 and has included the development of conventional forces, of nuclear weapons and of land and sea-going potential on an equal scale, the planning of economic development has hardly progressed beyond the stage of planning in mixed economies. Since the USSR has, nominally at least, abandoned the market mechanisms prevailing in non-socialist economies, it is at a great disadvantage in the economic field. As Michael Kaser demonstrates, even though the isolation of the USSR in the thirties simplified the operations of planning, planning processes then, as much as in the post-Stalinist era, were far from perfect. In particular, 'a general policy of taut planning . . . has not always ensured that micro-economic financial plans were met . . .'[10] Moreover, the frequent changes in plans, which were necessitated by many factors (inflation, excess money, overinvestment in industry) often rendered planning ineffectual. Kaser stresses the fact that despite the planned economy,

the documented sources in fact show an excess of expenditure over income in the sixties and early seventies. The excess of cash creation is indisputable and has been demonstrated in the familiar manner of retail shortages, shopping queues, and waiting lists, preferential supply for favoured or privileged customers and parallel markets.

Such a state of affairs has led critics of Soviet-type systems to conclude that centralised planning is totally inefficient. But Kaser demonstrates that decentralisation may not be the answer either. When such exper-

iments were tried in Czechoslovakia and in Poland in 1958-9, they produced difficulties by upsetting the continuity of planning.[11]

Some authors make the point that planning suffers from an inbuilt
factor of 'ignorance'. Such ignorance is said to be inherent in the planning processes for the following reasons: in drawing up the plan, the
planners may not be aware of all the circumstances in the whole area
covered by the plan; secondly, the executors of the plan may not have
all the necessary data at hand; and, lastly, as the plan progresses, circumstances may change in a way which has not been foreseen by the planners. Instances of such 'ignorance' are frequent in Soviet economy,
where the supposed conflict between 'planner's preferences' and 'consumers' preferences' often arises from the simple fact that the planners
are unaware of the consumers' preferences.[12]

In addition, Soviet-type economies are constrained by the ideology
they have adopted. The maintenance of full employment, which is the
mainstay of socialist ideology, can prove to be an expensive undertak-
ing when the planners want to phase out less successful enterprises or
manufacturing processes. Consumer resistance to home-produced goods
reinforces such difficulties, as hard currency is spent on foreign-produced
goods. (A small but highly significant example of this is the production
of clothes and underwear. In Poland women's underwear of high quality
is only available in hard-currency shops; in the USSR denim jeans are
only bought if foreign-produced. Yet both countries have manufacturing
industries capable of producing such items in better quality and of better
cut than at present; the only obstacle seems to be the enterprises' resistance to changing their processes of manufacture.) Factories in Soviet-
type economies suffer from low productivity partly as a result of overmanning. In Poland such overmanning is notorious. Yet the unions do
not allow the management to dismiss any workers, a policy fully supported by the party and the state. Virtually the only reason for which
management can dismiss the labour force is for action amounting to
armed revolt, as in the 1976 food price riots. A cynical observer may
comment that the wholesale arrests and subsequent dismissals of a large
work force in many Polish factories were not unconnected with the
urgent need to improve productivity.

To combat such difficulties, the smaller countries of the socialist
bloc, Poland, Hungary, Czechoslovakia and Romania, have adopted a
system of more flexible financial and economic planning. The problem
about such flexibility is that the responses may be too quick (i.e. a
change may be introduced when a plan appears to be unsuccessful, without giving it a chance to work its way through the system) and hence

this may undo any advantages of long-term planning. Therefore, if one
wanted to be controversial, one could supplement the statement that
'The existence of a formal plan is not a prerequisite of planning . . .'[13],
by stating that the Soviet-type economies have formal plans which may
be almost totally ineffectual.

If financial planning and economic planning in the socialist bloc have
proved difficult to implement and imperfect in practice, one is forced
to look for some other fields in which planning has succeeded. One such
field, that of defence planning, has already been mentioned. Another is
the field of social planning. Social planning, like full employment, is an
ideological commitment of this system. The full weight of party and
government pressure has been placed on social planning since the inception of the USSR and, later, of the Communist regimes in the Eastern
European countries. To prove the importance of social planning, one
need only quote the system of points which penalises the children of
middle-class parents in higher education, while aiming to give better
opportunities to the children of workers and peasants. Yet, despite
such drastic remedies, this aspect of social planning has not so far succeeded. The reason for this is only partly because the middle classes are
determined to retain the best opportunities for their children; it also
depends on the rural/urban dichotomy and on environmental advantages
enjoyed by children brought up in the cities in middle-class homes. To
abolish the dichotomy would require a much wider industrialisation than
even the USSR has considered necessary, and would, moreover, deprive
state-owned industries of a supply of cheap labour from the countryside. Hence, the advantages of nationalised industry and the possibility
of long-term social planning have to be weighed against the disadvantages
of attaining the economic status of developed countries: a small rural
population and an expensive industrial work force.

There are some aspects of social planning, however, which lend themselves more easily to the socialist commitment. This should apply in particular to the planning of higher educational facilities. Some years ago,
writing about the development of Polish universities, the author was
struck by the attention paid to this. The universities at that time (1965)
worked to a central plan, 'with a foreseen number of places, as well as
an expected number of graduates; these numbers being harmonised
with the needs of the national economy, prescribed by fixed plans of
economic development, as well as social and cultural development.' It
was also said that:

The 'planning' has several aspects. It should predetermine that the number of applicants for university places is fixed not only to the existing university places, but also to the expected number of posts for graduates; candidates for a university education should be chosen not only for their abilities, but also because they have social features which are desirable in Polish society. Planning also requires that students should be trained professionally, in accordance with their future employment, and that they should complete their studies in a prescribed period of time.[14]

Had such manpower planning been adhered to, there would have been little difficulty in producing trained cadres where and when necessary. Yet a paper in this book points out that one of the main reasons why the Polish administrative and planning reforms of the seventies appear to be failing is precisely the lack of trained cadres.

The problem of acquiring properly-trained cadres for the new offices, and most particularly, highly-trained personnel, has not been overcome. As a result the new administrative and planning offices suffer from lack of personnel . . . institutions of higher education do not take into account the training of appropriate specialists . . . it takes a minimum of five years to train an urban planner . . . There was a marked lack of teachers of planning in the institutions of higher education.[15]

Similar accounts from the USSR and other Eastern European countries are commonplace. Hence it must follow that higher education planning has not been a success. However, it is noteworthy that such planning does exist and that, given the correct application of the right data, it could work better than the erratic system applied in the UK. Here, despite statistics which were pointing to a diminishing school-age population in the seventies, the training of teachers continued on the same scale as in the fifties and sixties. The resulting glut of teachers demonstrates poor social planning. This is even more apparent in the fact that in some fields (i.e. science and technology) there is a shortage of teachers, accompanied by a large number of vacant places for students of these subjects in the universities. Mistakes in planning are here compounded by lack of concertation between planners.

One of the contributors to this book blames this situation in the UK on the 'deep suspicion that planning results in dictatorship', coupled to the belief that plans must be rigid. The author very rightly comments that 'no British explorer would have set out without at least a sketch map, close questioning of the locals, and some idea of the direction in which he was going.'[16] But the planners in the UK do not themselves trust in the benefits of planning! Yet the position on social planning is no better in France, which this author recommends as an example. In his discussion of social planning in France, Bruno Jobert points out that despite lip-service paid to social planning, statistics are very poor and inadequate. Moreover, there is extreme fragmentation between the agencies of social planning, each very jealous of its autonomy. In addition, there are only weak links between the budget and the plan.[17]

It would therefore appear that neither the socialist economy, nor the mixed economy, nor an 'étatist' solution, provides a real answer to the problems of planning. Each looks to the other for the positive or the negative aspects of planning, without being able to apply them because of political, financial or economic constraints. While generalisations are too facile, it may be cautiously stated that planning in socialist systems does tend to be too rigid and hence is often discarded, while that of the mixed economy is usually far too erratic to deserve the term 'planning'. The 'étatist' system depends on the same factors on which it had depended for over a century: a strong central administration, rather than a large degree of participation and voluntarism. It may be that the comparisons between the systems could produce a better application of planning techniques everywhere. One could demonstrate this by some positive aspects of planning in the socialist systems.

Such pointers could be found in the important field of maternity and child services. The provision of crèches and kindergartens is ample in all socialist countries. This is not only because there is an ideological commitment to 'free all women from the kitchen sink', to use Lenin's words, or because there is an economic necessity for all women to work. There is also a strong social preference to work, particularly in the case of middle-class women. Peasant women, whether still in farming occupations or already in industrial occupations, have no hesitation; women in agrarian countries have traditionally worked alongside the men and they consider it a natural state of things.[18] A study carried out by the author into this aspect of social planning in a region in Czechoslovakia confirms the great care with which such matters are treated. Another aspect of social planning which receives priority treatment is cultural policy. In the course of the same study, a comparison was made between Czechoslovakia and the UK, concentrating on an industrial region in each case. It was found that the provision of sports facilities, libraries, theatres, cinemas and concert halls was much greater proportionately in Czechoslovakia than in the UK and that it was reinforced by the accessibility of these facilities (such as low prices of tickets, special quotas of tickets for manual workers, widespread use of travelling theatres and cinemas in rural areas, and others) to the population.[19] There is clearly an ideological reason for the broad provision of cultural facilities in socialist states but this does not nullify the positive aspects of such policy. Moreover, it stops the unwarranted withdrawal of irreplaceable cultural facilities, on the grounds that they are not sufficiently profitable—a frequent occurrence in market economies.

There are also aspects of socialist planning which attain positive results through the application of negative motives. This is the case of the official policy to keep down the number of private motorcars. It has the incidental effect of keeping down pollution from traffic fumes in the cities and in reducing the consumption of fuel. Another result is that public transport in the socialist economies is cheap, often good and usually plentiful. Taxi services are also cheap and ample. Such results seem to be desirable from a national point of view, though it may be argued that they do not override the convenience of private transport.

However, in many instances, centralised planning is unable to provide a satisfactory overall result. This appears to be the case in the field of environmental protection. The reason is that the planning authorities are subject to ministries which are simultaneously concerned with industrial production. Industrial production is the first priority of the socialist systems and environmental protection is neglected, till the damage is irreversible. Barry Hills has demonstrated how wilful neglect reduced an ancient and well-preserved town in Czechoslovakia to the status of a highly polluted area;[20] very similar results are shown in the study quoted above.[21] The preceding chapter indicated the existence of similar conditions in Poland, though in some instances local initiatives can be applied to remedy the pollution.[22]

In each country of the socialist bloc, one can quote instances of serious damage through pollution. The preponderance of economic growth over environmental protection has been so intrinsic to the system that, despite the absence of the capitalist-type of profit motive, it is very difficult to impress upon the economic agencies the necessity for such protection. Paradoxically enough, it is in the mixed economies that it has been easier to put environment before the profit motive. And in the period since the mid-sixties, the socialist economies have also been applying some, though often half-hearted, measures of protection. Nevertheless, it is far too early to speak of concerted action on a continental scale. In this, Europe is far behind the United States, where a continental agency has existed for some time. The US Federal Environmental Protection Agency, spanning all of the North American continent, with the exception of Canada, enjoys considerable powers, and is able to pursue its activities freely, without any conflict of interests. A modest beginning for planning on a continental scale in Europe could be the setting-up of just such an agency.

There are some advantages in centralised state planning which are implicit. These are the public ownership of land and industries. Should the state decide to pursue one type of plan, there is little opposition from private interests, though such opposition may be forthcoming from various pressure groups. Additionally, and perhaps even more cogently, the planning is very rigid at the central level and this often makes it necessary to modify it at the local level. The very large local government apparatus at lower levels and the broad participation of the public in local government provide a feed-back and an instrument of pressure which is often absent in the less participatory local government systems in mixed economies. In the absence or near-absence of a pluralist political system, the lower levels of local government provide a real alternative to pressure from political parties; a type of pressure which is divorced from political ideology and may therefore approach an objective view.

These advantages contrast starkly with 'piecemeal' planning in mixed economies. Stephen Young demonstrates that in the UK, even in cases where the central government intervenes, it does so in an *ad hoc* fashion:

> there is little integration of such planning activities as there are in different policy areas . . . The progressive refining of industrial policies through the detailed provision of advisory services or selective financial aid often becomes an end in itself.[23]

In such circumstances, it is hard to expect any feed-back from the public, except on issues of burning local importance, such as the building of a motorway or a nuclear power station, particularly in view of the traditionally apathetic British response to local government activity. A mixed economy is therefore handicapped on two counts: firstly, because of the frequent lack of a national plan and the absence of a conviction that a national plan would be beneficial; secondly, because of an almost complete lack of participation and feed-back from the population affected by 'piecemeal' planning.

Despite such apparent advantages of planning in socialist economies, the socialist states do not appear to use them as well as they might. Such arguments have been quoted in favour of 'piecemeal' planning or the complete abandonment of planning. They must be treated as fallacious. The papers in this book generally support the view that a large measure of planning is not only desirable but indispensable in European conditions. One should therefore concentrate on the ways in which centralised planning machinery could be set up where it does not exist and improved where it does exist. In this way full advantage may be obtained from integrated plans, long-term forecasts and a wide range of publicly-owned amenities. The mixed economies can impart some valuable lessons to socialist economies as well. Their greatest advantage is a multi-party political system which ensures—in the main—that the central authority does not abuse its powers. There are some indications that the socialist systems are, albeit reluctantly, discarding their belief that the 'dictatorship of the proletariat' (understood as total government control) is necessary in a non-capitalist economy. If this were to continue, it would be possible for such systems to develop a pluralist political society. It would then enable them to have the best of both worlds: a nationally-planned economy and political freedom.

Other advantages of mixed economies are that, despite various problems, their system allows for much more flexible planning. Provided basic requirements are established, the disadvantages of political change, with the accompanying change of programme, can be minimised. In the European mixed-economy systems such basic requirements concentrated on family allowances, old age pensions, unemployment benefits. This assisted a growth in population, longer life expectation and less poverty than before the Second World War. However, there were inbuilt disadvantages to such 'piecemeal' planning. Because of technological progress, labour-intensive industries were replaced by machine-intensive industries. The growing European population found it more difficult to obtain jobs. And, as the expectancy of life increased, fewer older people could find employment. Old-age pensions and unemployment benefits, while taking the edge off starvation, were yet insufficient to provide a high quality of life. The recession of the seventies and the accompanying inflation showed that the effects of such sectoral policies were in sharp contrast with the intentions of the planners. Instead of the benefits of development, European population experienced a high level of unemployment, particularly among the large young population and the large middle-aged population, and an inflation which devalued old-age pensions and unemployment benefits. Instead of discussing ways of producing employment, social planners began to discuss what were the 'permissible' levels of unemployment.

Such attitudes appear to turn the whole concept of planning upside down. A flexible economy should be capable of preserving full employment, which is cheaper than unemployment in social and economic terms. A flexible economy should be capable of keeping the size of population down to a level which would ensure such full employment. If lack of flexibility in planning produces overmanning, but guarantees full employment, then perhaps the time has come to ask why flexible planning cannot attain a better objective. Part of the answer lies in the fact that 'in pluralistic politics there is seldom any clear, overriding, collective purpose to which public action can be subordinated', whereas 'in communist polities it is taken for granted that the reverse will normally be true.'[24] Yet at times of national danger, even pluralist polities can follow a national policy for public good. Does it really need a war before European states begin to think in terms of the greatest public good, a term well known to Republican Rome but somewhat neglected of late?

Planning in Europe—Possible Objectives

The essays in this book have demonstrated that planning in Europe, both in socialist and in mixed-economy systems, is not rational. The main difficulty seems to be one of definition. Planning is generally interpreted as 'planning for development' or 'planning for conservation', without the understanding that these are only two sides of the same coin. Such misunderstanding can stem from ignorance or misinterpretation, as for instance in the following statement from a planner in a socialist state, who says:

> From the social point of view, experience during the thirty years of the development of the Polish People's Republic has shown that the highest socio-economic and civilisational progress has been achieved in large industrial urban centres and their suburban extensions. That is why the acceleration of the development of such conurbations is considered an essential factor in promoting the more dynamic economic development of the country.[25]

Similar statements could be found among the speeches of captains of industry in the capitalist or mixed economies.

On the other hand, exactly the opposite view is being expressed by the conservationists. At a Conference on Regional Problems in North-West England and North-Rhine Westphalia, held in Manchester in June

1977, concerned with planning and local government, one participant sounded this note of warning:

> As a scientist, I cannot forget that we live on a finite planet, and we appear to be planning as though it was not finite. We must plan so that we shall have *not* what we would like, but what we *need* and what we *can* have.

Both sides are apparently unable to see that they represent narrow viewpoints, lobbies for special interests, industrial or environmental. The appalling problem is that both sides are right. The reason why they collide is that planning has become a political weapon, which serves sectoral interests. Unless this position is remedied, unless planning becomes an objective and not a subjective activity, little can be done. But when it is removed from the field of political infighting, it might really be the case that 'as the general standard of values is so commonly accepted, the functions of the state become so technical as to make politics appear as a kind of applied statistics.'[26] In such a system, planning would serve its real purpose: for the benefit of all.

Planning is a relatively new discipline in general terms. It is not yet an acknowledged necessity on a global scale, yet it is essential in contemporary circumstances. As one advocate of planning defined it, it

> assumes that modern industrial society requires public intervention to achieve national goals; assumes that such intervention must touch all fundamental social developments; must be goal-oriented, and effectively co-ordinated at the centre; must be anticipatory rather than characterised by *ad hoc* solutions and timing dictated by crisis.[27]

These sentiments were not expressed by a socialist planner but by an American scholar, writing at the express wish of a conservative American president. It is on the American continent, with its specific problems, that the need for planning is really understood. The progressive view is that: 'The creation of . . . planning machinery . . . is the next major task in economic design', while the conservative view reinforces it by stating that

> Planning (once) was equated with Plato's philosopher king, and in some circles even with socialism. That mythological image is behind us. The planner is being pushed, willing or not, to the front line of

the struggle to guide the catastrophic forces shaping the American city.[28]

Certain kinds of planning have become an accepted part of European politics as long ago as the nineteenth century. These concerned the planning of transport, including railways and roads, the planning of city development, and, more recently, the planning of airports. The preservation of agricultural land has been the concern of politicians and pressure groups since the inception of industrialisation. More recently, social planning has become respectable, though its objectives are sometimes dubious. There are, however, still certain political brakes on planning. One such obstacle is the view of *laissez-faire* industrialists, who wish to develop industrial complexes wherever they are most convenient and where the labour force is cheapest. In this they are at one with the socialist industrial bosses, who have the same aim. But such views are becoming less and less common. Politicians of all shades of opinion are beginning to recognise that planning is a science of survival, not a partisan weapon any longer.

There is one state in Europe where planning has not been tied up with political ideology to a great extent but where it has been an acceptable part of government machinery irrespective of which government was in power. This is, of course, France. However, two French contributors to this book, Jacques Leruez and Jean Carassus, point out that the French have relaxed their planning processes during the current Seventh Plan, partly as a result of world recession and partly because they feel unable to plan on a long-term basis in a climate dominated by unplanned economies and large industrial interests.[29]

Though planning may have suffered minor setbacks in the last few years, it is the discipline of the future. Graham expressed this new viewpoint in the following words:

for our survival, Planning must be effective. To harmonise with our national values, it must also be democratic. We wish to drive a hard bargain if liberty must yield to security, if elites are given more responsibility for the public direction . . . At the May 22 (1975) conference on planning held in Washington, one heard the full range of predictions in answer to this question. It was apparent that . . . even those who call for change are troubled by its possibilities . . . A few business leaders, while drawn to the idea of more predictable and rational public policies, expressed the old fears that perhaps Planning was a Trojan Horse with socialism inside . . . Some observers grimly

forecast that the new political economy would be dominated by the
corporations, even the multinationals. A slide into fascism was
glimpsed by a few alarmed participants. . .[30]

Graham is right in saying that those who oppose planning are merely
opposing change because it may upset their own values, just as the US
naval personnel opposed new firing techniques. There is no rational
reason why planning should be regarded as a political weapon of a particular system, except that some systems have adopted it on a national,
centralised scale, and these systems happened to be authoritarian or
semi-totalitarian. On the basis of such emotional responses, one ought
to reject all democratic parliamentary systems because the first such
systems in the modern world were generated by the American and
French Revolutions. This reasoning is reminiscent of the reasoning of
the old ladies who, on seeing the first trains, crossed themselves and
refused to ride in them, convinced that they were constructed by the
Devil; otherwise why were they full of fire and steam? Like trains, planning is a useful and important innovation and employed properly is calculated to produce a better quality of life. The converse must be that,
unless one plans on an integrated scale, a continent like Europe will
soon be a prey to political, economic and environmental chaos.

In Europe there is no single body concerned with all-European planning, and the functions of the Economic Commission for Europe are
confined to advisory ones. It seems likely that this body, if provided
with a larger budget and some additional powers, would be capable of
drawing up an integrated plan for Europe. In order to avoid political
controversy, the Commission's brief would have to be very limited. The
most likely point to start at would be environmental planning, providing
an admirable beginning for the protection of rivers and air in Europe.
If such a beginning were successful, the Commission could then be given
more powers. It could proceed to physical or social planning and could
then extend its powers to the field of economic planning. The results of
the European experiment could then be applied in other parts of the
world, under the auspices of the United Nations Organisation.

A United Nations Organisation devoted to planning for survival and
improving the quality of life on a global scale may seem like an impossible dream. This would be *a priori* confession of failure. To rephrase
Hayward: while it may well be humiliating that the decision-makers do
not often take the advice or guidance of social scientists, it is incumbent
on the social scientist not only to proffer it, but to impress upon the
decision-makers the risks of not applying it.[31] Since the political will to

apply such advice is still lacking, the social scientist must look at ways of generating public support for his rational views. This support is necessary because the majority of planners still refuse to endorse any measures which do not conform to their own political views. There is also a large number of opponents of planning, for whom it is a politically unacceptable activity, even though they would be appalled at the abandonment of the national budget—a venerable form of short-term planning. There are also the proponents of development 'at any cost'. Such groups meet and abuse each other at all enquiries into new airports, nuclear reactors and motorways all over Europe. They are vocal in the United States. They are less obvious, but equally strong in the socialist bloc. Their weapons are irrational; they use emotive arguments to support their points of view. The victory in such cases goes to the strongest, not to the most rational side.

The majority of the population in all those countries (all of which maintain that they are democratically governed) listens to the arguments uncomprehending, unable to commit itself, as there is generally only inadequate machinery to express its views. In any case, it is not educated to make decisions. Yet such decisions affect the population as a whole; with the continent itself being swiftly eroded, its rivers and seas poisoned, its air polluted, the heritage of their children is disappearing. Not so long ago Europe pioneered in the formation of democratic political institutions and of modern science and technology. It was a potent drive towards a better quality of life which drove the Europeans to invent the steam engine, just as they invented the parliamentary system. One wonders whether such feats exhausted them to the point at which they are unable to devise a way of saving the continent from possible extinction.

A single planning agency for Europe may be a step towards remedying this state of affairs.[32] Such an agency would be removed from political decision-making and only concerned with the improvement of the European way of life. It must be realised that the market forces have failed Europe, just as much as state socialism has failed it. They belong to the past century, with different problems. At this point in time one needs new attitudes to new problems. Integrated planning on a European scale may provide such an answer. Such planning can only be achieved by the people of Europe. It is to them that this essay is addressed.

Notes

1. *Human Settlements in Europe. Post War Trends and Policies* (United Nations, New York, 1976), p. 1.

2. Ibid. p. 1.

3. Tom Forrester, 'Do the British Really Want to be Rich?', *New Society,* 28 April 1977, describing the results of an ORC opinion poll. A recent book by an economist supports this view and suggests that orthodox economic theories are unable to deal with such shifts of opinion. See Fred Hirsch, *Social Limits to Growth* (Routledge and Kegan Paul, 1977), particularly pp. 2-4.

4. See above, p. 10.

5. See above, p. 14.

6. See above, p. 14.

7. B. Ward and R. Dubos, *Only One Earth. The Care and Maintenance of a Small Planet* (Penguin, 1972), p. 193.

8. Shon's study of the US Navy, quoted by J. Brand, *Local Government Reform in England* (Croom Helm, 1974), pp. 155-6. The experiments concerned a new and more efficient method of firing guns.

9. See above, p. 23.

10. See above, p. 72.

11. See above, pp. 73-4.

12. Michael Ellman, *Planning Problems in the USSR* (Cambridge University Press, 1973), p. 53.

13. See above, p. 11.

14. O. Narkiewicz, 'Polish or Socialist?', *Universities Quarterly,* September 1965, p. 356.

15. See above, p. 165.

16. See above, p. 110.

17. See above, pp. 119 and 127.

18. See figures given in Narkiewicz and Hills, *Planning in Western and Eastern Europe: A Case Study of Stoke-on-Trent and Pardubice,* forthcoming, ch. 8: Health and Social Services.

19. Ibid. ch. 7: The Uses and Misuses of Cultural and Sports Facilities.

20. See above, p. 141.

21. Narkiewicz and Hills, op. cit. ch. 5: Housing and Environmental Policies.

22. See above, p. 166.

23. See above, pp. 96-7.

24. See above, p. 12. Also, Hirsch, op. cit. on conflicting elements of an individualistic society and the 'public good', particularly ch. 13.

25. A. Karpinski, 'The Geography of Poland's Tomorrow', *Poland,* no. 7, 1975, p. 17.

26. See above, p. 14.

27. Otis L. Graham Jr., *Toward a Planned Society: From Roosevelt to Nixon* (OUP, 1976), p. xii.

28. Ibid. quoting J.K. Galbraith and Robert C. Wood, p. 281.

29. See above, pp. 26-50 and 53-65.

30. Graham, op. cit. pp. 304-5.

31 . See above, p. 9.

32. See Wayland Kennet, *The Future of Europe* (Cambridge University Press, 1976).

SELECT BIBLIOGRAPHY

Belanger, P.A. *Bibliographie générale sur la planification nationale en France*, Grenoble, Grenoble University Press, 1974

Benveniste, G. *The Politics of Expertise*, London, Croom Helm, 1973.

Bornstein, M. (ed.) *Economic Planning, East and West*, Cambridge, Mass., Ballinger, 1975.

Faludi, A. *A Reader in Planning Theory*, Oxford, Pergamon Press, 1973.

Glinski, B., Kierczynski, T. and Topinski, A. *Zmiany w systemie zarzadzania przemyslem*, Warsaw, PAN Publishing Co., 1975.

Graham, O.L., Jr. *Toward a Planned Society: From Roosevelt to Nixon*, London and New York, OUP, 1976.

Granick, D. *Enterprise Guidance in Eastern Europe*, Princeton, Princeton University Press, 1975.

Gross, B.M. (ed.) *Action under Planning: the Guidance of Economic Development*, New York, McGraw-Hill, 1967.

Gunsteren, H.R. van *The Quest for Control. A critique of the rational-central approach in public affairs*, London, J. Wiley and Sons, 1976.

Hall, P. *Urban and Regional Planning*, Harmondsworth, Penguin, 1974.

Hayward, J. and Watson, M. (eds.) *Planning, Politics and Public Policy. The British, French and Italian Experience*, London, Cambridge University Press, 1975.

Hirsch, F. *Social Limits of Growth*, London, Routledge and Kegan Paul, 1977.

Jantsch, E. *Perspectives of Planning*, Paris, OECD, 1969.

Lindberg, L. *et al.* (eds.) *Stress and Contradiction in Modern Capitalism*, Lexington, Mass., Lexington Books, 1975.

People and Planning: Report of the Committee on Public Participation in Planning, London, HMSO, 1969.

Planification et Société, Colloque d'Uriage, Grenoble, Grenoble University Press, 1974.

Podolski, T.M. *Socialist Banking and Monetary Control*, Cambridge, Cambridge University Press, 1972.

Schultze, C.L. *The Politics and Economics of Public Spending*, Washington DC, Brookings, 1968.

Shonfield, A. *Modern Capitalism*, London, OUP, 1965.

Sik, O. *Czechoslovakia: The Bureaucratic Economy*, White Plains, New York, International Arts and Sciences Press, 1972.

Vernon, R. (ed.) *Big Business and the State. Changing relations in Western Europe,* Cambridge, Mass., Harvard University Press, 1974.

Ward, B. and Dubos, R. *Only One Earth. The Care and Maintenance of a Small Planet,* Harmondsworth, Penguin, 1972.

Warnecke, S.J. and Suleiman, E.N. (eds.) *Industrial Policies in Western Europe,* New York, Praeger, 1975.

CONTRIBUTORS

The Lady Bowden of Chesterfield held the posts of Assistant Under Secretary of State in the Department of Industry and Regional Director for the North West Economic Planning Region, till her retirement in 1975. She serves on numerous government, local government and voluntary bodies.

Jean Carassus is a senior official in the Urban Studies Division of the French *Ministère de l'Equipement.*

Jack Hayward is Professor of Politics and Dean of the Faculty of Social Sciences at the University of Hull.

Barry Hills is at present completing a Ph.D. thesis at the London School of Economics.

Danuta Jachniak-Ganguly is at present working at the Centre for Environmental Studies, London.

Bruno Jobert is a researcher at the *Centre d'Etudes et de Recherche sur l'Administration Economique et l'Aménagement du Territoire, Institut d'Etudes Politiques,* University of Grenoble.

Michael Kaser is Reader in Economics at Oxford University and Professorial Fellow of St Antony's College.

Jacques Leruez is a researcher at the *Centre d'Etudes et de Recherches Internationales, Institut d'Etudes Politiques,* Paris.

Olga Narkiewicz is a Senior Lecturer in European Studies and Modern Languages at the University of Manchester Institute of Science and Technology.

Stephen Young is Lecturer in Government, University of Manchester.

INDEX